W9-BYO-780

Amazing
Fireside Talks

Intriguing Thoughts To Awaken YOU

Based on Real Life Situations

Dr. Charles N. Toftoy

Amazing
Fireside Talks

Intriguing Thoughts To Awaken YOU

Based on Real Life Situations

Dr. Charles N. Toftoy

*"A good editor understands what you're talking
and writing about and doesn't meddle too much."*

- Irwin Shaw

EDITOR'S NOTE

"A very compelling book; a must read for everyone...young, old, men, women, youths.

The author's extensive research and study took over three years. This included personal one-on-one live interviews, live small group discussions with people of diverse backgrounds, books, journal articles, internet articles and posts, and email correspondence.

Dr. Toftoy took a risk by changing genres from mystery/thriller to self-help/motivational. He tackles many important life issues...all in one book. Using the same four characters of his Alpha Team from his previous two novels, it is written as though you are present at their weekly Alpha Team fireside talks—as if you are a part of the discussion.

The thoughts provided are helpful and key in dealing with personal difficulties. Selected quotes, sayings and poems blend in wisdom and add depth to the particular topic under discussion.

His strategy in writing this book is very clever and unique. To my knowledge, there has never been such a book written covering all of the topics this one does, nor using characters from the author's other books.

As Dr. Toftoy's primary editor, I didn't meddle too much as far as topic content; however, we did work closely together to insure the outcome would be a top quality book.

It will be a useful tool in understanding and prevention of the topic matters for anyone, as we are all subject to the possibilities of them occurring to us or a loved one, no matter our backgrounds.

Highly recommended reading."

Cindy Bauer
Primary Editor

ENDORSEMENT

"There's an amazing conversation going on over by the fireplace and you're invited to join in…but be advised this chat just might change your life.

The topics are current and ancient; basic life issues and the most profound human troubles; even sacred customs and rituals, honored by ancestors and heroes of old, are part of the fireside exchanges.

Rarely has the deeper issues of our lives been addressed in such an enjoyable, readable and truly useful way."

Sgt. Jeffrey Duvall
US Army (Ret'd)
Disabled Combat Veteran, Vietnam

In memory of those who sacrificed
their lives in fighting for our country.
Because of them we have our freedom.
May they rest in peace.

CONTRIBUTIONS BY THE AUTHOR

The author will donate a portion of the profits on this book to the Disabled American Veterans (DAV) organization and to the Wounded Warrior Mentor Program (WWMP).

The DAV helps disabled veterans of the United States Armed Forces and their families in many ways. Its motto is *'Fulfilling our promises to the men and women who served'*.

The Wounded Warrior Mentor Program (WWMP) helps thousands of injured warriors and their families.

> "I encourage my readers to visit DAV's website at www.dav.org and the WWMP website at www.woundedwarriormentor.org."

- Dr. Charles N. Toftoy

Note: *Dr. Toftoy is a disabled Vietnam veteran with TWO purple hearts and he is a mentor for soldiers in the WWMP.*

In Memoriam

"Nelson Mandela's funeral is today. My manuscript is complete; however, I felt that a special tribute to him is important. So I developed four parts to this book with four of his most famous quotes on each of the parts I, II, III, and IV opening pages. These selected quotes fit in with the book's theme.

I know that Nelson Mandela would have liked the purpose of this book—to inspire and help people."

- Dr. Charles N. Toftoy

Nelson Mandela
1918 – 2013

Author's Opening Comments

"Please read this book slowly. It is not intended to be a quick read. Many of us speed read through most novels, however, this is a book for you to markup—underline sentences, use magic markers, or tab pages for handy reference. It doesn't belong lost in shelf space with your other books.

There are quotes, sayings, poems and other readings that directly relate to the topic under discussion. This provides depth to the content. For example, to gain the wisdom from a quote or poem you may have to read it two or three times before you continue.

To fully grasp the core meaning and full value of the thoughts, I suggest that you keep an open mind and read objectively. Give yourself time to let these common-sense approaches to life become embedded in your mind—sort of an osmotic process of assimilation and absorption.

If any part of this book helps to inspire you, then my efforts were worthwhile. After all, I wrote this book for **YOU**—the reader."

- Dr. Charles N. Toftoy

"The creation of a thousand forests is in one acorn."

- Ralph Waldo Emerson

Cast of Characters

"In case you're not familiar with the Alpha Team, this is an introduction to these four main characters. Consider this as a warm-up to understanding these team members from my novels, *It's In The Eyes* and *Eyes of Cold Case Killers*, available at most major bookstores."

- Dr. Charles N. Toftoy

Lars Neilsen: Norwegian heritage. Professor at George Washington University, part-time sleuth. West Pointer, 3 Vietnam tours, hardcore Ranger-paratrooper. Distinguished Service Cross, three Silver Stars, two Purple Hearts. Father was a Sergeant Major in the Military Police. Wife and daughter killed in a head-on collision near the Pentagon. Looks like Christopher Reeve—Superman.

Brenda Little: Criminal reporter for *The Washington Post*. Studied Criminal Justice at the University of Maryland (4.0 GPA). Father was a D.C. Metro policeman—killed in the line of duty. First in her class at Springfield HS. Eidetic memory. Black belt in Tae Kwon Do. Looks like Lisbeth Salander played by Rooney Mara in *The Girl With The Dragon Tattoo*.

Nathan Greene: Ex-Sergeant, US Army. Two Vietnam tours, served one tour with Neilsen, Distinguished Service Cross, Silver Star, 3 Purple Hearts. Helped father in family owned funeral home business in his hometown of New Orleans. Associate Director of Murphy Funeral Homes in Arlington, Va. Aunt drowned due to Hurricane Katrina. Nickname "Tiger". Looks like Eddie Murphy, the movie star.

Doris Wagner: Former FBI profiler—known as the best in the country. Works part-time teaching wannabe FBI agents at Quantico. Clairvoyant, into Astrology, clinical psychology, medium-ship. Husband died in 9/11 World Trade Center. Provence, France influence-paintings, décor, piano, classical lady. Looks like Veronica Lake, top movie star in the 40's, with the peek-a-boo hairstyle. Recently remarried to Lars Neilsen.

Part I

Rolling Along With Inspiring Thoughts

Importance of Life
Sacred Space
Vision Quest
Anxiety
Depression
Rescue Yourself
Initiation, Ordeal, Reintegration
Dark Shadow

"Everyone can rise above their circumstances
and achieve success if they are dedicated
and passionate about what they do."
– Nelson Mandela

Charles Robert Darwin
(1809 – 1882)

English naturalist and geologist, best known
for his contributions to evolutionary theory.

"The man who dares to waste one hour of time has not discovered the value of life."

- Charles Darwin

Fireside Talk #1
The Importance of Life

Charles Whitcomb recognized the area where Doris lives…the *Salona* historical part of McLean, Virginia. Dolley Madison fled here in 1814 when the British troops set fire to the White House.

He parked his black SUV in the driveway and before knocking on the door, Charles walked around the 2-acre lot. He visualized a touch of *Provence, France.* All kinds of trees—cherry, cedar, crabapple, crape myrtle, dogwood. Many of them. Some large, some medium. Shrubs and bushes—Azaleas, Hollies, Nandinas, Rhododendrons…all over the front and backyard.

Whitcomb, an ardent gardener, knew plants very well. Took courses at *Merrifield Garden Center*. He noticed at least eight Hemlocks, some Cedar and Oak trees. Two patios and a waterfall with Koi fish. A sign stating Backyard Wildlife Habitat, certified by the *National Wildlife Federation*, hung proudly off a Tulip Magnolia next to the waterfall.

Down below, off the lower patio, stood a cute little cottage. Whitcomb counted over 30 terra cotta planters of all sizes, about 8 hanging baskets, at least 12 birdhouses and 6 bird feeders. Beautiful grasses and Pachysandra coupled with English ivy formed much of the ground cover. Doris even had two upside down suet feeders, especially for woodpeckers.

He noticed little signs that portioned off the rear garden into separate sections for flowers, butterflies, hummingbirds, and herbs. Yes, Doris must have spent some time in *Provence*. The ambiance is so therapeutic creating a calmness and serenity.

That was the outside—now the inside of her home completely floored Charles with its gentle, classical elegance. Living room, dining room, sitting room—all in French Victorian style.

Double end sofas and chairs with elaborate exteriors of gingerbread scrollwork. In mahogany stained with deep brown and cherry hues. Curved moldings, angular lines coupled with ornate tassels and fringes galore on sides of chairs and below the cushions on sofas.

The upholstery is rich, lush, dark velvet, which blends with the deep stained brown wood floors. The fireplace reminds you of a country inn fireplace…huge with a one-foot ledge out front. Big enough for three people to sit in. Lars is responsible for having the fire roaring at meeting time each Thursday evening at 7pm.

The setting for the fireside talks is with three sofas forming a U with the fireplace at the open end and an ornate table in the middle. Nice and cozy for freewheeling discussions.

In the corner of the living room sits a country French baby grand piano. Louis XV style, in white. Beautifully carved. 1916 vintage. Doris's husband played classical music. He died on 9/11 in the World Trade Building.

Large paintings adorn the walls and along the hallway. The copies seem real, encased in two and three inch elegant gold frames. *Leonardo da Vinci - The Last Supper, Pablo Picasso - Tragedy, Claude Monet - Water Lilies, Van Gogh - Sunflowers, Rembrandt - Man In A Golden Helmet.*

The Alpha Team arrived. Whitcomb noticed what the team members were wearing. He hadn't met them yet, but Lars described them about a week ago. Tiger: Levi Strauss jeans, Redskins sweatshirt and hat, orange Nike gym shoes. Looks like Eddie Murphy. Brenda:

Tight black slacks, Jhoon Rhee T-Shirt, UGG black boots, hair in a bun. Looks like Rooney Mora who played Lisbeth Salander in *The Girl with the Dragon Tattoo*.

Then there was Lars: Corduroy pants, long sleeve polo shirt, New Balance running shoes. Looks like Christopher Reeve, Superman. 6'2", 210. Doris: Classical boutique wear, purple knitted skirt, flowing blouse. Obviously Neiman Marcus products or from a specialty boutique for petit women. Peek-a-boo blond hair. Only 5'1". Looks like Veronica Lake.

Tiger quips, "The problem with dying is you're dead too long! I gar-ron-tee you dat."

"But are you really dead?" argues Brenda.

"Hey! Hold on! That's why we're here—you guys are jumping ahead of us," scolds Lars. "Before we start our first session tonight, let me introduce Lt. Colonel Charles Whitcomb, who was the Chief Chaplain at Ft. Myer. Reverend Whitcomb has agreed to attend some of our fireside talks, as he wishes."

The reverend said, "I appreciate the opportunity to be with the famous Alpha Team. You all have such a grand reputation for assisting local police with tough criminal cases."

"To start with," interjects Lars, "let me give you a snapshot of our team members. As you know, we've helped solve three cases in the local area. The last one was with a cold case killer named Taurus."

"Yeah! Rev—that was a lulu!" quipped Tiger.

"We have all agreed to meet on Thursday nights here at Doris's house in McLean, since there are no cases which currently need our involvement."

"Actually, Lars, it's our house since we got married last year, remember?" stated Doris.

"Yup, that's right. A quick run down on us. Doris is my wife, a former profiler with the FBI and…"

Brenda interrupts, "And known as the top FBI profiler in the country."

Doris blushes and pulls back her peek-a-boo curl.

"Anyhow, Doris teaches wannabe FBI agents at Quantico. Her first husband died in the World Trade building during 9/11. In addition to her profiling expertise, she has helped on cases using medium-ship. So you know—medium-ship is where Doris talks to dead people. It doesn't work every time."

"Now Brenda…"

"Whoops! Don't forget to mention that Doris looks like Veronica Lake, Doc!" announces Tiger.

[Many elders remember Veronica Lake, who was a top movie star in the 1940s. She was the number one box office draw. Beautiful, with long blond hair that fell over her right eye causing a peek-a-boo look. That was her trademark, which drove men crazy at the time. Lake appeared in over 30 films and has a star on the *Hollywood Walk of Fame* on Hollywood Boulevard.]

"Back to Brenda. She is a criminal investigative reporter for *The Washington Post*. She has forced several murderers to come forth due to her newspaper articles that get to their core. Causes them to make mistakes. Buddhist and a karate black belt holder, which she has used expertly in two of our cases.

Tiger was my platoon sergeant in Vietnam. He has the Distinguished Service Cross (DSC), second highest award to the Medal of Honor for bravery, and two silver stars with two purple hearts. He was born in New Orleans and…"

"You mean the Big Easy, Doc." Lars tips his chin.

"He worked in the New Orleans Police Department and assisted his father with his family-owned funeral business. He is an Associate Director at the local Murphy Funeral Homes in Arlington."

Lars swigged his hot apple cider, swirling the cinnamon stick. "Let me tell you all about the reverend. He went to Princeton Theological Seminary and switched to Duke University's Divinity School."

"Excuse me, Lars—let me butt in. I left Princeton because I disagreed with the head honcho."

Everyone laughs. Tiger whispered, but all could hear, "I knew I was going to *like* this dude!"

Brenda rolled her eyes. Doris shook her head, however she couldn't conceal a mild grin.

"Then the reverend went to several military posts and retired at Ft. Myer with the Old Guard as a Lt. Colonel. So now, Reverend, that's us. Here's what we are here for. Our purpose is…"

"Wait," interjects Tiger, "What about you, Doc?"

Lars shrugged.

"Well, I'll tell you, Rev. Doc did three tours in Vietnam, two DSCs (Distinguished Service Cross), three silver stars, three purple hearts and more. Both of us were Airborne-Rangers. He teaches at the Business School at George Washington University; wins many teaching honors there. He knows the street and how murderers think because his Ph.D. is in Behavioral Studies. And he's a West Pointer."

"Enough, Tiger. Enough. Anyway, I flunked out of West Point after two years and went to Officer Candidate School to become an officer." Lars scratched his head.

Everyone headed to the kitchen to refill their tea or snag another cup of coffee.

In the kitchen, Lars mentioned that what will be good about our suggestions is that they will be applicable to anyone, from teenagers to the elderly.

Brenda agreed, adding that teenagers will like some of our discussion points, quotes, and poems. Brenda reminded them that she teaches karate after school at Washington & Lee and Yorktown High Schools nearby.

The books they like to read are: *Gone, Harry Potter and the Sorcerer's Stone, I Am Number Four, Revolver, The Maze Runner, Holes, Ender's Game, The Lightning Thief.* TV shows they watch are: *Teen Wolf, Awkward, Pretty Little Liars, Glee, Gossip Girls, The Vampire Diaries, Cake Boss.* These youngsters read books more than you think. I've seen them returning as many as eight books, stacked under their arms to Arlington's Central Library. So, yes…they'll be interested in our important life messages.

[Tiger hip bumps Brenda telling her that is good to hear and that she's more up to speed with the teens than we are.]

"Now you understand us fairly well. So, we can get on with our purpose, which is to *inspire* people that need to overcome anxiety, depression, or any other matter. We plan to choose a subject area for each week so everyone has time to develop their thoughts. I really like the reverend with us to…"

"To keep us honest, right Doc?"

"Yup, that's it, Tiger."

"Excuse me; do you all mind if I snag another brownie?" The Rev grins.

"I told you; I *love* this guy," Tiger chuckles.

"Brenda is always our note-taker, so why don't you take minutes for us, Brenda?"

"Glad to, Lars."

Tiger stammers, "That's good because this journey is going to be *amazing*." He makes a face at Brenda.

Again, Brenda full-circled her eyes and said, "Sure, Tiger…Sure!"

Doris cleared her throat. Lars shook his hands like runners do sometimes to loosen up. The reverend was into deep breathing by this point. Lars rocked forward in his chair.

"Hey! Wait a minute; that's a good idea to have Brenda take notes because these talk sessions are directed at **YOU**, the reader, to arouse your curiosity about *rubber-meets-the-road* issues you face.

"You know, I've just come full-circle on this," snapped Brenda. "Knowing this team, we'll come up with **intriguing thoughts** to *awaken* people. I just know it."

"That's the spirit, Brenda," said Lars.

The reverend added, "This is a magnificent concept."

"As the so-called captain of this team, I think we're all fired up and ready to go," barked Lars.

"Let's roll," yelled Tiger. "Let's roll, baby."

***

Rev:

I don't mind starting. Of course, you know what I'm going to say about what's the most important thing in life. Faith in God. Going to the seminary for three years coupled with my Chaplain experience all over the world, to include Iraq and Afghanistan, leads me to that response.

But since we're being very frank and open here, let me tell you what I mean. Without faith, you are shallow. Faith gives you depth. I don't mean the kind of person that goes to church twice on Sunday or every Sunday and appears weak, timid and lame. As a matter of fact, those kinds of people are too gooey and turn people away from attending church services.

I've met with several highly skilled people, having a lot of experience in their field of endeavor, but still if they lack faith, it shows up in their character. I hope you understand what I'm trying to say.

[Rev. Whitcomb picks at his ear.]

My bottom-line is that if you are missing faith in God—find it. Lars told me a few years ago that faith pulled him through in several close-combat actions in Vietnam. The seed of God is within every person. It's up to you to grow it. You can do it.

Frankly, life is rather random. I'm taking off my reverend hat here to suggest that life controls us through luck, timing and fate. So **YOU** need to appreciate each day because life has a lot of background noise like smelly, stagnant backwater in a beautiful lake or pond.

Brenda:
That's a good jump-off point for me, Rev. The most important thing to me in life is to have total harmony within myself. You have to strive for inner peace.

Maybe that's the Buddhism coming out of me, but without it, you've missed the meaning of life.

[Tiger raises his hand.]

Just remember, Tiger, everybody dies, but not everyone really lives. To sweeten this up a little, Norman Mailer said: *'I don't think life is absurd. I think we are all here for a huge purpose. I think we shrink from the immensity of the purpose we are here for.'*

[Mailer was a novelist, journalist, and filmmaker. He wrote *The Naked and the Dead* in 1948. He was an innovator of creative fiction and founded *The Village Voice*, a weekly arts and political newspaper distributed in Greenwich Village.]

DR. CHARLES N. TOFTOY

Tiger:

Awesome, Brenda. To me, it's having a genuine friend or friends. Someone you can trust—not a gossiper or liar. Like you said, Brenda, about the fact that everyone dies, but also some people miss life by not having a real friend. That's sad.

I want someone who can talk straight and that I can confide in. You know…somebody I can munch on chicken wings with up here in DC and crawfish in New Orleans. *Nurture a solid friend.* That's my advice to **YOU.**

[Tiger stands up in a preacher's pose.]

Oh! And guess what? We are lucky. We have our Alpha Team bond. Everyone here has killed somebody while solving our assigned cases by the local police. That's Doc's concept of justice: take no prisoners.

Lars:

You saved my life in the Hawthorne case, Tiger.

Tiger:

Yeah, Boss! But, you saved my life twice in 'Nam.

[Tiger scratched his right ear lobe. Half of it was ripped off by a bullet that grazed the right side of his face. Result of a Viet Cong ambush along a trail near Bien Hoa. Brenda noticed and gave a sympathetic nod. The Alpha Team knew the whole story about the frightening firefight. Twelve of his recon-buddies were killed within thirty seconds. Tiger sure knows the importance of life.]

Lars:

I guess my professor hat will show on this, but I think the most important factor is having goals. But you should only have one or two goals so you can keep the focus. Once you've accomplished a goal, then bring forth a new one. The question is what do you want to accomplish?

Just remember what Lao Tzu wrote: '*A journey of a thousand miles begins with a single step.'*

[Lao Tzu was a philosopher and poet dating back to the 6th century in ancient China. He was the founder of Taoism.]

Naturally, our spouse, family and others are important in life. But that's not what we're talking about. These are points we offer to **YOU** in order to help you cope with difficulties.

Our fireside talks are for everyone: a wounded warrior missing limbs, someone getting out of rehab or prison, a high school student having difficulties with bullies, someone on drugs or alcohol, those that are grieving, and so on. The works.

Doris:

You guys forgot me. I like the attribute of humility: that nobody is better than anyone else.

[Everyone cheers Doris.]

And that you have to be yourself. Don't try to copy someone. And Lord knows, don't take on a sports figure, entertainer or rock star as a role model.

[Doris flips her curl again, which drives Lars crazy.]

Just remember, you are worth much more than you think, regardless of your medical condition or anything else that appears to be inhibiting you. In short, always be yourself and let the chips fall where they may!

Remember what George Bernard Shaw said: *'Life isn't about finding yourself. Life is about creating yourself.'*

[An Irish playwright, Shaw was a co-founder of the London School of Economics. He won the Nobel Prize for literature.]

Lars:

This was a good first round. We're trying to keep these meetings to a one-hour limit, Rev. Of course we could say that breathing is the most important thing in life. Without breathing, none of us would be here.

[Everyone bursts out laughing.]

Okay, next time we offer thoughts on SACRED SPACE.

Rev:
That sounds interesting. I'll be here next Thursday night.

Tiger:
Root beer for the road, Doc?

Lars:
Yup. I've never turned down a free soda. But put ice cream in mine. I've liked root beer floats ever since I was a kid.

Brenda [grinning]:
Make that two.

Tiger [whispers to Doris]:
Brenda reminds me so much of that actress in the movie, *Girl with the Dragon Tattoo.*

Lars:
As I've said, our thoughts are for **YOU**. Edward Gorey, an American writer and illustrator, who wrote more than 100 books, mostly humorous, said: *'The helpful thought for which you look is written somewhere in a book.'* We hope you'll find a helpful thought or more as a result of our ***Amazing Fireside Talks.***

***

In the kitchen, everybody admired Doris's Parisienne Éclairs au Chocolat. Then they pounced on them like starved animals. Tiger gave Sasha a small dog bone as a treat, as he dug in leaving dark chocolate smeared all over his face. For at least an hour, the team chatted about the topics to be discussed in the next few weeks. They were very excited. Decaf coffee flowed. The Rev, Lars and Tiger talked about local sports. Brenda and Doris talked about facial crèmes and whether they really reduced wrinkles.

All gave high-5s, and then the noise level in the house was reduced 100% as Tiger and Brenda departed.

Joseph Campbell
(1904 – 1987)

American mythologist, writer and lecturer,
best known for his work in comparative
mythology and comparative religion.

*"Your Sacred Space Is Where You Can
Find Yourself Again And Again"*

- Joseph Campbell

Fireside Talk #2
Sacred Space

Whitcomb arrived early, as planned, so he could ask questions about Doris's landscape design and other features. They stood on the upper patio out back drinking a cup of Tully's extra bold decaf a' la Keurig. Both gripped their cups tightly. It was chilly.

"I must admit, Doris, I scanned your backyard with envy last week. I'm sort of a gardener myself. Now that we're in the fall season, I can't make out what flowers or plants you have." He raised a brow.

"I can't remember all the names, but for the butterfly garden I grow mostly cone flowers, milkweeds, butterfly bushes, Black-Eyed Susans and various honeysuckles. I must admit that Lars works up the butterfly and hummingbird gardens. I take care of the flowers and herbs," she responded, smiling.

"What kinds of butterflies visit these plants?" Whitcomb's curiosity was growing.

"Eastern Tiger Swallowtail, Cabbage White, Monarch, Red

Admiral, and Silver-Spotted Skipper."

With growing interest now, Whitcomb asked, "What flowers do you and Lars grow for the hummingbirds?"

Doris grinned. "Bee Balm, Cardinal Flower, Trumpet Creeper, Salvia, Crimson Columbine, Bleeding Hearts and Zinnias. But Lars knows more about these. Oh! I do grow Lavender all over the place—front and back. *Love* the aroma. I spent two years in Aix-En-Provence, so I try to bring that wonderful region here."

"I thought so. I feel like I'm in Provence." He stood looking at the wonder of it all.

Doris continued. "The birds that are attracted to my bird feeders are Finches, Chickadees, Nuthatch, Titmouse, Sparrows, Cardinals and Mourning Doves. The Woodpeckers love the upside down suet feeders because they are the only bird that can feed upside down, except for an occasional Chickadee. I admire the Woodpeckers. Mostly Red-Bellied, Downy, and Hairy Woodpeckers. By the way, most of my herbs are Parsley, Basil, Chives, Oregano, Rosemary, Thyme and Mint. Lars and I use a lot of herbs in our cooking."

"I've learned a lot about gardening from seminars at Merrifield Garden Center, and they also have webinars and instructional videos. Sorry to have asked you so many questions. It's just that I love this setting." He was noticeably impressed.

Everyone has arrived so the two garden enthusiasts go inside to warm up around the fireplace.

"Where y'at, Brenda?" Tiger asked

"Is that the New Orleans slang again? What mean, brother?" Brenda giggled.

Tiger rolled his eyes. "It means how you. The reverend knows that. He's had Café du lait with beignets at Café Du Monde too, I bet."

"You're right. Plus Cajun and Creole cooking. Gumbo, too. Can't beat it." The reverend sips his Easy Thai Tea. "Ah. What is in this tea? It's incredible."

Doris readily filled him in. "Cardamom seeds, cloves, black peppercorns, cinnamon sticks, milk, black tea bags and honey. It is a great mixture."

They take their places and the meeting begins.

***

AMAZING FIRESIDE TALKS

Lars:

How can we help someone as far as Sacred Space is concerned? There's been enough socializing already.

[Lars wants to speed into the evening's topic.]

Doris:

Well, we're talking to **YOU**, the reader…right Brenda?

Brenda:

Yup!

[Everyone snickers since this is Lars's favorite response.]

Doris:

I'll start. For me, it's a place where you can think. I actually have a space *within* a Sacred Space where I sit outside looking at our waterfall. My mind becomes clear as soon as I enter my Sacred Space. I block out everything. I mean *everything*—and watch the birds, squirrels, chipmunks and fish. It's my heaven. You need to find **YOUR** Sacred Space.

Rev:

My sacred place is sitting by a window in my den. I know you all thought that it would be somewhere in the church. The church is blissful for me, but my creative spirit comes from my sitting in that special spot. My mind clears up and I see a clearer perspective.

Doris is right—you need to find a Sacred Space for yourself.

Lars:

My place is a little hut below our house. I've turned it into a den. It is quiet. I'm all by myself. I turn on Tchaikovsky. I've got all the Tchaikovsky CDs. It's where I grade my student papers and I meditate there. It's sacred to me.

I guess what we're saying is to find your place and own it. My Sacred Space is where I generate creative ideas.

DR. CHARLES N. TOFTOY

Tiger:
And where you flunk students!

[Tiger gives a hee-haw bark, Doris groans and Brenda rolls her eyes—her trademark in response to something stupid.]

Lars:
Also, I do deep breathing in my Sacred Space. You've got to have a place like this to keep in touch with your inner self. Cell phone off. No disturbances. Even if it's a little corner in your home, barracks or dorm—it doesn't matter. Just so it's yours.

Actually, it's a way to heal yourself; maintain your well-being. It gives me balance to life. I feel good going to my hut, while I'm there, and refreshed after I leave.

Brenda:
With Sacred Space, you are hitting a home run with me. I will give you some good ideas. But first, realize that the earliest example of Sacred Space is from Buddhism—the stupa. It is a symbol of the enlightened mind or the awakened mind. I switched to Buddha because they see things the way they are and that's the kind of person I am. In Buddhism, a stupa is a commemorative building usually housing sacred relics associated with important saintly figures.

Tiger:
That's fo' sure.

Brenda:
Buddha said, *'All that we are is the result of what we have thought. The mind is everything. What we think we become.'* That's the best quote from Buddha; I have a hundred other ones.

My sacred place is special. It is a corner of a room in my apartment shielded by a colorful divider. I have a small Buddha statue there on a table. But for you, it could be something that means a lot to you and is unique: seashells, candles, incense, picture of a pet, drawings, teddy bears, a stone or stones, or other mementos.

I have a Buddha friend that has a spot in her garden with terracotta

30

pots filled with her favorite plants and flowers. Her spot. Hers only. She says that her sacred spot allows her to connect with her inner-self. She escapes her busy work at Raytheon.

That is what your Sacred Space is: an escape for you.

These ideas might help you to customize your Sacred Space. You should feel comfortable and relaxed in that special spot.

My Sacred Space grows on me. It allows me to breathe. I search for real meanings. Who am I? What am I doing? Where am I going? You can ask these questions yourself. Also, not to get too heavy here, but where did we come from and why are we here?

Sometimes I practice a little bit of karate in my space, but normally I do that at Jhoon Rhee's facility. However, your Sacred Space could be where you practice Tai Chi, Pilates or Yoga. If you're in a wheelchair, you can take some of my ideas and your own to form your refuge place. Again, customize it to fit your need. Mine borders on being slightly spiritual, but it doesn't have to be as you have heard.

I've taken too long, but it is a place to bolster your self-esteem, confidence—where you feel the most comfortable. This leads to healing and it eases your mind.

[Everyone stands up and applauds.]

Tiger:

Tough act to follow, Brenda! Sometimes I'm down on myself; maybe it's the Post Traumatic Stress Disease.

Lars:

You know, I have PTSD too.

Tiger:

I know, Doc. My wife keeps telling me that I don't know the wonderful qualities I have inside myself. Maybe you don't either, but a Sacred Space will bring that forth. It is your awakening.

My special place is a bench in a park nearby my home. That spot is sacred to me. I forget about the funerals, preparing the dead for burial, talking to those that are grieving. That is all blocked out. My advice to you is to learn the art of blocking. It doesn't mean to ignore things—

just block so you can focus.

I was a 90% free-throw shooter in high school. It was me and that basket—period. So in your Sacred Space, you need to block everything out.

I always carry the dog tags of Sergeant Marvin Sawyer who was killed in Nam. A mortar round landed between his legs and blew his body parts up into the top of the trees in the Michelin Rubber Plantation. Nothing left of him. He was right next to me. Somehow, we recovered his dog tags. I keep them with me everywhere. Maybe you have a token, stone, beads or something that means a lot to you so that when you travel, your Sacred Space moves with you.

Lars:

Like a mobile Sacred Space, huh Tiger?

Tiger:

Exactly, Doc. That's it. I hope this inspires you to never give up. When you've got PTSD, you might feel like giving up sometimes but struggling through it, is what builds character.

Rev:

It seems as if life is a mystery. Whether you feel that God put you here doesn't matter. We're born into a mystery and we leave in a mystery. In between those two—is life. We really aren't sure where we're going, so you need to concentrate on your existence now. You need to be clear on what you're doing now or what you want to do because you don't know how you're going to end up.

One of my sacred spots is at Arlington Cemetery where my mother and father are buried. It's quiet and I'm alone.

One more thing. We haven't mentioned group settings as a Sacred Space. It could be an Islamic Mosque, sweat lodges, Buddhist Temples, Hindu Ashrams, or your church. These places help to renew and purify yourself.

Brenda:

Not to interrupt, Rev, but, my Buddha meditations coupled with being in that special corner of my apartment helps me to drop down to a deeper place within myself. Hopefully, your Sacred Space will give you that feeling.

Lars:

This was powerful tonight. I just thought of something while looking at the fireplace. That's therapy in itself. There's a calmness to the fire that helps a person to think deeply.

Doris:

I leave it up to Lars to clean the fireplace. He's my logger guy!

[Everyone laughs. Tiger slaps Lars on his shoulder.]

Tiger:

Hey, Doc! It looks real, too.

Brenda:

Remind me, Doc. What's up next week?

Lars:

We're going to cover VISION QUEST. The session will help with ways to receive a vision that will guide you for a lifetime.

***

The team sat around the kitchen table sipping their favorite from the Keurig machine. Doris- cappuccino, Lars- extra bold decaf, Brenda- lemon zinger herbal tea, Tiger- dark chocolate cocoa, Rev- hot apple cider. They tapped their mugs together as one and listened to Lars. He reminded the team and readers that this reads like a novel. The characters interact with one another before and after the fireside talks. Like they did in the novels, where the characters...that's us...were used in full story essence inspired by true events.

Doris surprised everyone by serving an opera cake that she baked that afternoon. She feels that by providing some French deserts at the end of the discussions will loosen up everybody. Especially since some of the life issues are tough problems.

Brenda wanted the recipe. Doris told them that it is composed of thin slices of almond sponge cake soaked in coffee, layered with ganache, coffee flavored buttercream frosting, topped with chocolate glaze. She told them that the opera cake dates back to the 1600's to the court of Versailles. Even to this day, it is served at the *Dalloyau Restaurant* in Paris. In about 30 minutes, the entire cake was devoured by the Rev and the team.

After everyone left, Doris teased Lars about shoveling snow. She bought him a new lightweight shovel at Cherrydale Hardware…Lars favorite store…to replace the one he broke the handle off last week. Six inches of snow is expected tomorrow, so now Lars is prepared.

Lars sat on the couch alone, staring at the fire. He drifted off, having flashbacks of Vietnam combat situations, especially the battle where his unit was surrounded. Doris let him be, realizing that his dreams are a haunting for him and that he has to work it out by himself. Much progress has been made during the last year.

Anna Eleanor Roosevelt
(1884 – 1962)

American politician—longest serving
First Lady of the United States, holding
the post from March 1933 to April 1945
during her husband President Franklin
D. Roosevelt's four terms in office.

Fireside Talk #3
A Compelling Vision Quest

Tiger texted Doris. Fender bender. Will be a little late. In the meantime, everyone enjoys Doris's mulled cider. Brenda asks her how she makes it while wiping her mouth with her sleeve. Apple cider, mulling spices, orange zest, and ginger. Also, Doris adds a slice of a Granny Smith apple. Tiger arrives, explaining how you have to watch out for the other guy. Icy roads tonight, but Tiger has 4WD in his four door Jeep Wrangler.

They all talk about the grueling weather…snow, black ice on roads, temperature—24 degrees—wind chill 16. Tiger stands in front of the huge fireplace with the fire roaring, rubbing his hands together. He marvels at the mulled cider, cuddling his cup in his hands.

***

Brenda:

I should start this one since everyone has been to my apartment and seen my Southwest décor – Kachini dolls, storytellers, native play dolls, bows and arrows.

Tiger:

Yeah! One night I thought Brenda was going to shoot me with one of those arrows.

Brenda:

That's because you told a terrible joke, you half-wit!

Tiger:

So I'm a half-wit?

[Tiger stands up clenching his fist. Grinning.]

Lars:

Don't get in an uproar, Tiger. Squat down. We want to hear Brenda.

Brenda:

I'm really living my life…as of 5 years ago. I went to the nearby Shenandoah Valley for 2 days with nature. It was a remote quiet place in the midst of Mother Nature. I drowned out the busy, social world and let myself sink into inward reflection. I ended up having dreams that helped me to make life choices. To me, your life really doesn't begin until you've seen your vision. You have to think deeply to get a crystal vision of your life's purpose.

The Lakota Sioux call it *'crying for a dream!'* The Indian quest involves staying at his designated spot in the wilderness without food, water or sleep for one to four nights. But in this modern age, you can do it by yourself for one day. I think you can find your vision in the peace and solitude even in a National Park. If you're in a wheelchair, someone can take you to your spot and leave you for several hours. Even though it violates the tribe's type of Vision Quest arrangements, you should bring a bottle of spring water. Normally, the Sioux bring nothing to the spot they've chosen…not even water.

Oh! Before I close off…a little trivia. Some of the members of the

Lakota were: Sitting Bull, Red Cloud, Crazy Horse and Rain-in-the-Face, who fought at Little Bighorn. For the Indians, the Vision Quest is the most sacred ritual. For you, it can result in developing a compelling vision that will get you on the right track. And lastly, just remember a key point: your future is not pre-ordained. The Indian tribes, especially the Ojibwa, believed that way.

Lars:

The Vision Quest can help you. If you're feeling flat and shallow, this will pick you up. It helped a wounded warrior that I mentored. He lost a leg and an arm in Iraq. He found his meaning and purpose of his life.

I was lucky; my vision came to me. Doris is the only person I've ever told this to. I was in my second year at West Point. Had three roommates. I lost the fingers flip game and was awarded the top bunk. To get right to it…one night, rather early morning—probably about 2 AM, a bolt of lightning hit our room. I sat up straight and was looking at Jesus Christ—all in white and sparkling. His arms were held out in front towards me with his palms open. Then he was gone.

[Everyone's eyes are wide open, to include their mouths. Tiger was obviously dumbstruck.]

It wasn't a dream. So, I determined that I was a chosen servant and that I needed to make sure that I also took care of others…for my life's purpose. But as a young guy, I was confused. However, it has helped me through tough times.

Billy Graham came to the Military Academy and talked to us in a small auditorium. Afterwards, I told him about the events. He said: *'You have been chosen'.*

Brenda:

I have a question. Did your roommates wake up?

Lars:

No. They heard and saw nothing. Sound asleep as babies. It was sort of like my inner-eyes were opened. It was amazing and powerful.

The vision is compelling. It stays with you forever. We aren't talking about a company's vision that we teach in The Business School at the University. The strategy formulation process includes vision, mission statement, goals, and so on. This is *entirely* different.

Brenda:
I agree. Not even close.

Lars:
I had another sort of vision awakening when I went bass fishing at Lake Anna, near Fredericksburg, Virginia. I let my mind drift away and again, I discovered my purpose. It led me to teaching. That was the calling in my heart for years. I just never took the time to be alone, surrounded by nature, which gave me the calling. I found that I'm really here to benefit and help others. That includes animals.

YOU really ought to do it. Especially, like we've said before, if you're in a bad fix—like suffering through periods of fear, depression and boredom. Your Vision Quest will pull you out of pitfalls like drug abuse, alcoholism and other medical addictions.

Tiger:
Don't forget, Doc got his Doctorate in Strategic Planning so he knows the difference. Helping my father in the funeral home as a kid, to the New Orleans Police where I got run off, to the Army as an infantry airborne-ranger, like Doc, fulfills my dream.

Now back to the funeral business. My quest for a vision just evolved. It was my calling. I fell for the departed. When I prepare them, I'm their last friend to respect them and maintain their dignity. I'm the last one to close their eyes for good.

[Tears swell up in Tiger's eyes. Ditto for everyone else.]

Many times, I was alone in the wild as a ranger and I was haunted by the calling—to care for those who lost loved ones and to care for the deceased person. I've seen it all—from babies to those over 100.

When I'm preparing the person, I talk to them in a calming way. New Age music is playing. I found my niche. That's a business term and it's corny. I'm living my vision. I can feel it daily. **YOU** can live your vision, too. It will tell you what you're here for, which will help you resolve some predicament or anything that's eating at you.

Doris:

Lars pulled me out of the depths. I was drinking too much due to losing my husband in the World Trade Building. And memories of being abused by a Catholic Priest when I was 14 kept haunting me. Long story short—Lars went to AA with me and switched me to the Episcopal Church.

I'll never forget the first church service at St. Paul's in Georgetown. I was nervous. Half-way through, I leaned over to Lars and whispered, *'I'm here'*. In other words, after leaving the Catholic Church, I found a new home…the Episcopal Church. I quit the FBI. Gave up. Then I saw the light. I guess that's my vision. I was on a quest—ended up training recruit FBI agents at Quantico.

It is more about doing what you're meant to do, rather than doing what you want to do. And you need to love it. I agree with everybody here, you can really pick yourself up via a Vision Quest.

I've studied Astrology for many years, so look up your sign and play on the positive aspects of your sign. See, there's good in everyone. You're better than you think. Let me end with a quote from Charles R. Swindoll. He said: *'When you have vision it affects your attitude. Your attitude is optimistic rather than pessimistic'*. My mother had this saying posted on our refrigerator. Strong beliefs.

[Swindoll is a Christian pastor, author, and founder of Insight For Living. His uplifting comments via radio broadcasts to over 2,000 stations worldwide in 15 languages.]

He sent me an email and wants me to read his message, so here goes:

'I went to a sweat lodge when I was a captain in the artillery. It was a life changing experience because I switched branches to the Chaplain Corps. A group vision quest is perhaps what might be a good choice. But even then, it was on that quest being alone in the natural

environment with great scenery when my dream popped right out of nowhere. It happens—just like that. For the more spiritually motivated person, I suggest you try one of the groups. It is a life changing experience. On the other hand, the vision quest is a solitary pursuit. It can consist of an hour sitting in the nearby woods to days in the wilderness. It is working wonders for wounded troopers and people with PTSD.

My last tip is that when you find out (and you will) why you're here in this life, then integrate it into your life—like I did.'

[Everybody said Amen. Lots of chatter about going to a sweat lodge together.]

We all need to find out who we are.

Tiger:
Ten-4 on that!

Brenda:
This is super stuff.

Lars:
I agree. Don't forget, next week is about ANXIETY, so study up, gang.

Tiger:
Yes, Prof.

***

Tiger scrambles to the kitchen to fetch more mulled cider. Doris mentions that the team is going to Wolf Trap in the near future to see the Gipsy Kings and Josh Groban. Everyone is excited about that. Tiger says that one of his buddies works for the U.S. National Park Service who are responsible for Wolf Trap National Park for the Performing Arts. Brenda adds that she knows a lot about it because she used to work there as a summer student. It has 130 acres with a 7,000-

seat theater. And that it is the only National Park dedicated to the Performing Arts. They all give high-5s and Tiger skips out the door yelling, 'Hee-Haw'.

Gautama Buddha

Gautama Buddha, also known as
Siddhārtha Gautama, Shakyamuni, or
simply the Buddha, was a sage on whose
teachings Buddhism was founded.

"Anxiety Shortens Life."

- Buddha

Fireside Talk #4
Thwart Anxiety: Run to the Roar

Reverend Whitcomb called to let Doris know that he would be 30 minutes late...conducting a baptism. While waiting for the Rev, Lars reminisced about Doris and his wedding last year. A double wedding with Carl Mercer and Dena Kendrick who both helped the Alpha Team on their last criminal case. In pursuit of Norman Lattimore, known as Taurus, a genius type of cold case killer.

Lars reminded everyone about how Father Taylor, of St. Paul's Church in Foggy Bottom, walked the two couples around the Stations of the Cross prior to returning to the altar for the wedding vows. They stopped at each Station, really the Way of the Cross...symbolic of the *Lord's* pilgrimage from *His* beginning to end. A prayer said at each Station. It really moved the attendees. Most had ever heard of the Stations of the Cross ceremony usually performed during Lent.

Lars seemed a little choked, since the next week would be their first wedding anniversary. The wedding reception was held at the

Army-Navy Country Club in Arlington. Doris giggled when she reminded everyone about when Tiger said, *'I'll do the honors'* in pouring a cup of punch for Doris. Three of his fingers became numb and he spilled the grape flavored sparkling apple cider all over Doris's beautiful wedding gown and his white tuxedo shirt. Doris was shocked for a few seconds, then laughed, followed by laughter from everyone at the reception. She danced all night with the purple stain streaking her dress from her waist all the way to the bottom.

Reverend Whitcomb arrived just as Lars finished telling about his fond memory.

***

Lars:

I sure ran to the roar in Vietnam. Every time I went out in the jungle, we got into a firefight. One time, when we hit the ground after making a combat jump, the Task Force Commander got an anxiety attack—curled up, shaking at the bottom of a crater. As a captain, I had to take command. It was embarrassing.

I had a prostatectomy due to Agent Orange by the same surgeon that removed the prostate of a famous general. The general had an anxiety attack as they were wheeling him into the operating room. It delayed the surgery.

In all my fields of endeavor (military, corporate, academia) the people that have anxiety problems usually make mistakes. Panicked leaders make rushed, poor decisions. You've got to stay calm.

Tiger:

I agree, Doc. I've seen it in combat, too. I know troopers that are six feet under right now because their anxiety took control, leading to poor decisions or judgments.

And in the funeral business at Murphy's, I've been faced with everything you can imagine. While in the midst of making funeral arrangements, people have thrown up, had the shakes—you name it. One grabbed me so tight suddenly, that her nails dug into my back.

Events can cause anxiety, but I think we are talking about the over-anxious person in which anxiety is a detriment to your state of well-being. Some people just 'pole vault over mouse droppings', making big things out of little things.

I think you should face your problem head-on and not run away. Instead, *run to the roar.* The problem is causing the roar and your anxiety is killing you inside, but to no avail.

[Tiger is all pumped up, rocking his left leg back and forth. Out of habit, Tiger scratches his left earlobe. Part of it is missing as the result of a claymore mine explosion during an ambush in 'Nam.]

Yeah. Ya gotta' put the past behind you and keep looking forward. It's easy to say, but you've need to do it or you fall into the anxiety trap. To me, being a humble Catholic, anxiety and depression are the soul talking to me.

Lars:
I think what Tiger is saying is to stop being bound to routine and status quo. Or just wait it out—whatever it is. Be bold and take action. Nathan Greene picked up the *Tiger* nickname in Vietnam because of his fearlessness in combat. Otherwise, you just become anxious. Is that a Roger, Tiger?

Tiger:
Roger that, Sir. Or I mean, Doc.

Doris:
Looks like you can take the man out of the military, but you can't take the military out of the man.

Tiger:
Yeah! I mean as Sergeant Nathan Greene, I used to report to Captain Lars Neilsen in 'Nam.

[Everyone chuckles.]

Brenda:
Good stuff so far. Since I'm our African travel guru, let me compare all of this to the lions on the hunt. When I visited Botswana

and Tanzania, I saw this in action. Maybe this will enlighten **YOU**, so that anxiety takes a back seat from now on. Lions can run at 35 mph with bursts up to 50 mph. Gazelles run at 30 mph with bursts up to 60 mph, but they have more stamina than lions. Lions are low on endurance. So, how do the hunting lions catch the gazelle? They *run to the roar.*

Here it is in a nutshell. The oldest lions in the pride with slow legs, some teeth missing, and little hunting skills lay ahead in the brush in wait. The younger lions chase the gazelles toward the oldest lions that still have a deathly roar. The gazelles or antelopes panic and flee in the opposite direction, where the younger strong lions are waiting in the tall grass.

In short, this lesson tells you to *run to the roar* to overcome your anxiety. Just remember the lions. Lastly, Buddha believes anxiety relates to self-centeredness. Think about it.

Doris:

I just think that worrying saps your strength. What I mean is you should take one day at a time. Worrying about tomorrow takes away from what you need or want to do today. It's a waste of mental energy. I've learned this the hard way. Charles Darwin once said, *'A man who dares to waste one hour of time has not discovered the value of life.'*

[Charles Darwin was an English naturalist and geologist and the top expert on the biological theory of evolution. In 1859, he wrote his masterpiece: *On the Origin of Species.*]

I have friends that really let anxiety control their lives. It's sad to me. Losing sleep, food has little taste anymore, and breaking out in hives. Sally feels like her life is destroyed. And Jan tells me that her life is revived. Now, I did help Jan by telling her to check with another doctor about her medications. Lo and behold, her meds were causing her anxiety. That's something you should check, if applicable. It might solve the anxiety problems.

Some of my other friends have minimized their anxiety by limiting coffee, sugar, alcohol, and by exercise. Diet too. But we all can read about those treatments or steps to cut anxiety, at least in half. My way is deep breathing. Two or three times a day, I do deep breathing exercises. It works great. I breathe in through the nose, pushing the abdomen out, then exhale through the mouth. Ten repetitions. I do it just before my class starts at Quantico. I enter the classroom as cool as a cucumber.

My other tip is that if you have a phobia about heights, bridges, elevators, or crowd gatherings—just stay away. And stay away from people that put you on edge. Like Lars and Nathan, [Doris refuses to call him Tiger] they should avoid situations that remind them of the original trauma. I know that Lars won't visit Vietnam because it reminds him of the past. Although he likes the Vietnamese people, he can't cope with it. So why do it? By the way, your verses have helped me already, Reverend Whitcomb—there's no point in being anxious, especially about something that you can't impact.

To sum up, I used to be a worrywart, but then I learned it's wasteful and has negative undertones.

Rev:
Some of the readers of Brenda's notes will be believers in God. Others may need to be spiritually motivated. Whatever the case, I've provided you all tonight with certain verses I've selected from the Bible that may help you. Realize that God doesn't want you to be weary, but to put your trust in Him.

[Reverend Whitcomb passes his handout to the Alpha Team members and begins reading the verses below to everyone.]

Luke 12:25
And which of you by being anxious can add a single hour to his span of life?

Proverbs 12:25
Anxiety in a man's heart weighs him down, but a good word makes him glad.

Matthew 6:25-27
Therefore I tell you, do not be anxious about your life, what you will

eat or what you will drink, nor about your body, what you will put on. Is not life more than food, and the body more than clothing? Look at the birds of the air: they neither sow nor reap nor gather into barns, and yet your Heavenly Father feeds them. Are you not of more value than they?

Philippians 4:6-8
Be anxious for nothing, but in everything by prayer and supplication with thanksgiving let your requests be made known to God. And the peace of God, which surpasses all comprehension, shall guard your hearts and your minds in Christ Jesus. Finally, brethren, whatever is true, whatever is right, whatever is pure, whatever is lovely, whatever is of good repute, if there is any excellence and if anything worthy of praise, let your mind dwell on these things.

Matthew 6:31-34
Do not be anxious then, saying, 'What shall we eat?' or 'What shall we drink?' or 'With what shall we clothe ourselves?' For all these things the Gentiles eagerly seek; for your Heavenly Father knows that you need all these things. But seek first His kingdom and His righteousness; and all these things shall be added to you. Therefore do not be anxious for tomorrow; for tomorrow will care for itself. Each day has enough trouble of its own.

1 Peter 5:6-8
Humble yourselves, therefore, under God's mighty hand, that He may lift you up in due time. Cast all your anxiety on Him because He cares for you. Be self-controlled and alert. Your enemy the devil prowls around like a roaring lion looking for someone to devour.

These selected verses are special and may help you to renew your faith. No matter who you are or what you believe in—we all need faith. If nothing else, you need to have faith in yourself. Without faith, you are living a shallow life.

If you believe in God—that's good. If you're not sure—on the fence so to speak, just remember: He makes all things possible.

The Bible verses about anxiety should help you to cope with your worries. I've talked to hundreds of soldiers and civilians, over many years, who have felt that nothing is quite settled. Worry takes over their mind and they become obsessed with these anxious matters. Sometimes you may find yourself worrying about the wrong things to a point where it takes over your life. This can lead to panic attacks. If you've had panic attacks, give the Bible verses a chance. Otherwise, your soul can be poisoned by constant worries that lead to a disease, named depression—anxiety. It can ruin your life and we don't want that to happen to you.

That's why the fireside thoughts all of us are offering you to consider, could change your life. Hopefully the verses will ***inspire you.*** That's the best I can offer.

Lars:

For those of you who are atheists or you're on the fence about believing in God, hopefully our *thoughts* will help you. Those who are spiritually motivated will appreciate the reverend's Bible verses. I know that I do and so does Doris.

Next time we'll cover DEPRESSION. I'll give you an example of my own experience that drove me into deep depression and is the causative factor of my PTSD.

Doris:

I've got a good one too that I can share with you. It's heart wrenching.

Tiger:

Next time, bro's and sisters. But for now—let's all snare one of Doris's famous brownies!

Rev:

Amen.

***

In the kitchen, Brenda commented that greed wasn't covered during the discussion tonight. She feels that it is at the heart of most of the problems in the world. Tiger agreed saying that when people don't get what they want, they get anxious…sometimes leading to an unnecessary anxiety attack. Many of them are spoiled and complacent. They haven't had to sacrifice. They don't know what sacrifice means. When you are away, fighting for your country, separated from your family for a year…you understand sacrifice. Tiger said he heard that only 1% of the general public know about how the military operates. When people are shooting at you, and you are shooting back…that's the real thing.

Lars added that greed is one of the 7 deadly sins: lust, envy, sloth, wrath, gluttony, and pride being the others. We all need to back away from any of these sins.

Doris picked up on Brenda's broader approach, by stating that it takes only 3 weeks for a member of Congress to make what the average American makes in one year. Doris stressed that if you have a greedy, self-serving Congress, then the country mirrors them. It looks as if many of them are guilty of most of the seven deadly sins, leaving the rest of us to feel anxious. It's sad and sickening.

The reverend closed by saying that he enjoys the brief informal sessions before and after the main fireside talk topic discussion each evening.

As they departed, Tiger stuffed a whole brownie in his mouth and placed two in a napkin. Of course, one is for Beatrice.

Albert Ellis
(1913 – 2007)

American psychologist who, in 1955,
developed Rational Emotive Behavior Therapy.

"You largely constructed your depression. It wasn't given to you. Therefore, you can deconstruct it."

- Albert Ellis

Fireside Talk #5
Depression: The Soul's Call for Reinforcements

Everyone was sitting at the kitchen table sipping Doris's honeyed cocoa...cocoa with honey and a pinch of kosher salt. Reverend Whitcomb knew that Lars had visited his Wounded Warrior (WW) last Monday, so he asked Lars to explain the Wounded Warrior Mentor Program.

Lars discussed the set-up at the Walter Reed National Military Medical Center at Bethesda, Maryland. He explained that his assigned WW, Sergeant Frank Buckingham, his wife and two children, live in an apartment in Building 62, which hosts several suites for the WWs. The apartment includes two bedrooms, a kitchenette, washer and dryer, and lounge room. It is home to multiple amputees and long term recovering patients. Some have had as many as 50 surgeries.

Lars told the team that many WWs have a wide range of psychological and emotional difficulties. Some have trouble sleeping, feel withdrawn and irritable. Thus, many suffer from depression—the

53

topic for tonight's fireside talk. Frank lost both legs and is blind in one eye, yet feels that he does not have PTSD.

"As mentors in the WWMP, we help the WW's transition to a new life. Mentors are 100% volunteers, not paid, and the WWMP does not solicit funds. It is different from the Wounded Warrior Project, which provides programs, services and events for the WWs. The WWP requests donations, however, the WWMP is a non-profit organization, under Section 501(c) (3) of the Internal Revenue Code.

As mentors, we meet with our assigned WW usually each month, coupled with telephone calls and email correspondence. I'm sort of a sounding board for Frank and his wife, providing guidance during his recovery and rehabilitation. Like a personal advisor.

Mentors help to insure that their WW understands benefits, educational and job opportunities, and is aware of available internships. We make sure that our WW applies for things due to him or her, such as Social Security Disability and Tuition Assistance Programs.

I make sure that Frank takes the VA Aptitude Test and takes advantage of the VA Vocational/Rehabilitation and Employment Program. Also, the G.I. Bill and insurance.

There are too many things to cover here, but as Frank's coach, I try to make sure that Buckingham, his wife, and both children are taken care of."

Lars went on to tell the team that there are many persons and contacts for coordination, covering all the issues of concern to the WWs.

"As mentors, we even have a Nurse Case Manager to advise us as needed. We try to be good listeners and ascertain what is important to the WW. Usually a close bond develops based on mutual trust."

Lars also said that he and Tiger, also a mentor, immediately bond with their WW because of both having purple hearts.

Tiger chipped in, saying that his WW, SP4 Tommy Crawford, lost his right leg above the knee and had some internal injuries. He's had 26 surgeries. Tommy was injured in Sangin, Afghanistan. Tiger mentioned that he likes to meet Tommy in the Warrior Café, Building 62, which has a grill, salad bar, sandwiches, drinks...a nice meeting place. Tiger found out, over lunch with Crawford, that he likes fly-fishing. Tiger got him into a program called Healing Waters. A shuttle bus takes WWs to Rose River Farms in Virginia for weekends…to fly fish. It's Tommy's main love of life.

When Tiger determined that Tommy liked the outdoors, wilderness, and nature, he suggested that Tommy try a Sweat Lodge since Tommy felt that his livelihood was being strangled. Crawford was struggling early on, being only 19 years old and Tiger realized that the Native American approach might help Tommy transform himself from combat to non-combat.

Part of Tommy was still in combat. Tiger went with Tommy to the Sweat Lodge. He told everyone in Doris's kitchen that it helped to purify Tommy's spirit. It minimized his stress and pain; it was sort of a cleansing, which is far better than using drugs or psychiatric care.

Tiger told everybody that the first WW he had, a few years back, transitioned to his new life as a result of going to the Boulder Crest Retreat in Bluemont, Virginia. A touch of nature can do wonders.

Lars jumped in to say that depression is a key topic for tonight because some WWs get depressed, feeling that they can't get hired— that the person *doing* the hiring may feel that the WW may 'break' somewhere along the way. That assumes that the WW has a form of PTSD but in reality, not *all* WWs have it.

Thus, the WW feels that those hiring probably feel that WWs really can't do anything.

Sometimes the WWs go to KFC, McDonald's, or Cracker Barrel with their family and someone always pays for their meal. This is good, but often the WWs feel as though they are like a charity case.

Lars added, "Just to end this, Reverend, since you wanted the program explained, we have follow-on mentors throughout the country. When a WW leaves the medical center here, a mentor is assigned wherever the WW goes. Now, let's get on with tonight's topic: depression."

***

Doris:

Nathan is going to explain how to pronounce New Orleans, then we can begin tonight's fireside talk.

DR. CHARLES N. TOFTOY

Tiger:

Hey! It's N'awlins, my dear. N'awlins—my hometown with Seafood Creole, File Gumbo, Crawfish Etouffee, Creole Red Beans and Rice.

Brenda:

Maybe the entire Alpha Team should go there together!

Tiger:

Man! I'd bring you guys everywhere, but especially Preservation Hall to hear the jazz band...on St. Peter Street. The hall building dates back to the War of 1812.

Lars:

I'm going to relate something that I've never shared with anyone. It was the battle of Dong Xoai, or ten days of horror. Trauma occurred hour after hour, but I'm only going to give you three occurrences that later kept haunting my soul—deep depression.

As a battalion advisor to a Vietnamese paratrooper battalion, we were flown in by helicopter to save a US Special Forces camp and to find two missing regular Vietnamese (ARVN) battalions. After storming the camp, I bent over the body of a US Special Forces trooper, blackened from a Viet Cong flamethrower. His dog tags disintegrated in my hand—ashes.

We moved north towards the Than Loi rubber plantation and found the remnants of the ARVN battalions. Bodies stacked neatly on a road. We evacuated them by helicopter. As I carried a body to the helicopter, it blew up on me because of being bloated. A discouraging task for us.

Later, we got caught in an ambush by 2,000 Viet Cong— surrounded. We were targets like on a firing range at Ft. Benning, sometimes called a mad-minute. We could only retreat. There was only one way out—over a fence. About 75 of us made it out of 350. Over 500 were killed within one hour—total of both sides. As we were retreating, I could hear single shots ringing out, meaning they were shooting our wounded troops in the head as a coup de grâce. A helicopter picked us up. I thought we would be dropped at Dong Xoai so I could organize a counter-attack, but instead we were taken somewhere else.

This last event, I just described, haunts me to this day. Hearing those single shots and not being able to do anything—I lost a few hundred friends during the Vietnam War; 50 were lost during that 10-day battle at Dong Xoai.

I think depression is like a living wound. The wound becomes worse over time if not attended. My treatment was self-imposed blocking, so I block out those days of the largest battle in the history of the Vietnam War. My reason for providing this story is to help you learn how to block. You may have been faced with trying to save someone from a fire, drowning, auto accident, or other traumatic event and it keeps sticking with you—like mine. Blocking can save you from certain misery. It helps you to move on.

[Everyone is in tears, to include Tiger and the reverend.]

Brenda:
Let's take a short break.

[The team uses breaks to catch up with each other and get their minds off the evening's main topic for a few minutes.

Brenda talked about her co-worker, Mark, at *The Washington Post*, who switched from smoking traditional cigarettes to electronic cigarettes. Mark told her he feels much better since the e-cigarettes avoid the tars and gases of regular cigarettes. The battery-powered cigarettes deliver nicotine through water vapor rather than tobacco. Brenda told the team that it is a $1.5B business. And that the US smoking rate has declined from 42.4% in 1965 to 18.1% in 2012. It may cause some smokers to gradually quit. None of the Alpha Team members smoke.

Upon their return, Doris sips her hot chocolate with toasted marshmallows and continues the session on depression.]

Doris:
I'll make my story short too, Lars. In a nutshell, I was sexually assaulted by our Catholic Priest when I was 14. After that traumatic

incident, I refused to go to church. Later, I told my father. The priest was quietly moved to another church.

Depression #2 was when my husband died on 9/11 in the World Trade Tower. I gave up on myself. Began drinking. Met Lars, by coincidence, at Sunrise Assisted Living at Bluemont. My father was in the Alzheimer's ward and Lars' uncle was there, too. Lars supported me at AA and so I am completely healed. And now I'm an Episcopalian—all thanks to Lars. I've mentioned this previously to you all.

Brenda:
Not only did you become an Episcopalian, but his wife too, Sister!

Doris:
Yup! That too.

Brenda:
My main depression stemmed from coming home one day to my apartment and seeing my roommate hanging from the alcove. Huge trauma. I joined a group and it was clear that a death brings forth a normal process of depression. So it wasn't me; it was normal. Lars and Doris's depression was normal, too. We just have to beat it—like the three of us have done. We have to heal that living wound. **YOU** have to unclutter your thoughts. One saying that I taped to my refrigerator was written by Corrie ten Boom, *'Worry does not empty tomorrow of its sorrow. It empties today of its strength.'*

Rev:
I know about Corrie ten Boom. Born in Amsterdam, Netherlands, she and her family were strong Christians. They hid out Jews who were being hunted by the Gestapo. She and the other local social workers saved over 800 Jews. I've used one of her sayings in some of my sermons. *'If you look at the world, you'll be distressed. If you look within, you'll be distressed. If you look at God, you'll be at rest.'* It's one of my favorite quotes, Brenda.

[Everyone says Amen. Lars and Doris cross themselves. Most

were thinking about the unfair treatment to Jews during World War II.]

Doris:

Think about it! I gave up a top job with the FBI. I was in a fog. Isolated. But later, I began to read novels, joined a local book club. Boy! That helped a lot. **YOU** can do the same thing. Like join an art club, take a cruise, go on an African safari, join a study group— whatever you like. It breaks you out of the rut. I took it one day at a time. By talking to someone about your depression, you gain relief from the stress that's built up if you hold it inside too long. It's called venting, not whining.

Brenda:

I read about diet and made sure I took Omega-3, per most doctors' advice. All that information is available. My key points to **YOU** are to exercise. And get a pet. I have a Border Collie and an African Gray Parrot—both are my saviors. Doris is right; take one day at a time and reward yourself.

Tiger:

Like Doc, I went through a lot of trauma in Vietnam. One time, I heard that a helicopter hit a telephone line and crashed in a lake near Fort Bragg. I raced my jeep to the scene, swam out to the chopper and dove down to free the two pilots who were trapped inside the cockpit. The fuel churned up, burning me all over. Made several diving attempts, but I couldn't get inside—the broken glass cut my hands and arms. I saw them inside. That haunted me for a long time.

My friends came to my aid later. So try your friends, even though you may feel ashamed or guilty. Doris and Brenda have good ideas for you if you're depressed.

Another way I came out of depression was through cooking… *N'awlins* style. Making up recipes, stealing ideas from others and concocting modified recipes like Crock-pot Jambalaya, Shrimp and Andouille Sausage Gumbo, Shrimp Ragout, Chicken Fricassee, Artichoke Oyster Soup, Baked Red Snapper. Hey! I could go on, but you get the point. Try something you like or even something new. Depression needs to take a back seat to you in the driver's seat—

otherwise, it can take control.

Doris:

Not to go into a TV series but on *Downtown Abbey*, my favorite, good advice was given to Mary by Mr. Carson, the head butler. She was suffering from deep depression, having lost her husband in an auto accident. She was miserable for six months. Then Mr. Carson said something to her like '*You've been living the life of the living dead; now you need to join the living.*' It took Carson with that intriguing thought to awaken Mary. Remember: a damaged heart *can* be mended.

Rev:

Like Helen Keller said, '*The world is full of suffering; it is also full of overcoming it.*' I'm not going to get on the God kick here. My living depression is after I've been with troops in Iraq and Afghanistan when they are minutes away from death. Looking at that 20-year-old when he's only got 2 or 3 minutes left in this world—it's tough. It's like a black cloud hanging over me as a Chaplain, yet I know that I must push through and clear up that fog, and turn it into a rainbow. Struggles are meant to be in this earthly life, but each struggle we overcome builds our character and makes us stronger.

Albert Ellis said, '*you can deconstruct your depression*'. I believe it. Dr. Ellis was a psychologist who developed REBT or Rational Emotive Behavior Therapy. He is rated as the second most influential psychotherapist in US and Canadian history…Carl Rogers is first and Sigmund Freud is rated third.

Lars:

You may not know it, Rev, but I'm our Aristotle, Plato, and Socrates guy; Brenda is the Buddha and Confucius guru, and Doris has studied Darwin. From time to time, we may pop in a quote or saying that relates to our fireside talk topic for that particular evening. Aristotle said, '*Suffering becomes beautiful when anyone bears great calamities with cheerfulness, not through insensibility but through greatness of mind.*' Aristotle was the first genuine scientist in history and is the most influential person who ever lived. He was a pupil of Plato and taught Alexander the Great. Aristotle died in 322 BC, in

AMAZING FIRESIDE TALKS

Euboea, Greece.

Next time is a tough one. It's on RESCUE YOURSELF. Before we leave the important subject of depression, I want to give you all a copy of Lao Tzu's saying. He was a philosopher and poet of ancient China, during the Zhou Dynasty. He founded Taoism.

> *'If you are depressed, you are living in the past.*
> *If you are anxious, you are living in the future.*
> *If you are at peace, you are living in the present.'*

Doris:

If we help just one person, and hopefully that person is **YOU**, the fireside talks will be a success.

Rev:

I'm looking forward to next time. Wow! Rescue Yourself. Maybe I'll get some ideas for a sermon.

[Everyone chuckles.]

***

Even though the discussions are over, Lars piles on two more logs. Most of the team like to hang around for a while after the fireside talk to chat and enjoy refreshments. The team has a solid bond.

Doris invites everyone into her kitchen. Sitting around the long worktable, she gives them a mango tart. She told them that she got the recipe from a pastry shop in Paris called, *La Pâtisserie des Rêves,* the pastry shop of dreams.

The team members depart in a happy mood, even though the discussion topic tonight was a tough one.

Alice Sebold
(born September 6, 1963)

An American writer. She has published three books:

Lucky (1999)
The Lovely Bones (2002)
The Almost Moon (2007)

"You save yourself or you remain unsaved."

- Alice Sebold

Fireside Talk #6
Rescue Yourself

As Lars was loading more logs on the fire, he thought of how proud he was of the Alpha Team. All of them are so 'up' all of the time. As their leader and founder, he feels very special about these elite team members. Lars is responsible for getting the fire roaring before the fireside talk session begins. He chops his own wood and has it stacked neatly in the backyard. Sometimes a team member will get up and stand near the fireplace. The arrangement for the fireside talk sessions was excellent. The sofas form a U with the open end being the massive fireplace. It was large enough to hold all four Alpha Team members.

According to the Farmers' Almanac, it was to be a long cold winter in the Washington, D.C. Metro area. It lived up to that and more. Since it was late November, it was getting cold already. Team members will be wearing winter clothes for about four months, then spring wear. But the fireplace will still be at the center of it all…drawing out amazing thoughts from the team. He felt that the discussion tonight will be incredible on rescuing yourself or *helping* yourself.

***

Tiger:

To be frank, you have to get yourself straight before you can help others; so **RESCUE YOURSELF**. Like a friend of mine asked me that wanted to be a great father—his wife was due soon. I said that he needed to get himself on track before he could launch into being a great father. My remark stunned him, but later he said it was the best advice he ever heard.

Doris:

That reminds me of the White Knight syndrome.

Tiger:

What dat?

[Brenda rolls her eyes. Doris snickers because here goes Tiger again, putting on the New Orleans talk.]

Doris:

The White Knights are usually men who are attracted to helping women, mostly damaged people who are thought to be beyond help. Often they are men surfacing the internet, who are single and lonely. Please, if this shoe fits... please get out of it. It is not healthy for you because they will bring you down with them as you roll along, ignoring your well-being. A lot of times I learned in my study of this topic, the guy oftentimes contradicts himself and takes the woman's side because he thinks he might have a better chance with her.

I'm not talking about a chivalrous act where you save an elderly woman from being kicked into the street. I think you know what I mean, so I suggest that you shed the White Knight armor, if it applies to you or someone you know.

Lars:

Others are faced with circumstances worse than your situation.

Many of them are stepping up to the plate and swinging hard. Think of the 26-year-old soldier who was the first service member to survive the loss of four limbs. He received a double arm transplant at John Hopkins Hospital.

Brenda:

I covered that story for *The Washington Post*. I remember what he said two days before the multi-hour complex surgery: '*Holy Mother of God, I was just told I might be having my transplant tomorrow.*'

Later he said, '*Wow, what a day. I'll be going to Baltimore tomorrow morning for pre-op and having my transplant Tuesday!*'

Now, Lars—you talk about rescuing yourself. That's got to be a good example of what it means. And what an attitude. I remember that he lost both legs above the knee, his left arm below the elbow and his right arm above the elbow. It's like Helen Keller said—*overcoming suffering*.

Lars:

And per Aristotle, doing so with cheerfulness. I often refer to Aristotle's teachings in my classes at the George Washington University.

Tiger:

Man. That's hard to do cheerfully. But **YOU** should try to do it.

Brenda:

And just think—his main goal is to get his fingers moving, then one of his arms. He was provided with prosthetic arms, including new hands and fingers. I'm sure whatever struggle you're facing that you can overcome it with willpower. It's up to you.

Tiger:

You're right, Brenda. We are all our own 9-1-1. Instead of dialing 9-1-1 because we're facing a tough life situation, we should call on our own *personal* 9-1-1. Slip into a self-preservation mode or a survivor mode.

Doris:

To *save* yourself, just try to *be* yourself. Don't try to be someone else. I think Nathan's idea about our 'inside 9-1-1' is an intriguing thought. We can't keep expecting others to pull us up. Here's sort of a Darwin thought for you, but it's really mine.

Think about this—it's outside the box...pretty far out, but true when you think about it. It deals with the moment we are born. When you enter this world and take your first breath, you don't know who or where you are. You could be born of royalty or in a slum; you could be white or black; from the West or East; Irish or Scandinavian; male or female, and so on. We don't know. Be honest; think about it...you really don't know. But lo' and behold here you are. **YOU.**

The bottom line is that you had no control over your birth. You are you. Therefore, you need to appreciate yourself more...and others, too. Be respectful and respect others. *Everyone* is their own individual.

My point is that we should not be belittling one another or fighting and killing each other. In the grand scheme of things, that is absolutely ridiculous. Just remember Newton's laws of motion: *For every action there is an equal and opposite reaction.* Thus, we should be aware of the consequences of our actions before taking action. This is one of my biggest points in trying to be helpful.

Brenda:

Great point. I've never heard it expressed that way before. So true. Since I've studied the Middle East, let me blow this up on a global scale. Again, as you said...we should not be fighting amongst ourselves.

Maybe this is a poor example, but consider the Sunnis versus the Shiites. Mohammed founded the Islam religion in the 7th century. There are two branches with different beliefs about Mohammed's successors. Shi believe Mahdi, the rightly guided one, has already been here. Sunnis believe he has yet to emerge. There is more to it than this, but these two branches fight repeatedly.

We shouldn't want to kill each other because of different beliefs or what you think is right or wrong. Murder cannot be justified because people don't believe in what you believe. You don't have to agree with how anyone else thinks or feels is the correct way, but I feel that you should respect that everyone has the right to their own beliefs. To receive this kind of respect ourselves, we need to also extend that respect to others. They have as much right to their belief as you do. If everyone lived this way, we wouldn't have senseless squabbles or in a global sense, we wouldn't have fruitless wars.

Tiger:

I think those people with different beliefs have diminutive mentalities. A sane person would not kill for a belief that can't be proven in this life. What is right for one may not be right for another. ***Killing other human beings is never right, for any reason.*** Two wrongs don't make a right. Killing someone is not going to fix any situation...it's only going to add to the problems in the particular situation.

Anyhow, there should always be room for compromise.

Rev:

Amen, Tiger.

Lars:

Unfortunately, Tiger...most of those doing the killing are radical extremists.

Doris:

Also, I don't like the way they treat their women...it's so archaic. After all, some of these extremist men could have been born as women. That's how I started this simple dialog. Which leads to the main point: everyone needs to practice humility, even the radical extremists; then they would understand that what they are doing is wrong.

Humility is like a shining light, which radiates dignity. I feel sorry for them. They are so far off base in what they are doing. It's a joy to be humble. There's no joy in killing because someone doesn't believe the way you do.

My Darwin guy's key thought is that you should appreciate that you are who you are and make the best of it. Just remember the grateful paraplegic soldier who feels that life is a gift. My last thought for you is just remember that you are worth more than you think. Always.

Tiger:

I jotted down a witty statement made by Oscar Wilde: *'Be yourself, everyone else is already taken.'*

Being the Alpha Team comedian, I thought I'd toss that one in. I gar-ron-tee you—Wilde was sharp. He was an Irish writer and poet in the 1890's and London's most popular playwright. He wrote *The Picture of Dorian Gray* and *Salome* in French.

Rev:

If you are damaged, you have to repair yourself from the inside out. That's my idea on rescuing yourself. William Shakespeare wrote, *'God has given you one face, and you make yourself another.'* Like Doris said, don't try to be something you aren't or try to be someone else. Be yourself. Only **YOU** can change your life. **YOU** can only be **YOU**.

And this is just one of my things—that if you don't like who you are, then decide what you should change about yourself. To be who you want to be. But you have to be you, no one else. Now, you can try to be like someone you admire, but again—you can only be yourself.

Some people are complainers. You know who I mean. Some are fixers. Complainers like to voice their complaint about what's wrong, but have no intention of doing anything about it. Fixers are people who see a problem and do what it takes to fix it instead of wasting time complaining about it time and time again. A total waste of energy.

I suggest that if you don't like something—fix it—but please, stop grumbling about it. That won't fix it. It takes positive action to fix something that is wrong. So are you a complainer or a fixer? Time to look in the mirror and be honest with yourself. By the way, I hope you like who you are. *I bet you're a better person than you think.*

Most of you studied Shakespeare but as a reminder, he is considered the greatest writer in the English language. He was called England's 'National Poet' and labeled as the 'Bard of Avon'. He wrote over 38 plays, including *Hamlet, King Lear*, and *Othello*.

AMAZING FIRESIDE TALKS

Tiger:

Let me read a quote from Marcus Aurelius: *'Very little is needed to make a happy life: it is all within yourself, in your way of thinking.'* This backs up my idea of your inside 9-1-1. It's there—you just have to call on it. Aurelius was a Roman Emperor from 161 to 180 AD. One of the best stoic philosophers of all time.

Rev:

Let me tell you what will really help. Just take 10-15 minutes each day to meditate or to just to relax and listen to your inner-self. Many troops have done this, coupled with ridding themselves of toxic friends. A complete turnaround—they rescued themselves. You can do it, too. I was just the catalyst who led them to realize that they had the courage to make a positive change. I told each one of them that I was betting on them. I won 80% of my bets. If you don't change, then nothing else will change. The best rescue is self-help. Don't wait for a rescuer or winning the lottery. These are cop-outs. It takes **YOU** to do it.

Lars:

I've got a good follow-up to Reverend Whitcomb's thoughts. I guess that I haven't realized that something that I do is actually a rescue of myself in real-time. I have a list of 10 activities that I want to share with Wounded Warriors. Here's my list: Washington Nationals baseball game, Kennedy Center event, fishing in the Chesapeake Bay, help in physical fitness, picnic along the Potomac River, visit monuments in DC, restaurants, aquarium in Baltimore, movie theater, and have them play with my two Yorkshire Terriers at home. I keep this list updated and check off each time an activity is completed. You can do the same thing. Make up a list of things you want to do…and do them over a certain period of time. We all need something to look forward to whether we are physically able or in a wheelchair.

Doris:

I agree; to rescue yourself, you have to be able to change. In my studies of Darwin's theory, he said, *'It is not the strongest of the species that lives, nor the most intelligent that survives, it is the one that is the most adaptable to change.'*

Brenda:
Rid yourself of denial, frustration, depression, impatience, anxiety. Get rid of your baggage. Don't keep carrying it around. Rescue fantasies. My friend, Ed, wanted to bump into Anderson Cooper in a men's room. Just to chat with him. And be asked to be on his 360° show. Fame and fortune. But my friend dropped that rescue fantasy because he needed to get on with real life. A re-focusing was in order for him.

You need to change. Forget the lottery, someone giving you a great job or a new car. Drop the fantasies. They're a waste of energy.

Lars:
You need to look at things right now—at this moment. And make changes. You have to rescue yourself because it takes **YOU** to get out of a negative situation. **YOU CAN DO IT.**

Tiger:
Don't let yourself fall into a common trap: that an opportunity will come 'out of the blue' and save you. My mother died at 36, I was 14. I finally realized that my subconscious really undermined me. It helped me back until I realized that I needed to move forward.

Doris:
Some people are obsessed in that they ride a white horse going from one person to another that needs rescuing. In the end, the White Knight becomes unhappy. That's the bottom line. Sometimes the rescuers need to be rescued because they become more unhappy than the person in need of rescue—who is in financial distress, or has other issues such as: substance abuse, abusive relationships, medical conditions, or a terrible past. As we've said here, that person has to work at it, so divorce yourself from an obsession to rescue other people.

Brenda:
'When the Reader's Digest crew shows up at my door with a big

check, then I'll be able to...' Bunk. Forget this and throw the sweepstakes stuff in the garbage. Your chance of winning is more than one to six million. By playing with lotteries, you are kidding yourself and wasting precious time. When you realize that you must discover yourself, all of a sudden you look at life differently. It causes a ray of enthusiasm and hope for you. A regeneration of yourself. It works, so I suggest you try it.

Otherwise, you are just playing games with yourself. Again, a waste of energy. As Sun Tzu said, *'You have to believe in yourself.'* Do you know that even today, some military leaders use Tzu's strategic lessons. As a Chinese military general, he wrote *The Art of War*. He died in 496 BC.

Rev:

My humble advice is don't try to be someone else. Be yourself. You have to work hard to be yourself. Follow your instincts. Another quote by Shaki Gawain: *'Every time you don't follow your inner guidance, you feed a loss of energy, loss of power, a sense of spiritual deoclues.'* This has happened to me several times in guiding troopers. I failed when I strayed from my gut instinct. So I don't do it anymore. I go with my inner guidance and common sense. Perhaps this will work for you. I hope so.

By the way, Gawain is a *New Age* author. Her books on 'personal development' have sold over 10M copies. Best-known book is *Creative Visualization: Use Power of Your Imagination to Create What You Want*.

Brenda:

Hey. I have a quote, too. Did my research, Tiger!

[Tiger blows her a kiss.]

'When one is pretending the entire body revolts' is a fabulous statement by Anais Nin. When you are faking, it tears up your insides. Anais Nin was born in Spain. She wrote short stories and essays. Best known as a diarist.

Lars:

That reminds me of what cadets are endeared with at West Point. It's part of the Cadet Prayer: *'Make us to choose the harder right instead of the easier wrong, and never to be content with a half-truth when the whole can be won.'* I live by that code.

Tiger:

Yeah! Doc also lives by: *'Duty, Honor, Country.'* Right, Doc?

Lars:

Yup.

Brenda:

The Buddhists believe that you use adversity as a path to cultivating a better situation. But we are impatient and want the change to occur right now. My best thought for you on rescuing yourself is to not worry about what people think of you. It's wasteful energy. Like Gawain, *the New Age author* said, *'follow your inner guidance.'*

Lars:

We will discuss patience later on. A huge issue to come to grips with. Since Tiger is making a beeline for the kitchen, I'll just say that next time will be a challenge: INITIATION, ORDEAL, REINTEGRATION.

***

In the kitchen, Tiger is the first one to tackle Doris's famous chocolate mousse. Reverend Whitcomb brings up a good point in regards to rescuing yourself. What about rescuing others? The Nigerian girls? We just can't let Boko Haram get away with kidnapping 276 girls with threats to sell them into slavery.

Since Brenda wrote a front-page article for *The Washington Post* on the international tragedy, all agreed to listen to her commentary.

Brenda's main point is that it will take the Nigerian people to save their girls. She mentioned that Boko Haram has killed thousands of people in the past. They have attacked schools, churches, police stations, newspaper offices and others. They've attacked schools with male students and murdered them.

The Nigerian government is ineffective. They know where Boko Haram operates, but the Nigerian army and security agencies have severe flaws and lack resources. Brenda told the team that the Muslim countries should take the lead.

Tiger adds his two bits by saying that the Nigerians should rise up and overwhelm Boko Haram and rescue their girls. Tiger stated that the Italians rose up and slaughtered Mussolini…hanging him upside down in a public square. But the Germans did nothing about Hitler. And the Iraqis did nothing about Sadam Hussein.

Lars said that this brief session is a beneficial add-on to our earlier discussion tonight.

They finished up the chocolate mousse with Tiger licking his plate. Brenda rolled her eyes. Before departing, everybody high-5s each other—the Alpha Team tradition at departure time.

Alexander Graham Bell
(1847 – 1922)

Eminent scientist, inventor, engineer and innovator
who is credited with inventing the first practical telephone.

*"When one door closes, another opens;
but we often look so long and so regretfully
upon the closed door that we do not see
the one that has opened for us."*

- Alexander Graham Bell

Fireside Talk #7
Initiation, Ordeal, Reintegration

Prior to the first meeting of the fireside talks, the Alpha Team underwent a four-hour brainstorming session. They agreed to all of the topics. The discussion topic for tonight was Lars's idea. He was worried that nobody would fully understand the topic: Initiation, Ordeal, Reintegration. To Lars, we are all faced from time to time with these three interwoven aspects of life. We are placed in a certain situation, go through the challenges or struggles it places upon us, then we return to our regular routine.

Examples are: the Boy Scouts, Girl Scouts, youth camp, fraternity, sorority, military boot camp, rehab center, or other similar organizations. Lars was pacing, thinking in front of the fireplace, waiting for everyone to arrive and be seated so he could begin.

***

Lars:

A good topic for me to present. I have a real-life example to explain our topic. Let me start with West Point. Cadet Basic Training begins near the end of June and ends in mid-August. It's called Beast Barracks. Real hell. It's a culture shock, full of anxious moments.

The first day I was yelled at and that night I asked myself, *'What am I doing here?'* But you're so tired each night that time passes and before you know it—you're hooked. You have to ask for permission to talk and meals are about 5 minutes. Start at 5:30am, poop out at midnight.

In the meantime, firsties (seniors) and upperclassmen are asking you to recite all kinds of stuff.

Examples are:

'Mr. Neilsen, how is the cow?'

'Sir, she walks, she talks, she's full of chalk, the lacteal fluid extracted from the female of the bovine species is highly prolific to the nth degree.'

[Lars explains: the nth degree means the highest degree or infinity...a West Point slang word.]

'Dumbsmack Neilsen, how are they all?'

'They are all fickle but one, Sir.'

'How many names on Battle Monument, Mister?'

'2,230 names, Sir.'

Anyhow, the hazing goes on and on:

'How many lights on Cullum Hall? How many gallons in Lusk Reservoir? What is the definition of leather? What do Plebes rank? All right for the lights? Portland cement? What time is it? MacArthur's message. Scott's fixed opinion. The days. Principles of war.'

You have to know these by memory to the exact wording.

Perfection. If not, they really crawl all over you. *'Get that chin in, Mister. Squeeze it back.'*

If you've really screwed up, you get up on the alcove rail and swim to Newburg (a figure of speech) until your arms, flaying in the air, give out. That covers initiation and some of the ordeal. Part of the ordeal is the academic rigors. We were graded in every class—everyday. Lots of competitions since most of the guys are the smartest in the country. Parades (perfection in marching), physical fitness high standards, and the everyday pressures from all fronts added to the ordeal or struggle.

As far as reintegration, we could look at it as a reintegration back into society...the real world. The cadet's journey has been one of isolation. Stuck in a fortress built on the side of a mountain overlooking the Hudson River. I don't mean this in a condescending way because West Point is the most beautiful campus in the country. Beautiful setting. But having graduated now, you are faced with commanding a rifle platoon of 39 men/women. A rude awakening, though cadets get field training and study tactics, strategy, and leadership. So that is my example of the three phases.

Tiger:

I can pick up from there, again using the Army. Basic combat training is the initiation. Drill sergeants are on top of you 24/7. Rules, regulations, uniforms, haircuts, and foot marches. You are faced with all kinds of challenges: extended foot marches, marksmanship, rappelling, weapons training, obstacle courses, night infiltration course, and physical fitness tests. Welcome to the Army.

After 10 weeks, you are sent to your first military unit. Even if you stay for the minimum period or make it a career, like Doc and I, you'll go through a lot of struggles. If you go to war then the ordeal is far greater. Most of this ordeal experience changes the soldier for life. Reintegrating yourself back into civilian life can be tough.

You really want to be your old self as before. But you can't...too much has happened, so just admit that to yourself.

Take the 'Wounded Warriors' that Doc and I mentor. After having several deployments, the transition back to home life is tough. My tip is to be patient and spend time talking to your spouse, parents, friends, children.

I'm no counselor, but Doc tries to get these guys suffering from PTSD into some educational program. Right, Doc?

Lars:

Yup. And as mentioned before, patience will be the topic later on. That is a key point in making the transition, Tiger. Patience.

Doris:

This topic is key because it pertains to everyone—not just the military. All of us have been faced with an initiation to something, gone through a struggle, then had to regroup.

When my husband died in the World Trade Building, I gave up. Retired from the FBI, and started drinking and taking drugs. Lars saved me by getting me to AA. But that was after I went through detox for about a week, followed by rehab—about 20 days. Now I'm fine. But if you're faced with this problem, it takes you to fight it off. There are plenty of treatment programs available. It's a saving grace.

Rev:

I gave last Sunday's sermon on '*Rescue Yourself.*' I emphasized many of the points you all made last Thursday evening about how it's up to you—don't wait for a rescuer to save you. Don't waste energy. Lots of good feedback from my parishioners.

Tiger:

Yeah, Rev. We do the good and bad to ourselves, right?

Rev:

Yup! God isn't responsible for horrific acts like occurred at Blacksburg, Newtown, and Boston.

[Serious looks fall on the Alpha Team's faces.]

Doris:

So if we cross a street and get hit by a car—it's the human mistake of us or the driver. Right, Rev?

Rev:

Absolutely. God has nothing to do with it. It's not in His game plan. Most mass killings are done by people with deranged minds, right, Lars? You're the expert.

Lars:

Yup.

Brenda:

But so many people suffer as a result. One of the worst feelings in the world is that knock on the door or telephone that signals that a tragedy has occurred.

Tiger:

Yeah, stomach ties up in knots. Heart's in your throat.

Doris:

Now, I'll let you all in on something. It strays from our topic for this evening, but since you brought up Newtown, I can tell you that Brenda can recite all the names of those that died there. She has a photographic memory.

Go Brenda.

Brenda:

Well, okay: *Bacon, Barden, Davino, Engel, Gay, Hockley, Hochsprung, Hsu, Hubbard, Kowalski, Lanza, Lewis, Marquez-Greene, Mattioli, McDonnell, Murphey, Parker, Pinto, Pozner, Previdi, Rekos, Richman, Rousseau, Sherlach, Soto, Wheeler, Wyatt.*

[Everyone applauds.]

Rev:

And may they rest in peace. They are our heroes and will never be forgotten.

[Everyone wipes their eyes. Tiger bows his head.]

DR. CHARLES N. TOFTOY

Doris:

I can brag more about Brenda. She actually has a photographic memory. I've talked to her about it. She can recall visual information and sounds with extreme precision. Sometimes it's called eidetic memory. That's why she can finish an article at *The Post* in two hours that takes others two days. And that's why she was the top student at Springfield High School, plus a 4.0 GPA at the University of Maryland.

Brenda:

Enough already. Let's move on, Doc.

Lars:

Yup! Let's move on. But God bless all those who have died in these terrible tragedies.

[Everyone gets up, holds hands, and responds with an Amen.]

Tiger:

When you talk about initiation, ordeal, and reintegration, I've got a short answer. Initiation—I went to Vietnam. Ordeal—all the combat I went through. Reintegration—nothing. I came home to nothing after putting my life at stake multiple times. So…you wonder why I have PTSD!

Heavy duty, Bro—but I block it out and fight through it. What I'm learning in these fireside talks is that you've got to keep moving forward. Not backwards. The past is done. You've got to move on.

Doris:

Bravo, Nathan! Robert Anton Wilson wrote: '*Beyond a certain point, the whole universe becomes a continuous process of initiation.*'

Wilson was one of the most important scientific philosophers of this century. An author, novelist, and philosopher, he wrote: *Quantum Psychology*, and *Prometheus Rising,* amongst other books.

Brenda:

I can echo that because one of my best friend's uncles is an ex-prisoner. He went through all three stages. The toughest one is social reintegration. He had lost his livelihood, family, personal belongings and friendships. Actually, his friends caused him to go off the deep end.

He tried to make a reentry, but that put him back with the old gang, who are all screwed up. Finally, an intervention program saved him. If you are faced with this problem, search out an intervention program that supports your transition from prison to the community and accomplishes it through care, whereby interventions continue all along the journey until reintegration is successful.

Lars:

I have to piggyback you on that one, Brenda. I did a study for the University on trying to set up education classes at a women's prison. To make a long story short, I was talking to an older black inmate, who told me that the prison is a revolving door for these young women.

She pointed out women who had been in and out several times. They go back to the same place and people, and just pick up from where they left off. I agree with Doris; you need an intervention to avoid these pitfalls.

T.S. Eliot, one of our most famous poets of the 20th century wrote: *'What we call the beginning is often the end. And to make an end is to make a beginning. The end is where we start from.'*

He won the Nobel Prize for Literature. In 1915, he wrote: *The Love Song of J. Alfred Prufrock.* It was called a masterpiece of the *Modernist Movement.*

Rev:

It seems to me that in reintegration, people want to hide, deny or repress their feelings so a return to society is difficult.

Lars:

Good take-off point, Rev, for next week. We will discuss our DARK SHADOW that seems to follow us around, unless we can turn it into a golden shadow.

DR. CHARLES N. TOFTOY

Rev:

I know it's time to shut down, but let me put my Rev hat on for a few seconds. God forgives those who forgive themselves. You are your own worst judge because you are harder on yourself. God will forgive you if you forgive yourself for an error in judgment. Put that under your belt and move on. A lot of our personal problems are self-inflicted that can actually be prevented.

***

Everyone made the short journey to Doris's kitchen. Brenda spent several minutes doing her stretches prior to joining everybody around the kitchen work table. Everyone knows about Brenda's past in regards to physical fitness. A black belt in karate, set the National High School record for the 100 meter dash by running it in 11.55 seconds at Springfield High School, college scholarships at undergraduate and graduate levels for athletics, batted fourth for Springfield in softball—hitting 29 homeruns in her senior year and stealing 10 bases in one game.

Doris brought out her authentic French meringues, which just floored everyone. They're made with egg whites, confectioners' sugar, all-purpose flour, hazelnut powder, and cocoa powder. Tiger downed five before you could say Jack Robinson!

Brenda was very interested in the US Army Ranger School. Here was a chance to find out since Lars and Tiger are both rangers. When everyone was seated she asked Lars and Tiger about it.

In their ranger class, Lars was the honor graduate and Tiger was the enlisted honor graduate in his class. Lars said that 60% of all failures are in the first 4 days. Tiger mentioned that the overall graduation rate is 50.13%. Before candidates can enter the School there are a lot of qualifying tests including: 49 push-ups in 2 minutes, 59 sit-ups in 2 minutes, timed 2 and 5-mile runs and other tests. Brenda said that she can do more than 49 push-ups in 1 minute.

[Doris and the Rev clapped their hands vigorously.]

Lars added that the Ranger training is the toughest training course in the Army. It is strictly a combat leadership course. Tiger said it gets you ready to engage in close combat. In the sawdust pits where rangers fight until the last man is standing…the yell is "Kill or be killed".

Lars and Tiger joined together to bring out the following points: The course is 61 days, broken down into 3 phases. Phase I - Ft. Benning, Georgia (Camps Rogers and Darby). Squad level tactics, physical stamina, mental toughness. Phase II - Camp Merrill near Dahlonega, Georgia. Mountaineering, rugged terrain, hunger, mental fatigue. Phase III - Camp Rudder, Eglin Air Force Base, Florida. Waterborne operations, stream crossings, swamps.

Lars said that the Ranger School started in November 1950. Graduates wear the ranger tab on the upper shoulder of the left sleeve on their uniform.

Everyone applauded the two rangers who were definitely proud to be rangers. Their enthusiasm and self-confidence was obvious to all. Brenda thanked them because she had always heard about the rangers, but didn't know anything about what Lars and Tiger covered tonight.

They continued to munch out on the meringues' and gave high-5s before leaving. Tiger stuffed three in his pocket as he departed.

Carl Gustav Jung
(1875 – 1961)

Swiss psychiatrist and psychotherapist
who founded analytical psychology.

*"To confront a person with his shadow
is to show him his own light."*

- Carl Jung

Fireside Talk #8
Lighten Up Your Dark Shadow

Brenda pulled her red and white Mini Cooper into Doris's driveway and just sat there for a few minutes with the heater on. It was 22 degrees—3 inches of snow on the ground. She played back her series of nightmares from last night. Her roommate who hanged herself in their apartment.

The hit man who was in her apartment as she entered. Running from him down her sidewalk and shooting him with her Taser®, supplied to all Alpha Team members by Lars. Lunged at by a man hiding in the underground garage at *The Washington Post*...as she was entering her car on the way home. How she gave him a karate kick in the chest, even with a Beretta pistol in his hand, which broke four ribs. And a second kick which resulted in the removal of his testicles.

At the RV rally in Colorado when she discovered her aunt, uncle and their two children dead due to carbon monoxide. They were late to breakfast. These were her nightmares although there are other events that haunt her.

She felt that the nightmares were due to knowing that tonight's topic was on the dark shadow that everyone has. Things she keeps to herself. The haunting dark shadow, full of unwanted memories...her baggage.

She hoped that tonight the team would have thoughts and suggestions to relieve her of the pain she endures inside herself. And she hopes to contribute her ideas too. So far, she has gained so much from their discussions but tonight is a big one for her.

***

Doris:

Our dark shadow leaves us empty, shallow, and causes us to lead a superficial life.

Brenda:

I think your dark shadow is all the stuff inside yourself that you don't want to let out.

Tiger:

For really bad things in your past, your dark shadow may be in a closet.

Lars:

That's the worst case.

Rev:

It's what we hide, deny, repress.

Lars:

So you need to reset yourself from within. Don't leave it up to a shrink. **YOU** have to find your old self and bring it out from within.

Tiger:

Yeah, Doc...at least work towards that goal. I mean, trying to be more of your old self even though you've been through a lot. I've never returned to my old self before Nam, but I've tried to get there.

We'll never be the same. But we can work at it.

Rev:

That's due to change. And change, changes everything—for better or for worse. If worse, then you have to overcome it.

Brenda:

I think you can be eaten up by your own dark shadow. We have to remake ourselves, which helps us to overcome obstacles. There's no life if there are no obstacles to overcome. Take a minute to think about this point.

Tiger:

Takes willpower, Brenda. Beatrice, my ever-loving wife adores Charles Dickens. Especially *'A Christmas Carol'* and *'A Tale of Two Cities'*. An English writer and social critic, he is considered as the greatest novelist in the Victorian period. He died in 1870.

Beatrice wanted me to pass on to you all a great quote from Dickens: *'There are dark shadows on the earth, but its lights are stronger in the contrast.'*

Lars:

In my study of American Indians, I found that they had to reset their warrior psyche from killer to becoming a peaceful tribe member again. You actually discover your shadow when tested during the ordeal, as we discussed last week. For instance, an Indian brave might kill a buffalo or Indians from another tribe. When he returns to camp, he's full of adrenalin. Yet worn out from close combat. The Indians did the sweat lodge thing followed by going up on the hill, meaning they would go up a nearby hill. The Indian needed a meditation time-out. This is like the Vision Quest we discussed five evenings ago. However, it will distance yourself from your dark shadow.

Like our Indian, I had been out in the bush, ambushing and on patrols for so long that I needed to go to a sweat lodge for a few days to be reset. When you are so engrossed in things you're doing, you can lose touch with reality. And when a person has been in close combat many times and killed enemy troops, later it comes back to haunt you.

That's one reason why some hard-core infantry troopers can't adjust well when they return back to society.

Doris:

When you're gone, the world moves on as if you never existed. So you might as well get the most out of this life.

Lars:

Too bad we can't all live the Nordic life. My heritage is Norwegian. Thus, I'm somewhat prejudiced.

Tiger:

Beatrice and I will never forget the opening ceremony of the 1994 Winter Olympics. To Beatrice, it was refreshing.

Lars:

I was in Lillehammer then. They decided to show a range of Norwegian culture such as: sami joik, folk dancing, fiddlers, telemark skiing, Norse mythology, and simulations of traditional weddings.

Actually, it was held at Lysgardsbakken Ski Jumping Hill. The people are great.

Brenda:

My take on Norway is via 'Lillehammer', Norway's most popular TV series. Steven van Zandt plays Frank 'the Fixer' Tagliano, a former Mafia gangster who wacked a powerful Mafia boss in New York. Goes to Lillehammer to start a new life. I give it five stars.

Doris:

Glad you mentioned that, because I'll start watching it. I like van Zandt from the *Sopranos*. I'll get the past seasons a' la Netflix.

Brenda:

I love the people, too, and the quaint villages. The country is clean and fresh.

What you can learn from this short discussion is that you can get more out of life by keeping things simple. Don't get too 'wrapped around the axle'. You need to move on with the world. The world isn't stopping.

Doris:

We got off on a tangent, but the learning points are there. You can get too tied up physically and internally. Keeping things simple will help you…like the Nordic way of life.

Tiger:

Roger that, everybody! How do we handle all of this, Rev?

Rev:

I hate to bring God back into the picture, but Lars invited me to be a guest to keep you all honest.

[Everyone chuckles.]

By the way, Lars and I served together in the 'Big Red One' in Vietnam. Been friends for many years. Oh! That's the *1st Infantry Division*.
When you bring God into yourself, your ego, greed and arrogance slowly disappear. These characteristics are useless and wasteful.

Doris:

I agree, Reverend Whitcomb. You should avoid inertia.

Rev:

That's it, Doris.

Tiger:

Right on, Doris. Right on. Don't get *wrapped around the axle*, per Brenda's comment.

Doris:

Since I studied analytical psychology along with medium-ship, astrology, and psychic behavior, I thought I'd share a list that I selected from sayings by Carl Jung.

He was a Swiss psychotherapist who developed 'individuation', which is heavy-duty stuff. It involves integrating the conscious with the unconscious. The dark shadow and dream analysis are some of his contributions. Anyhow, some of these selected sayings might help you understand yourself better:

'Everyone carries a shadow and the less it is embodied in the individual's conscious life, the blacker and denser it is.'

'As far as we can discern, the sole purpose of human existence is to kindle a light in the darkness of mere being.'

'Knowing your own darkness is the best method for dealing with the darkness's of other people.'

'Maybe the only thing each of us can see is our own shadow.'

'The shadow is a moral problem that challenges the whole ego-personality, for no one can become conscious of the shadow without considerable moral effort. To become conscious of it involves recognizing the dark aspects of the personality as present and real. This act is the essential condition for any kind of self-knowledge.'

'Taking it in its deepest sense, the shadow is the invisible saurian tail that man still drags behind him. Carefully amputated, it becomes the healing serpent of the mysteries.'

'We carry our past with us, and if such a person wants to be cured it is necessary to find a way in which his conscious personality and his shadow can live together.'

Brenda:

So the shadow is made up of all the things you want to deny, hide, and repress per the reverend's earlier comment. It is a part of us that we don't want to share with anybody.

Rev:

Okay, then the shadow realm is composed of all these dark feelings—our baggage that is inside us. Reminds me of what Blaise Pascal wrote:

> *'In faith there is enough light for those who want to believe and enough shadows to blind those who don't.'*

I know Lars studied Pascal's teachings at West Point and knows better than I, that Pascal was a famous French mathematician and physicist who invented the hydraulic press in the 1600s.

Tiger:

Hey! We're really rocking. This is good stuff for **YOU**, our reader. Brenda has put our thoughts together nicely into the book that you're reading now.

Just to let you know I did some homework on this subject, too. I made a list of things that you might be hiding, keeping it inside. That kind of thing. Holding stuff inside can lead to a breaking point. We don't want you to go there!

Like a pot of water coming to a boil on the stove. It builds up and finally boils up into bubbles then overflows if you don't watch it. It may be a combination of things…guilt, shame …but you need to let it out.

We don't want you to have a nervous breakdown or seizure as a result of holding things inside yourself too long. It comes to a boiling point.

Lars:

Shoot, Tiger. This is getting good.

Tiger:

Okey dokey. These are the kind of things that might make up your dark shadow. These are from real life events that we may want to repress, hide or deny.

To be honest, Beatrice helped me to come up with this list. One or more may apply to you:

DR. CHARLES N. TOFTOY

- ✓ Cancer
- ✓ MS
- ✓ Drug/Alcohol Abuse
- ✓ Out of prison or rehab
- ✓ Loss of limb(s)
- ✓ Sexual abuse (date rape, gang rape, and rape whether male or female)
- ✓ Grieving
- ✓ Traumatic event (hurricane, tornado, earthquake, fire, flood, bombing, bridge collapse, train accident, car accident)
- ✓ Betrayed by someone, like my first wife
- ✓ Schizophrenia
- ✓ Erectile dysfunction
- ✓ (and/or anything you did that you feel sorry for)

Brenda:

Wow! Great homework, Tiger. You could be the care provider for someone suffering from one of those you've listed. Or you could be the victim. But I think Doris will agree that whatever it is, it's added to your dark shadow baggage—kept inside you, causing internal pain and suffering. I explained some of my nightmares last night and two quotes by Victor Hugo sparked me up. *'To contemplate is to look at shadows', and 'To think of shadows is a serious thing.'*

I've seen *Les Misérables* nine times. I just love French history. Of course, Victor Hugo wrote it and *The Hunchback of Notre Dame* in 1831. France's best-known writer and novelist.

Doris:

I'd add Alzheimer's or any form of dementia. I watched my father go through the stages until the very end. As the care provider, I hid lots of dark stuff because I didn't want to talk about it. I didn't tell anybody that he urinated in the 50-gallon aquarium that all patients adored on the third floor of the Sunrise Assisted Living Facility. Many things were hidden. My feelings about my husband dying in the World Trade Building were buried, yet it's one of those things that gnaw away at me.

Then, along came Lars who opened me up about both of these

situations. Light came in and cleared out some of the darkness. That's what you have to do—open up and turn some of the dark parts inside you to gold. You become free.

Lars:

I didn't like to admit that I suffer from erectile dysfunction.

Tiger:

Me either, Doc.

Lars:

Tiger and I both had a prostatectomy due to Agent Orange. But that was a dark side until I opened up and told people. Sometimes, I think we hide things because we're embarrassed. What think, Rev?

Rev:

Pulvis et umbra sumus. That means we are but dust and shadow. It comes from Horace, *The Odes of Horace*. Thus, the shadow that we all have follows us to our grave.

Remember Ecclesiastes 3:20: *All go to the same place; all come from dust, and to dust all return.* Our shadow follows us to our dust end. To me, the less dark the shadow the better. You should be reaching for a golden shadow. The dark shadow is full of wasted energy.

All I can say is that if you're struggling with some things, component parts of your dark shadow, then it's time to lighten the load of the dark shadow baggage that you're carrying around. If you're fishing for tarpon and you get a shark on your line, you cut the line. You don't want to bring a shark inside the boat. Get it, Tiger?

Tiger:

I sure does, Rev. So if the situation isn't good, maybe it's best to cut bait and move on.

Doris:

'There is no darkness but ignorance.' A saying by William Shakespeare. I relate this to Reverend Whitcomb and Nathan's

comments. If you're being used by someone, drop the relationship.

Rev:

It seems that your soul wants you to face your dark shadow elements. Then you'll add light to your dark side and begin healing. But your ego can hold up this process since it wants to hide the darker subparts of your personality. We all have a dark side.

Brenda:

Seems like you've studied Jung too, Rev. If you can bring these dark subparts out in the open, into your consciousness, it certainly will bring light to your dark side.

When I covered the wounded warriors in a cover story, one Army Sergeant said: *'I'm tired of people gawking at me because I only have one arm and one leg. I feel like smacking them in the face.'*

Doris:

But even if it isn't a wounded warrior, this happens to anyone missing a limb. I see it all the time.

Tiger:

Those kinds of people have a pinhead of a brain! A pinhead mentality.

Lars:

So the Sergeant's and others' resentment to this attitude adds to their dark shadow baggage.

Rev:

You have to master yourself. Most of us don't. But when you do, truth will prevail and you'll discard the complications that have lived inside you for so long. It's an awakening. So you need to awaken to your own self. It's like getting rid of impurities in a body of water so that life (fish) can thrive.

If you develop peace inside, outwardly you will give others peace. It radiates. Egos and arrogance are negative impressions. They will disappear if your actions are good. Don't let the shadow darken because that just means that your anger, fear, sorrow and worries are winning. It's like a game. You have to win the battle. It brings out enthusiasm and that's what draws other people to you, whether it be a sports team or at your workplace. Of course, I must say that having a strong faith helps you to overcome almost everything.

Tiger:

I've got a strong faith. Catholic, but Rev—PTSD is a sub-part of my dark shadow. There are things I can never tell anyone. Meds keep PTSD somewhat stable but still, it's in the shadow. So I weaned off the meds. It helps. Make sure you try to wean off meds so you can own it—your shadow. Or it will own you. I'm a *rubber-meets-the-road* guy, like you all—but we gotta' move forward. Or why are we here anyway—in this life? Back to you Rev, how can we bring gold to the dark shadow?

Rev:

Let me stay away from religion, because you all are bringing practical thoughts to the reader to create an awakening as applicable. Your dark shadow can eat you up. You can go downhill. You need to reawaken yourself so you realize that you have the willpower to overcome your challenges and obstacles by yourself. So far during this discussion tonight, we haven't talked about willpower. The seed of willpower is inside us. It's up to us to fertilize it and let it grow. It builds our inner strength and doesn't allow it to be siphoned off by taking the easy way.

Like Lars said earlier about choosing the harder right instead of the easier wrong. Just think of the trooper who lost all four limbs He's looking forward to the day when his fingers move on one of his hands. God bless him. And I mean God bless him. He's trying to overcome. You can, too. Willpower will lighten the load of your dark shadow baggage. That's done by converting negatives to positives—that energy transforms the dark shadow to a more golden-like shadow.

Lars:

In The Business School at GWU, I taught students about the strengths and weaknesses of companies. Strategic Management.

Similarly, I think you can understand your inner strengths and weaknesses by facing up to the sub-parts of your dark shadow. Then you begin to discover your real personality, in my view.

Rev:

Those are good points, Professor! Many of those hidden sub-parts in the dark shadow baggage are actually positive attributes that exist within you. A good idea would be to make a list of, say…ten of these, and bring more light to your dark shadow, thereby decreasing the weight of the baggage you are carrying around in your subconscious. I sound like Carl Jung.

Doris:

Very good. You know, our shadow follows us everywhere. If we confront it, we can discover good things about ourselves that we didn't know existed before we made an exploration of our inner self. An example is our soldier without limbs. He's probably discovered that he has more determination than he ever believed existed within himself. Now he wants to just see his fingers move. That's moving forward. That's willpower, as mentioned by Reverend Whitcomb. He's doing it, so whatever you're faced with—you can overcome it too by moving forward—reaching for a golden shadow.

Lars:

I think I understand Jung and some of the other psychotherapists' views on the dark shadow. However, in the real world some of the darkness remains inside you. I'm a good example. So many horrible things happened during battles in Vietnam that I have to block them out forever—keep them in my dark shadow closet. But you have to understand the art of blocking, or all the subparts in your dark baggage will weigh you down.

Tiger:

I've got lots of sub-parts that make up my dark shadow. So do young troopers who have killed people as part of their job—like Doc and I did in Nam. It affects you. Civilians don't understand it at all. They fly flags, yellow ribbons and have parades to show appreciation, but that's all superficial. No disrespect intended. But until you've been in close combat, dodging bullets and mortar rounds and firing back—they have no idea of what it's like.

What I'm saying is the young trooper has a dark shadow building up from one battle to the next. Doc was responsible for killing over 400 enemy soldiers, some at close range. I had my share of that, too.

Lars:

It seems that what we are saying tonight is for you to work on that willpower seed that's inside you. And to face your dark shadow. That way you'll bring light to the shadow.

Sudden outbursts or irritability are probably caused by your dark shadow. Hopefully our thoughts can assist you to cope with your current difficulties. I found these thoughts at this session to be truly amazing.

Tiger:

Me too, Doc.

Doris:

Let me quickly add one more thing from Walt Whitman: *'Keep your face always toward the sunshine-and shadows will fall behind you.'*

Brenda:

I needed that, Doris. As a journalist student, I studied Whitman. In his poetry collection, he wrote *'The Leaves of Grass'.* As an American poet and novelist, he volunteered as a nurse in the American Civil War. I know we are about to close, so let me pass on a viewpoint from August Wilson. He was a Pulitzer Prize winning playwright who was self-educated. *'Confront the dark parts of yourself, and work to banish them with illumination and forgiveness. Your willingness to wrestle with your demons will cause your angels to sing.'*

Lars:

Last week Brenda emailed us the list of all the topics we agreed on to discuss during our entire fireside talks' journey. They are not in any order, but it helps to guide us.

Tiger:

Yeah, Doc. I even jumped ahead by doing some research on our next topic: TRUST. It seems like trust will be our most important fireside talk. Without trust, you have nothing. Anyhow, I'm looking forward to next week's discussion. Ooh Rah! Ooh Rah!

***

They all gave each other high-5s, per tradition at the end of each session. Tiger headed to the kitchen to get another piece of applesauce spice cake, followed by Brenda with her empty plate. Brenda was feeling much better. The discussions definitely lightened up her dark shadow. Smacking his lips, Lars dove into his third piece of applesauce spice cake. Doris grinned.

Part II

Pursuit of More Intriguing Thoughts

Trust
Hope
Happiness
Love
Denial
Patience
Dignity

"Hope is a powerful weapon, and no one power on earth can deprive you of."

– Nelson Mandela

Johann Wolfgang von Goethe
(1749 – 1832)

German writer and statesman.

"As soon as you trust yourself, you will know how to live."

- Johann Wolfgang von Goethe

Fireside Talk #9
Trust: The Key to Life

Even though team members eat supper prior to the 7pm meetings, Doris decided to surprise them tonight by making minestrone soup. Last week's fireside talk was cancelled due to a wintry mix…6 inches of snow and ice. Tonight's temperature was 19 degrees, with a 6-degree wind-chill.

After everybody arrived, Doris brought out a bowl of soup for each person. All of them ate two bowls full! Tiger and the reverend ate three bowls each because they both missed supper. Everyone lauded Doris, the gourmet chef, and demanded her recipe.

There were too many ingredients so she read from her list: Chopped onion, cannellini beans, cubed potatoes, chicken broth, parsley, elbow macaroni, Parmesan cheese, tomato paste, shredded cabbage, diced tomatoes, garlic, dried oregano, basil, pepper, bay leaves, dried sage and thyme.

All of them remarked how tasty and healthy the soup was. All gave

Doris a rousing applause. Doris felt good because she knew that the soup would lift the team's spirits before they tackled another tough issue of life.

***

Brenda:

I think trust is the most important thing in life. I don't know why this wasn't our first fireside talk topic!

Lars:

Our topics aren't in any priority order. But the substance of them all, are to help **YOU**, our reader.

Rev:

You know, I try to make practical points rather than emphasize the Godly arena too much. My mother-in-law used to watch Lawrence Welk.

One time he said, *'Never trust anyone completely, but God. Love people, but put your full trust only in God.'*

[Welk, a famous bandleader, led his own musical show from 1955 to 1982.]

As a man of the cloth, I do put my trust in God. You should, too. You'll see a difference, but there are several other people that I do trust completely.

Tiger:

Yeah! I trust my wife. My first wife was a waste, but now I'm squared away with Beatrice. When I was a platoon sergeant my men had to trust me…my decisions…and I had to count on them.

Lars:

I agree, Tiger. When you're in real close combat, there's no time to doubt people. That's why training is important…to build confidence, and now I can see how it builds trust, too.

Never thought of it that way before. You've got to be able to trust the guy next to you in the foxhole and vice versa.

Rev:

When you think pure thoughts, trust develops along with other good traits. If you think pure thoughts, you are a benefit to the universe. I sound like one of the old philosophers, but it's true.

Doris:

The Catholic priest that raped me when I was 14 couldn't have been thinking pure thoughts.

[Doris looks down, snorts in disgust. A scowl on her pretty face.]

Rev:

Don't worry, Doris, he will pay for that later on.

Tiger:

I wish I knew where he is now. I'd git him good, right Doc?

Lars:

Yup.

Rev:

Let me jump in here and remind you of Romans 12:19: *Beloved, never avenge yourselves, but leave it to the wrath of God, for it is written, 'Vengeance is mine, I will repay, says the Lord.'*

Lars:

Yup. Anyway, we need to get back to this trust thing that Brenda feels is the most important of all.

[Brenda's thinking of the one-night stand she and Lars had at Ocean City while they were tracking down two hit men. But Lars was only casually dating Doris at the time.]

Brenda:

I find it hard to trust people, because I have girlfriends who break promises all the time. And they lie. Plenty of guys, too.

Tiger:

Whoa! Once someone lies to you—it's done. You can never trust them again completely—as the Rev says.

Lars:

When you hear Doris's story—it's just shameful. We had a teacher who used his position to sexually abuse students. Finally, when the 'powers-to-be' found out about it, he was fired that day.

I hate it when people are taken unfair advantage of. You should never take unfair advantage of anyone. I'll bring in Shakespeare again, *'Love all, trust a few.'*

Tiger:

Back to my earlier point, if someone lies to you, you can't trust him or her again. You may be able to later on, but it's tough to trust again.

Brenda:

I like that one, Tiger. And you're right. Been there!

[She wrinkles her nose.]

Rev:

Doris's story reminds me of post-World War II horrific crimes. The Russian troops ravaged German villages, even raping nuns. Think of those nuns. Probably having trust in everyone, especially in God. And then to be tormented like that. Some couldn't live with it and committed suicide.

Lars:

Suicide is one of our fireside talks later on.

Tiger:

You know, you read about some politicians' wives who stand by their man even though he's being openly unfaithful. Think about it;

she's home maybe reading a book one evening and at the same time, her husband is being unfaithful.

I hate to say it but I feel, like many Americans, that you can't trust anyone in The White House or Congress. Many of them lie, cover up, betray, and conspire. I know I'm just a former Infantry sergeant, but I think that nobody should be elected President that hasn't served in the military.

Brenda:
Incredible how the wives dumbly stand by them.

Rev:
Well, there's zero trust there. That's for sure. Because when there's no trust inside you, there can't be trust outside.

Lars:
Those kinds of people need to knock it off. Just like Reverend Whitcomb said, *'think pure thoughts.'* They must despise themselves inside because of what they're doing. Thinking in real world terms.

Tiger:
They should, but they're so active in what they're doing, they probably don't give a darn.

[Tiger gives the power arm thrust.]

Lars:
Some people let power go to their heads so they feel that they can take liberty with anyone.

[Lars takes two big chugs of his decaf latte and scratches his chin.]

Brenda:
I'll swing Buddha back into action. He said, *'Believe nothing, no matter where you read it, or who said it, no matter if I have said it, unless it agrees with your own reason and common sense.'*

DR. CHARLES N. TOFTOY

Doris:

I have a saying of my own...*If I don't hear it with my own ears, see it with my own eyes, or say it with my own lips, then I may not believe it at all.* I don't listen to gossip. It demeans trust.

Tiger:

See, I come from the school that believes if you let me down by lying or cheating—that you've dropped down a few notches in my 'trust meter.' I read this statement somewhere: *'I've learned that it takes years to build up trust and it only takes suspicion, not proof, to destroy it.'*

Rev:

Think about this. *'IN GOD WE TRUST.'* It's engraved on our coins and printed on our paper currency. We live with that every day. We carry it around in our wallet or purse.

Brenda:

I know the history on it, Rev. The quick version: *'IN GOD WE TRUST'* was engraved on the two-cent coin in 1864. That was the first time the motto was used. Added to paper currency for the first time in 1957. And it is the motto of the State of Florida. Likewise, *'En Dios Confiamos',* or In God We Trust, is the motto of the Republic of Nicaragua.

Tiger:

I told you Brenda was smart. Hee! Haw!

[Tiger drinks what's left of his hot apple cider and gobbles down the slice of apple. Doris pours him another mug full.]

Doris:

Hmm. To me, if you can't trust someone, you can't love them. To trust your partner, you need to be able to talk about intimate things freely: past personal history (skeletons in closet—or the dark shadow sub parts), fears (of height, water, claustrophobic situations), issues (gay, Syria, North Korea, Middle East wars, abortion, gun control, money, caregiver frustrations…like the severely handicapped wounded warrior), compromising (give and take). Everything is built on trust. George MacDonald wrote: *'To be trusted is a greater compliment than being loved.'* All I'm saying is that trust comes before love. Love can come and go, but trust is everlasting. MacDonald was a Scottish author and poet.

Things might be made clearer about love and trust when we discuss love three weeks from now.

Rev:

He was a Christian minister, too.

Lars:

I used to teach a course in leadership to our university MBA students. Oftentimes, I would refer to Stephen Covey, author of *The Seven Habits of Highly Effective People.* He wrote: *'Trust is the glue of life. It's the most essential ingredient in effective communication. It's the fundamental principle that holds all relationships together.'*

Tiger:

That's what I've been searching for, Doc. The glue. That's it. Without trust you have a shallow, empty life. For our reader, you need to ask yourself a frank question: *'Are YOU trustworthy? Really trustworthy?'* If not, please work on it. We all need to work on it. And I might add, *'who deserves YOUR trust?'*

Lars:

I have a quote here from Aristotle that I didn't think I'd use tonight, but now that you said what you just did, Tiger, here it is: *'Even that some people tried to deceive me many times…I will not fail to believe that somewhere, someone deserves my trust.'* I told my students that integrity is the core of trust—the foundation that bonds leaders together and inspires them. As a matter of fact, I would have my students study some of the teachings of Aristotle. The Greek philosopher had many practical thoughts that are useful today. He taught Alexander the Great and was recognized as the first genuine scientist in history.

Brenda:

Got a good one to follow you, Doc. So, we don't confuse you about integrity and trust.

A person may have a plan to do for you whatever was agreed on. But something avoided accomplishment of that plan. It was unintentional.

On the other hand, my landlady told me to never loan money to anyone unless you can afford it. I did that...lent $500 to a friend and harassed him continually to pay it back, to no avail. My landlady said your chances of repayment are 1 out of 10. Needing a loan in the first place means they are rather tight in their finances. That's the way to lose a friend. I wrote him off. In summary, here's my take on integrity and trust:

Integrity: the quality of being, and the honest having strong moral principles; moral uprightness.

Trust: firm belief in the reliability, truth, ability, or strength of someone or something.

Doris:

This is timely for a passage I read somewhere, Lars. I think it fits in right here.

A little girl and her father were crossing a bridge.

The father was kind of scared so he asked his little daughter: Sweetheart, please hold my hand so that you don't fall into the river.

The little girl said: No, Dad. You hold my hand.

What's the difference? asked the puzzled father.

There's a big difference, replied the little girl.

If I hold your hand and something happens to me, chances are that I may let your hand go. But if you hold my hand, I know for sure that no matter what happens you will never let my hand go.

AMAZING FIRESIDE TALKS

Brenda:

The moral of that beautiful story is that you need to reach out and hold the hand of those you care about rather than waiting for them to reach out to you.

Tiger:

Back to what someone said before…a true relationship can't exist without trust. Love comes in second place. Without trust, love is doomed in my opinion. Trust is the brick and mortar.

Doris:

Breaking Bad…the TV series is a good example of violating trust. Bryan Cranston, as Walter White, developed the world's purest crystal meth. It was to provide for his family's future. He became a desperate dad, lying to his pregnant wife, disabled son, and just everyone. He went from hero to villain. Even his son called him a liar several times. All of this led to his death. I hope those watching, learned about trust.

Lars:

That's as straight forward advice as anyone will ever get. Maybe it will help someone out there, Tiger. By the way, for everyone's knowledge—Tiger got his nickname because he was fearless in combat. A real Tiger. The Tiger in him comes out now and then during these discussions. He sure displayed his fearlessness in our last criminal case.

Tiger:

I was with the South Vietnamese Airborne Brigade on my first Vietnam tour. Those Vietnamese paratroopers called me 'Tiger' because I would sometimes attack directly at the enemy and I always remained calm even when we were surrounded. It was just instinct, I guess. I trusted those guys and they trusted me.

Rev:

Once trust is broken, it's difficult to repair the damage. Your relationship with that other person changes. Like Tiger, I've seen this hundreds of times with troops.

Tiger:

Even if you forgive, Rev—it's still not the same. The forgiveness is a fake.

Lars:

Maybe you can forgive, but you can't forget. The trust factor has been violated. Over time, you might rebuild it but still, you can't forget.

Brenda:

In the workplace, I've found that someone who cheats on his wife will also lie to you. It's in their DNA. Or at *The Washington Post,* we have a few writers who promise to meet deadlines, but consistently miss. I can't trust these people. It's a broken relationship in the real world.

Rev:

My advice to you is to back up your word. Do what you say you're going to do or don't say it at all. And always be honest. This is important because trust is with you for a lifetime. It affects you forever in this life.

Brenda:

And surround yourself with people you trust.

Lars:

I wish we had a university course entitled: *Trust.* I don't think there is a course in trust anywhere, even a one or two hour course. And here we are saying it's the most important thing.

Brenda:

You're right. It's a missing link, treated very vaguely as a sub-set of something else. It may rear its head in a philosophy or ethics class, but with passing emphasis.

Doris:

You can ask yourself two questions: 1) Who do you really trust?

And 2) What's your relationship now with anyone who has betrayed you in the past?

Be honest with yourself. The main purpose in passing on our thoughts, that have been well researched and many based on real experiences, is to help **YOU**.

Brenda:

In my studies on Confucius, I remember his famous quote, *'Without Trust, Life is Not Worth Living.'* I remember that quote from years ago studying at the University of Maryland. I read a few days ago this longer quote about his politics: *'It is to provide food, protect people with armaments, and gain trust from people.'*

When asked which we should abandon first if our country is forced to abandon food, weapons, or trust, Confucius responded: *'Abandon weapons first, then food. But never abandon trust. People cannot get on without trust. Trust is more important than life.'*

Confucius was a Chinese teacher and philosopher in 551-479 BC. He put emphasis on personal and governmental morality, and strong family loyalty.

I also uncovered a recent research study conducted by the University of Notre Dame. It reported that those people who reduce the number of lies they tell improve their physical and mental health.

Rev:

I believe that. Good point. When you lie, it begins a decaying process inside yourself. You need to keep a strong inner-self. I know we're nearing the end of this great discussion. Let me point out Proverbs 30:5: *Every word of God is pure: he is a shield unto them that put their trust in him.* And Psalm 118:8: *It is better to trust in the Lord than to put confidence in man.*

As the reverend in our group, let me give you a simple thought: try to think pure thoughts and if you have trouble about whom to trust, then at least put your trust in God.

Tiger:

Let me give you an example about trust and confidence. We have a solid natural trust as infantry combat soldiers. Since the start of the

Iraq War, five troopers have sacrificed their lives by throwing themselves on a grenade. Two soldiers, two marines, one Navy Seal. Their self-sacrifice, by being a shield, saved their comrades, yet all five of them perished.

Lars:

Tiger is right. That bond that we have out there in close combat is the highest level of trust and confidence a person can have with another. It's automatic. Soldiers have a saying: *I would take a bullet for you.* Usually, it's a split-second decision. Just like in one of our criminal cases, our Alpha Team handled for the local police department...Tiger leaped in front of me to take a bullet, saving my life.

The point here is that you should be known as a person other people can trust. Furthermore, that you would fall on your sword to defend them.

For example, the Chairman of our Management Department at GWU would take the heat from the upper echelons by himself, allowing us to do our jobs unprovoked by busy stuff. It doesn't mean sacrificing your life like in combat, but this concept relates to everyday life; think about it!

Next Thursday evening we discuss HOPE. The state of the world today can impair our dreams or hope for good outcomes for all of us. Hope is a virtue that we want to pursue as opposed to despair. It's different from optimism, which is more like everything being ordered for the best.

Brenda:

This is going to be good, huh, Tiger?

Tiger:

You betcha!

***

After listening to Doris play Tchaikovsky's 1st Piano Concerto, they all waltzed into the kitchen. All of them talked about how the music made them tingle and that it was simply beautiful. Doris mentioned that this concerto of Tchaikovsky surpasses all concertos ever written, especially the first movement. Everyone was still wiping away tears, to include the reverend.

Reverend Whitcomb commented that most of the soldiers he's talked to, tell him that the Arab world doesn't trust us. These are mostly returnees from Iraq and Afghanistan. He feels that trust is in decay worldwide and that's why tonight's topic was so important. We trust based on actions, not words, and al-Qaida are a bunch of liars. Because of the Taliban and al-Qaida, many Americans don't trust Muslims. That's unfair to decent Muslims.

The Rev said that he has read the Koran and there's no support for indiscriminate slaughter in any of the verses. Most verses are taken out of context to serve the purpose of extremists. He continued, stating that the trust is not there since we know the Taliban exploits, kills, and brainwashes the weak minded. Many are uneducated youths who are recruited because of promised after-life rewards.

Also, there is no verse in the Koran that permits the killing of non-combatants, or the murder of innocent people. As a matter of fact, the Rev feels that Allah would oppose those activities. But Allah allows Muslims to stick up for themselves if an enemy attacks them.

Tiger injects that it seems that we cannot destroy their ideology and that the Taliban Warlords really rule in Afghanistan. The Taliban and al-Qaida will continue the Muslim War until Islam is spread throughout the entire world. That's their goal. Tiger pounds his fist on the kitchen table.

Brenda stated that her problem with all of this is that they seem to hate us, yet they come over here in droves.

Lars interceded saying that they come here to gain wealth. And to avoid bombings in their own country.

According to Doris, since nobody trusts each other, they should just stay in their own country. We all visit other countries for 7-10 days or more, but we return here. Why don't they visit the US and go back home where they belong. It's ridiculous.

Tiger followed up, acknowledging that Lars hit it on the head. If you want to get to the bottom line—they come here for the money. It's greed...one of the 7 deadly sins. Most Americans hate Muslims, according to surveys Tiger has read, and it's because they aren't trustworthy.

Doris said that they hate our secular ideology.

The Rev wrapped it up by saying that the violent Muslims believe that their religious beliefs justify their actions. He reminded the team to not forget that the radical Muslims are terrorists.

Lars said that trust is the key in anything. The tribes in the Middle East don't trust each other. Wars have gone back centuries—due to religious conflicts. It's not our affair. We are just in the way, yet our troops have done a great job in spite of the challenges they face.

Before departing, everyone fills their mug with their favorite hot drink via the Keurig machine.

Martin Luther King, Jr.
(1929 – 1968)

American pastor, activist, humanitarian, and leader
in the African-American Civil Rights Movement.

"We must accept finite disappointment,
But never lose infinite hope."

-Martin Luther King, Jr.

Fireside Talk #10
The Paths to Hope

Lars had a roaring fire underway in the huge fireplace. He knew to be ready since there was three inches of snow along with 15MPH winds outside. At 7pm…right on time, everyone huddled around the fire.

Tiger said that he and Beatrice saw the film, *12 Years a Slave*, last night. The team asked him about it. Tiger stated that it took place here in Washington, DC in 1841. A free African-American, Solomon Northup, was kidnapped and sold into slavery. He worked on plantations in Louisiana for 12 years. Hope was lost for most of the slaves.

They had to pick at least 200 pounds of cotton per day, or be beaten with a switch. Women slaves were raped at will. These people had no hope. However, Solomon hung on and he was finally freed. He held on to hope even though he, like the other slaves, was faced with terrible conditions. It was disgraceful.

Brenda piggybacked Tiger's comments by discussing the TV series, *Game of Thrones*. Daenerys Targaryen, the Mother of Dragons, sets out to free slaves and save women from being ravaged. Earlier in life, she had been physically abused and traded as a piece of property.

She knew the hopelessness of the thousands of slaves throughout the land. Daenerys worked hard to end the slave trade and in some areas, like Astapor, she freed every slave…giving them hope.

Daenerys was given three petrified dragon eggs as a wedding gift. The dragons protected her, understanding her determination and that she was ruthless against those who oppose others. She names her pet dragons Drogon, Rhaegal, and Viserion. Daenerys's efforts to free slaves allowed her to build up a huge army. One example of the way she made deals was when she sold Drogon, her largest dragon with his distinctive black and red markings, to Kraznys for his 8,000 slaves, or unsullied workers.

On the day of the deal, Drogon joins Kraznys, flying over his head nearby, and the happy 8,000 slaves cross over and join Daenerys. Suddenly, as Daenerys gives the command: *'Dracarys'*, Drogon spits fire at Kraznys, burning him alive.

Lars said that these are two good examples of giving hope to people. It shows that we are pioneers in developing new thoughts…outside the box to make our points. Too bad we didn't have Daenerys back in 1841. She could have eliminated the unfair slavery going on in our country.

Tiger added that *12 Years a Slave* had 199 wins and 398 nominations from film critic organizations, to include an Oscar for Best Picture at the Academy Awards gala.

Doris refilled everyone's mug with pumpkin spiced decaf latte. Now, they sat back waiting for the discussion on hope to begin. Tiger and Brenda had put them in a good mood.

***

Doris:

I read *The Diary of a Young Girl: The Definitive Edition,* three weeks ago for the second time. Anne Frank wrote, *'Where there's hope, there's life. It fills us with courage and makes us strong again.'*

Lars:

I don't know if we can add much more to that. It says it all.

Brenda:

Anne Frank was so brave by writing that diary. It's sad that she died of typhus in the *Bergen-Belsen* concentration camp.

Rev:

I've seen hundreds of people who have lost hope. They go downhill fast. The truth of the matter is that we can't live without hope. If you are hurting for one reason or another, it will instill a spiritual survival for you. I mean it. Seen it work, numerous times.

Brenda:

It's easy to lose hope. Just as it's easy to lose faith in God—sorry Reverend.

Rev:

Hey! I understand, Brenda. Quite well.

Brenda:

Some people out there are flailing about in despair for one reason or another. In many cases, some form of addiction has caused them to feel hopeless.

Tiger:

But look at the Wounded Warrior with no limbs. He has hope that his fingers will move one day, then his hand, later his arm. That's real, living, active hope.

Lars:

Yup! Their despair can cause them to lose the energy to fight it off. Fear can also douse the flame of desire. I've seen guys run the other way when faced with a close combat situation. For **you**, I say develop a pillar of hope that you can lean on all the time. Then you'll see that you're on the path to achieving your goals or expectations.

Doris:

Martin Luther, the great leader of the religious revolt of the 16th century in Germany, said, *'Everything that is done in the world is done by hope.'* So, you should switch from fear to hope in facing your difficulties.

Rev:

Let me add to that, because Luther was right on target. You should develop a spirit inside yourself that causes actions that result in what you are anticipating. **You** need to have faith in yourself, which I believe will quell any fears in the future. Hope overcomes fears. Back to my point in last week's session—about wasteful energy. You waste energy thinking about fears that you can override by building up expectations. You can do it.

I've talked to several survivors of Nazi concentration camps. All of them focused on being liberated one day rather than the horrific atrocities happening in the camp—to include death. Again, none of us can survive without desire. My tip to you is to start building up a strong hope base. You will be happier, too.

This reminds me of Proverbs 13:12: *Hope deferred makes the heart sick, but a desire fulfilled is a tree of life.*

Brenda:

Actually, hope breeds optimism. Frankly, I want my dreams to come to reality. Like, I always wanted to get a black belt in karate. That was my big hope. It was accomplished through my own actions. Hope drove me onward.

Tiger:

I like that, Rev. By the way, if a wounded warrior is reading this, here is an email address for the *Hope For The Warriors Organization*: info@hopeforthewarrior.org.

They help to restore a sense of self, restoring the family unit, and more. You can read about how they help with financial advice and professional development. I think people with difficulties should contact support groups, don't you, Doc?

Lars:

Yup! Don't feel embarrassed to reach out. However, hope building is up to you. As the reverend said, '*It takes you to build your inner faith.'* It's what carried me through many life and death situations. And I mean it.

Tiger:
Me too, Doc.

Doris:
When I was in dire straits a few years ago I always remembered what Lars told me when we first met. *'Never give up because there is always at least a ray of hope to buoy yourself up.'*

Brenda:
I brought in an article I read seven years ago by Annie B. Bond: *The Importance of Hope—A Buddhist Healing Story.* She is a green-living advocate and wrote five books on green living. It really gets to what we're talking about tonight. I'll read it now:

Many centuries back, a severe famine swept through a valley in Tibet. A father saw that he and his children would not live much longer since all their food was gone. And so he filled some bags with ashes, tied them with ropes from the ceiling, and told his children, 'We have lots of roasted barley flour in those bags, but we have to save it for the future.'

Find out what happened, and learn the powerful lesson from this Tibetan Buddhist healing story, here:

The father died of hunger, but the children survived until some people came to rescue them. Although they were weaker than their father, they lived because of their belief that they had food. Their father died because he had lost hope.

Hope gives powerful strength to mind and body. However, the truth as it relates to our lives is even more inspiring than the particulars of the story. Unlike the bags of barley flour, the purity of our inmost nature is not just a fiction aimed at building up confidence; it is based on the utmost truth.

When we truly grasp the perfection of our inmost natures, the door opens to positive life-changes.

Lars:

Let me toss another Aristotle wise passage at you all: '*Hope is a waking dream.*' Think about that one.

Tiger:

Hope has been essential for me since PTSD is a powerful force. I have a VA disability because of it and my other wounds. For us PTSD guys, hope is a PTSD ice pick. Without it, you can't crack through. To be up front, hope coupled with strong willpower has improved my health and outlook on life. I have several buddies who have committed suicide as a result of PTSD. They gave up hope of recovery.

Lars:

I'm in the same boat as you, Tiger. It has to be overcome in order to get on with life. We always need to move forward. Remember that song: *Time waits for no one; it passes you by. It rolls on forever...*

Brenda:

That song was by Helen Forrest from the film, *Shine On Harvest Moon.*

Tiger:

See, what did I tell you about Brenda? She's a memory genius.

Lars:

I agree, Tiger. Have you all heard Tom Bodett, the American author and radio host? He's the spokesman for the *Motel 6* chain. Ends the commercial by saying, '*I'm Tom Bodett for Motel 6, and we'll leave the light on for you.*' He wrote: '*They say a person needs just three things to be truly happy in this world: someone to love, something to do, and something to hope for.*'

Doris:

When things are uncertain for us, then we call on hope. We want things to get sorted out.

Tiger:

Of course we have to take actions to accomplish that. We need to diffuse the uncertainty. I had to do that as a cop in *The Big Easy*. That was tough duty.

Rev:

I have to resurface willpower again. Willpower gives us a *hope mindset.* This enables us to develop pathways to desirable thoughts, enabling us to reach out towards our goal or desired outcome.

Tiger:

Bravo, Rev! Hope helps us to see the forest instead of just separate trees. I think that those who have survived a traumatic situation or condition will tell you that the ray of hope brought them through. As the Rev said, you have to have the will to recover and construct paths of hope to get there. I did it. Therefore, anyone can do it.

Rev:

Remember, last week I said for us to have pure thoughts. Well, also we need to have hopeful thinking. It keeps you positive and spills off onto others around you in the form of happiness for them. It's sort of via osmosis. Undefined kind of thing. Hope in the Holy Bible means: *A strong and confident expectation.*

Doris:

All I can say is that you can face your problems easier by having a positive outlook. That's the bottom line.

Tiger:

Bob Hope visited troops at Christmas to keep their dwindling spirits alive. Sometimes it takes something to reactivate our hope.

Brenda:

We call on hope to help us get through difficult tasks or challenges we face. Easy tasks don't require hope. Agreed?

AMAZING FIRESIDE TALKS

Lars:

Yup. I agree. Gosh, hope is powerful. Gotta' have it. Your future in life depends on it. It's gotten me through some real tough times. To be honest, I look at hope in two ways:

1) A regular hope coupled with willpower and

2) A spiritual hope. Like Anne Frank wrote, '...*it makes us strong again.*'

Brenda:

You can't let anything or anybody deflate your expectations. I think hope is our strongest asset. It keeps us going. The Dalai Lama said it well: '*I find hope in the darkest of days, and focus in the brightest. I do not judge the universe.*'

Lars:

It has been stated that hope is our strongest human need. Think about what the Dalai Lama said about darkness. I think your candle is your desire in the darkness. Does that sound too corny? Regardless, I mean it. In other words, even if your situation is desperate, sort of dark, there is hope somewhere, (the candle), to bring you out of it. Think of this: hope gives you a powerful feeling, a silent burst of energy.

Tiger:

Jesse Jackson, an American civil rights activist and candidate for the Democratic Presidential nomination in 1984 and 1988, said '*At the end of the day, we must go forward with hope and not backward by fear and division.*'

This quote is super. Very inspirational for **you**. Think about it. To me, it amounts to never giving up and...

Brenda:

...*and* the realization that hope is essential for us to survive. Sorry to interrupt, Tiger.

Tiger:

No problem. Better said than I, Brenda.

DR. CHARLES N. TOFTOY

Brenda:

The maximum display of hope—the pinnacle of it has to be the 317 survivors of the *USS Indianapolis* disaster. The ship was struck on July 30th, 1945, by two torpedoes from an Imperial Japanese Navy submarine. It sunk in 12 minutes taking about 300 of the 1,196 crewmembers with it. The other 900 sailors were scattered in the Philippine Sea.

I know about this historical incident because it was my thesis while studying journalism at the *University of Maryland*. It is the world's worst shark attack in history. Sharks dragged dead sailors away. Most died from exposure, dehydration, lack of food and water, sharks, and drinking saltwater—those that did, died within 5 hours due to saltwater poisoning. Only 317 sailors survived. These men kept hope strong in their hearts. I interviewed several of them. The US Navy botched it up. Only hearing about the sinking four days later.

Think of yourself being in that water for 4 days. Sharks dragging off your friends. Others so thirsty that they gave up and drank saltwater. Some committed suicide.

This is a short version—my thesis was 150 pages long. But talk about HOPE! Again, this situation is one of the world's best examples of hope at its utmost—at the tip of the summit of hope.

Whatever your situation is—just keep hoping for the best.

Tiger:

Man, that's quite a story. I think hope keeps us alive. I remember hoping to make the *Fortier High School* football team in New Orleans. My girlfriend hoped to be a cheerleader. We hope, hope, hope. But it takes **YOU** to make things happen.

Brenda:

I agree, Tiger. Your actions turn your hope into reality.

Doris:

Then you move on to the next hope. The hope has to be realistic, right? Like, I couldn't hope that my father, suffering from Alzheimer's, would get better. But I could pray for him...to hope for less pain.

AMAZING FIRESIDE TALKS

Rev:

I have three Bible verses to make you feel stronger about all of this. By the way, hope makes you stronger. No doubt about that.

You will be secure, because there is hope, you will look about you and take your rest in safety. You will lie down, with no one to make you afraid, and many will court your favor.

Job 11:18-19

The Lord delights in those who fear him, who put their hope in his unfailing love.

Psalm 147:11

We are aliens and strangers in your sight, as were all our forefathers. Our days on earth are like a shadow, without hope.

I Chronicles 29:15

Those three sayings will help you to build a stronger mind.

Doris:

You just reminded me of a writing by Thomas Carlyle: '*A strong mind always hopes, and has always cause to hope.*' Carlyle was a Scottish philosopher and writer. In 1836, he published *Sartor Resartus,* first published as a serial in 1833–34 in Fraser's Magazine and one of his best works. To be happy, **YOU** should have something to boost yourself up. I know we're discussing happiness next time, but I think they sort of go together.

Brenda:

Here's something that Charles Darwin wrote which might help you: '*Let each man hope and believe what he can.*' I read a lot of Darwin's findings while I studied at the Research Center in the Galapagos Islands.

Doris:

We could end tonight's fireside talk with Anne Frank again: *'Think of all the beauty still left around you and be happy.'*

Lars:

   That's an unbeatable ending, Doris. Especially since next week's topic is on HAPPINESS.

Rev:

   Looking forward to that with gusto, because there are so many unhappy people out there.

***

   Suddenly, Lars slides off the sofa, falling on the rug. Sasha jumps off his lap quickly. Lars holds both hands against his chest. Doris races to the telephone and dials 9-1-1.

Annelies "Anne" Marie Frank
(1929 – 1945)

One of the most discussed Jewish victims of the Holocaust.
Her wartime diary *The Diary of a Young Girl* has been the basis
for several plays and films. It documents her experiences hiding
during the German occupation of the Netherlands in World War II.

"Whoever is happy will make others happy."

- Anne Frank

Fireside Talk #11
In the Pursuit of Happiness

All cheer Lars as he arrives from the Virginia Hospital Center. The doctor told him to take a week off to rest. The Echocardiogram and EKG indicated a mild heart attack. More like a dizzy spell due to atrial fibrillation. He was released from the VHC after two days of observation. It appears that Lars has ischemic heart disease.

Doris placed a large plate of butter crisp wafers on the table in front of the fireplace. She poured everyone a cup of fresh raspberry herbal hot tea. Now they were ready to tackle tonight's topic.

***

Doris:

The question is—are **YOU** 100% happy? Or a more fair question is—are you 100% content or satisfied? If not, you've got to do something about it.

Brenda:

It's all about feelings. To me, there is a continuum of happiness. It comes and goes in spurts. All of a sudden, something happens and it makes you happy. Along the continuum there is a spike. Then it recedes back to contentment, hopefully. It seems as if you need to check in with yourself. Are you glad, mad, sad, or scared?

Tiger:

I agree. It comes and goes. You make a three point shot with one second left which wins the game. You are happy—the spike. Then it all goes back to practicing for the next game. Or a place kicker missing a chip-shot field goal, thereby losing the game. Unhappy. Other teammates are unhappy, too, as they look at you in your clean uniform—theirs being dirty and maybe muddy.

Lars:

Or a relief pitcher who loses the baseball game in the ninth inning. Others have been playing the entire game. The pitcher only has to get three batters out. Again, nice clean uniform. Unhappy. Or happy if he retires the side. Likewise, if the place kicker makes the field goal, he is happy.

Rev:

What we're saying is that you can't be happy all the time, 24/7. But, you can be content coupled with irregular spikes of happiness. So, test your feelings. Are you glad, mad, angry or scared per Brenda's comment? If you're mad, angry or scared, then you need to change something. We should be glad that we're alive. Being mad or angry is wasteful energy. Change that. Think pure thoughts.

If you're scared, then you need help to overcome it. Being afraid of thunder and lightning is different than being fearful of your husband, for example. For the latter, you need to seek help. You shouldn't have to live with the feeling of being scared of somebody. You deserve more. Same goes for those being bullied.

Psalm 37:4 states: *Delight yourself also in the Lord, and he will give you the desires of your heart.*

Lars:

People that are leading a superficial life should stop feeling hollow, empty, shallow—that are the elements of leading a superficial life; instead, **YOU** need to unclutter your thoughts and move ahead in a streamline fashion. Like Dadi Janki has written, '*We need to free ourselves of wasteful or negative thoughts.*' Janki is a spiritual teacher, teaching wisdom in the art of living. Based in India, she has set up Brahma Kumaris Centers in over 100 countries.

Brenda:

I agree. For example, 55% of people are unhappy at work.

Tiger:

There goes our *brainy* Brenda again.

[Brenda rolls her eyes and glares at Tiger. Tiger taps his foot.]

Brenda:

To continue, my suggestion is to work at a business where teamwork is emphasized. In other words, everybody counts.

Doris:

That's true. Because everybody is important in this world. **YOU** are important.

Lars:

As I tell my students, you are worth more than you think you are. Work at something that you love to do.

Tiger:

You are kidding yourself if you're not truly happy inside. What I mean, is that outwardly you can display a state of happiness, leading others to think you are happy. In reality, you are being eaten up inside because of your situation or predicament. It could be considered as a phony front.

Sort of like Philip Seymour Hoffman, the versatile actor, who died of an accidental drug overdose. The public didn't know he had a heroin drug problem, but behind the scene it must have been a different life. Not a happy one.

Doris:

I remember Sandy Duncan, with her pixie hairstyle, who played the happy Peter Pan. She had to put on a happy face for every performance while her personal life was not satisfactory. She suffered from two failed marriages and the loss of vision in her left eye due to a tumor on her optic nerve. That's an example of a person showing happiness on the outside.

Brenda:

We, as a team, don't want you to be like that, so we're going to give you tips on how to be happy. Right, gang?

[All whistle the 'Fight Call!' Brenda brought her African Gray Parrot, Sancho, with her tonight. Sancho joined in whistling the 'fight song', too. His favorite whistle tune.]

Lars:

If you're not happy, then a change needs to happen. A change created by you.

Rev:

Obviously, you can't be a *happy camper* all of the time. It comes and goes, but you *can* be content more often. In other words, you need to have your mind at ease.

Tiger:

After all, you only live once—so why not try to be happy.

Brenda:

Like the Rev said, you're more satisfied, I think, when your mind is at ease.

Lars:

We'll sprinkle tips for **YOU** throughout this fireside talk as Brenda promised. I'm happiest when I'm around my pets. My Yorkie and fish. The life in the aquarium soothes me. And a dog is your best friend. If you don't have a pet—get one. Whatever you like: dog, cat, bird, fish, hamster…whatever. They appreciate you. I'm not trying to tell you what to do but if you have a pet, try to spend more time with him or her, or watching the fish. It will help make you more content and relaxed. Also, they depend on you, but the reward is 100 times in return.

Tiger:
Roger that, Sir! My dog keeps me happy. He's a therapy dog. Beatrice and I take him to hospitals, rehab centers, adult senior centers and other places. Butch does tricks and they get to hold him. He makes them smile. As a result, we are happy.

Beatrice has a magnet message on our fridge: '*Husband and dog missing. $500 reward for dog.*' She loves Butch, too. He's family!

[Everybody laughs.]

Brenda:
My African Gray parrot makes me happy, too. Talking and whistling. Tiger just came up with a good idea for you, if you're in a slump. Get a dog. Teach the dog to be a therapy dog and take your dog around to different places. Making other people happy will make you happy. It's always better to give than take.

Rev:
All of us face crises whether we are young, older, wealthy, or poor. According to Dadi Janki, '*When I have the power of peace, I do not allow the stability of my mind to be disturbed.*' She wrote a short book, *Inside Out*, which is a must-read for everyone.

You can't help crises that occur outside of yourself, but you sure can stop those you create inside yourself. Again, Dadi Janki stated, '*Allowing yourself to be unhappy is not useful.*'

Don't forget the past and don't worry what people think of you. This causes unnecessary worry. And others around you are affected negatively.

AMAZING FIRESIDE TALKS

Lars:

Your internal energy radiates goodness to others. That's why we live—to do just that. Goodness inside yourself breeds goodness outside.

Rev:

You need to keep pure, peaceful thoughts in your mind. Blow away negative thoughts just as you use a blower to blow away leaves on your lawn.

If we dedicate ourselves to achieve happiness it may be synthetic—not lasting, but rather a frustrating journey. In 350 BC, Chuang-Tzu wrote, *'Happiness is the absence of the striving for happiness.'* He and Lao Tzu founded Taoism. He was held in high regard because of his analytic philosophical background.

Lars:

One of my professor colleagues, David T. Lykken said: *'Trying to be happier is like trying to be taller.'* That we all have a *happiness set point.* He concludes that we can pursue happiness by putting aside anger, resentment and pessimism. And try to foster the positives, such as gratitude, empathy and serenity. I'll add to that—humility and compassion. By the way, Lykken was a behavioral geneticist and is well known for his work on twin studies and lie detection.

Doris and I have a butterfly garden. To get to the point, when I see a butterfly whether it be a Monarch, Swallowtail, Red-spotted Purple, or other feeding on a butterfly bush, I feel good. It produces a nice smile. But when that Monarch lights on my shoulder, I'm happy. So happiness does come and go. By the way, it's good luck if a butterfly attaches itself to you. Sort of a myth, but still a neat thought.

Brenda:

Can't beat that analogy, Doc.

Tiger:

I don't think happiness prevails. Things have to be somewhat grim for you to suddenly explode into being happy. That's because you overcame some obstacle.

Doris:

What makes **YOU** happy? Concentrate on those things. Stick with happy people. If you are around negative people, you'll be unhappy. Someone said, *'You are what you read.'* Similarly, you are who you hang around with. Everyday try to do something cool for yourself. Dig out humor in all things.

Brenda:

I like that, Doris. Be around happy people and find humor in all situations—as best you can. I have some other thoughts to help you on your pursuit of more happiness:

- exercise is the best mood changer
- deep-breathing (this really works; I mean it)
- take on new things: travel, yoga, tai chi, bird-watching, art, dancing…anything new
- don't go to sleep angry (as we have already learned, anger is a waste of energy)
- eat regularly, like every 3-4 hours (watch what difference it makes; you aren't so short-tempered or hyper as before; and get enough rest)
  AND
- this one is so obvious that I've set it apart from the other thoughts—start reading on a consistent basis (change genres; I used to read westerns for years; then I switched to World War II; now I read mysteries)

The bottom line is: please don't keep doing the same-old stuff. Sure, I keep going back to karate, but I have to in order to maintain my black belt rating. Each time is different because there's a new butt to kick. And guys, that makes me real happy. However, I do a lot of the other things I just mentioned to you, too.

Tiger:

And in our last two criminal cases, Brenda used her karate skills to save the day a few times.

AMAZING FIRESIDE TALKS

Lars:

Aristotle wrote: *'Happiness depends on ourselves.'* And I have one more tip for you. Carry pictures of your pets, or of anything that makes you smile. The iPhone photos are handy. You can show them to others as you're traveling about. Keeps me happy. Just another thought for you.

You should be happy, content, or satisfied. Whatever you do…enjoy it. I hope you do. Yes, you deserve to be happy. Makes others feel good—the result is you feel good. Synthetic happiness is short-lived. You need to be along the happiness continuum, per Brenda.

Rev:

If you love God, you're happy. But it's not for everyone. Those that love God know what I mean. A good Proverb for all of us is 10:12: *Hatred stirs up dissention, but love covers over all wrongs.*

Doris:

We all agreed to come up with a few movies that will make **YOU** feel happy or feel good. I know some of these are older movies, but you can get them at your local library or they can search for them and contact you when they receive them.

Or you can do it via Netflix. My favorites are: *The Wizard Of Oz, The Sound Of Music, It's A Wonderful Life, Enchanted* and *The Happiest Days Of Your Life.*

Keep these on hand for when you get down in the dumps. You can play them over and over.

Tiger:

Mine are: *Forrest Gump, Meet The Parents, Ventura: Pet Detective.*

Brenda:

I like these: *Desperately Seeking Susan, Hairspray, The Goodbye Girl, Little Miss Sunshine.* However, I like all the ones mentioned so far.

Rev:

I'll toss in my two bits: *Finding Nemo, Groundhog Day*, and *Amélie.*

Lars:

I guess I'm batting cleanup. My favorites to make you feel good are: *E.T., Chariots Of Fire, Casablanca.* Our purpose is to give you a menu of movies that you can watch, or provide for a person that you're assisting. Now, guess what our topic is for next week?

Tiger:

What dat, Doc?

Lars:

I've invited Dena Kendrick and Carl Mercer to discuss LOVE with us.

Brenda:

Gee. That will be great to see them again.

Lars:

In summary form for you, Rev; Dena and Carl helped us on our last case. Dena lost both legs in Iraq as an Army lieutenant. And Carl was an FBI agent for 31 years. They both helped us on our last case where we helped the local police departments chase down a cold case killer. More on this next time, but LOVE is our next topic. I'll leave you with another Aristotle gem: *'Love is composed of a single soul inhabiting two bodies.'*

***

The team crowded around Brenda in the kitchen to hear her explanation of Buddhism. She covered the following points: 2,500 years old, never any religious wars, more of a self-help religion—it depends on you, free thought, accomplish goals through your own efforts.

The main reason Brenda chose Buddhism was because it's a good religion for strong minded people. The basic prayer chant is: *Nam-Myoho-Renge-Kyo,* which is the law of life. Also, she likes the basic premise that all people can attain enlightenment regardless of race, gender, social status, or education. And that life is eternal.

Team members hugged Brenda and gave high-5s.

Since it was freezing outside, Doris gave everybody a nice surprise—a bowl of French Onion Soup Gratinée. She uses large red and sweet onions along with balsamic vinegar and Asiago and Mozzarella cheeses. Some other ingredients are: parsley, thyme leaves, bay leaves, black pepper and pinches of paprika. Doris makes slices of Gruyères cheese. When done, the cheese cascades down the sides of each crock.

The team digs in and later departs in a jovial mood. The soup set well with Brenda, Tiger, and the Rev, who now face a cold drive home.

As they headed to the door, Lars provided feedback on his follow-up visit to the cardiologist at Virginia Hospital Center. It was a dizzy spell caused by Sinoatrial Node Disease. His pulse rate suddenly decreased causing a loss of equilibrium. He told the team that his pulse rate must have dropped below 60 beats per minute.

Mohandas Karamchand Gandhi
(1869 – 1948)

Gandhi led India to independence
and inspired movements for civil rights
and freedom across the world.

"Where there is love there is life."

- Mahatma Gandhi

Fireside Talk #12
Love is Everywhere

Lars:

I hope that **YOU** won't mind if we pause here. We're about at the halfway point in our fireside talks' journey. I want to cover a few things to refresh and remind you of our team's mission and how we operate. This is a good time for that because our guests, Dena Kendricks and Carl Mercer are here, and this will enable them to understand our Thursday evening drill, too.

First of all, I want to introduce Dena and Carl to Reverend Whitcomb. Rev, I sent Dena and Carl your bio, so they've got your number already. Here's the short version of this highly professional duo.

Dena: Army Lieutenant. Lost both legs above the knee in a firefight in Iraq. With both legs gone, she kept her troops fighting. Awarded the Silver Star for bravery.

As Tiger knows, the Silver Star medal is awarded for gallantry in action. It's the third highest military decoration for valor. The first award of the SS was in 1932…just a bit of trivia.

[Everyone applauds Dena.]

My brother-in-law is the Arlington County Chief of Police. He recruited Dena from the Wounded Warrior Mentor Program to be ACPD's Chief Cold Case Homicide Detective. Since our team's last case involved pursuing a genius killer, Taurus, whom had over 20 cold murders to his credit, Cory assigned her to us.

Carl Mercer was added as a consultant to Dena and us. He had tracked Taurus for years and coupled with 31 years of FBI experience, he was a natural to join us. Also, he worked with Doris on two previous cases when Doris was an FBI profiler.

Doris:
You might add that last year we had a double wedding with Dena and Carl. Just a small point, Lars…so I thought I might toss that in here.

Lars:
Whoops! I goofed—thanks, my dear. I think I'm in trouble.

[Doris snickers. Brenda rolls her eyes. Tiger bites his tongue. The reverend grins. And Lars turns cherry red. Snapping out of it, Lars continues.]

Anyhow, we meet every Thursday. We have a list of important topics to cover each week. Everybody digs in and does a lot of research. That along with real-life experiences and experiences of others allows us to present the reader with down-to-earth practical thoughts that can be chosen to apply to real life.

Tiger:
Yeah. Not real gooey rhetoric. No fluff. All of us on the Alpha Team have walked the walk.

AMAZING FIRESIDE TALKS

Doris:

Not to be boastful, but I think we're supplying gems of wisdom for the reader. Useful tools through our thoughts, key quotes, sayings, and summaries of important articles by dedicated writers in these various fields. Even appropriate poems.

Lars:

I'm glad you said that, Doris. Our hope is that **YOU** get some inspiration whether your situation is medical, personal, business, at the workplace, or…

Brenda:

Or whatever situation you're faced with. So I don't think our thoughts are lame; they're on target.

Tiger:

Bull's-eye, Brenda. Right on target. It should be good for you because some of our comments are based on real events that have happened to us. Others, we've had first-hand knowledge about.

Lars:

Just to finish this break in the action, we have about 20 minutes at the beginning to socialize. We get caught up. Refreshments, like tonight we have Doris's famous chocolate chip cookies that melt in your mouth. In the kitchen, we have a Keurig machine. Tea and coffee. My favorite is extra bold dark magic decaf from Green Mountain. That with Stevia laced with Half and Half. Better than any regular coffee, I know. Regular coffee makes my heart palpitate somewhat. Boy, am I getting off course. But anyhow, you get the picture.

Reverend Whitcomb asked me if the Alpha Team is paid since they show up every Thursday and do heavy research. The answer is yes. They are paid via the endowment provided by Belissa Hawthorne. She gave us $500,000 to put forth as we feel appropriate. We worked on the case, which involved pursuing her daughter's killer. That was the case before the *Taurus* case. There are two books published that cover those two cases—done in fiction to protect the innocent.

DR. CHARLES N. TOFTOY

Tiger:

When the cops are clueless, Rev—they bring us in.

Lars:

That's right. Now, we have a break. No cases, so we all agreed to meet in an attempt to help others out there. Sorry to bore you with this review, but Dena and Carl needed to understand our mission and procedures.

Anyone chimes in whenever they want, so it's open for you two to spout off anytime. Glad to have you with us.

Oh! And our comments are directed to the reader—**YOU**.

Brenda:

It's like old times, having Dena and Carl with us.

Lars:

Now, onto love—our topic for tonight. Last week we all agreed to do some extra homework for tonight's fireside discussion.

Tiger:

Sounds like a Prof!

Lars:

We were all to choose a best romantic movie, a poem, and a quote or saying about love. The idea is for **YOU** to gain some inspiration by experiencing these best-choices of ours. Who's first? Let's start with movies!

Doris:

No doubt about it, *Dr. Zhivago* with Omar Sharif and Julie Christie. Gives me a chill just thinking about it.

Tiger:

Mine is *Casablanca*. I could watch it once a week. Humphrey Bogart and Ingrid Bergman at their best. Yipes! What a love flick. Intense. Oh la la!

AMAZING FIRESIDE TALKS

Brenda:

James Garner and Gena Rowlands tore me up in *The Notebook*. Real class act.

Rev:

You all know mine – the incredible *The Ten Commandments*. Charlton Heston never was the same after he made that movie. Great impression on him and us.

Lars:

Back to me. Mine is *Titanic* with Leonardo DiCaprio and Kate Winslet. Unsurpassable love story. A neighborhood girl saw it eight times.

Dena:

Carl and I didn't know about homework, but off the top of my head, my favorite is *An Affair to Remember*. Cary Grant and Deborah Kern were matched perfectly. Another foreign film I loved was, *Cyrano de Bergerac* because it was a heroic comedy, full of love. I suggest you try these, since we are talking to **YOU**—the reader.

Carl:

Caught unprepared, I've got to state that *Gone with the Wind* is the classical love story. Clark Gable and Vivien Leigh really let us know about the ins and outs of love. Gable was a dashing fellow!

Lars:

Well, that takes care of movies for you. We hope you watch all of these in the near future. These kinds of movies make you feel good. Perhaps you can get them via Netflix. Let's move on to poems.

Brenda:

I've got a beauty. We might warn you that sometimes poems have to be read three or four times to really sink in. So be patient. *Looking For Your Face* by Jalaluddin Rumi is one of the best ever. By the way, Rumi was a 13th century Persian poet regarded as the 'love poet'. Here it is:

DR. CHARLES N. TOFTOY

From the beginning of my life
I have been looking for your face
But today I have seen it

Today I have seen
The charm, the beauty,
The unfathomable grace
Of the face
That I was looking for
Today I have found you
And those who laughed
And scorned me yesterday
Are sorry that they were not looking
As I did

I am bewildered by the magnificence
Of your beauty
And wish to see you
With a hundred eyes

My heart has burned with passion
And has searched forever
For this wondrous beauty
That I now behold

I am ashamed
To call this love human
And afraid of God
To call it divine

Your fragrant breath
Like the morning breeze

AMAZING FIRESIDE TALKS

Has come to the stillness of the garden
You have breathed new life into me
I have become your sunshine
And also your shadow

My soul is screaming in ecstasy
Every fiber of my being
Is in love with you

Your effulgence
Has lit a fire in my heart
For me
The earth and sky

My arrow of love
Has arrived at the target
I am in the house of mercy

And my heart
Is a place of prayer

This Rumi poem is in a frame by my bedside. Very insightful. It should help you understand true love and that love still exists in our hearts. My favorite by far.

Doris:
That one is great, Brenda. Mine is shorter. The simplicity and clarity of *The Look* won me over. It's by Sara Trevor Teasdale. She was born in 1884 in St. Louis, Missouri.

Teasdale was a famous lyric poet and in 1918 won the Columbia University Poetry Society Prize, which later became the Pulitzer Prize for poetry.

She published volumes of poetry.

DR. CHARLES N. TOFTOY

Strephon kissed me in the spring,
Robin in the fall,
But Colin only looked at me
And never kissed at all.

Strephon's kiss was lost in jest,
Robin's lost in play,
But the kiss in Colin's eyes
Haunts me night and day.

[Unexpectedly, Doris jumped up and went into the living room. She wiggled into a good position on the piano bench and began playing Beethoven's *Moonlight Sonata*. The team gathered around behind her. They felt that the love poems' must be reminding her of her first husband whom she dearly loved. All eyes welled up. Brenda whimpered quietly; throat tight. Doris's playing was beautiful.

When Doris finished, she swung around on the bench completely dry eyed. Her pale blue eyes were radiant. To the team's surprise, she was completely composed.

Doris told them how the *Moonlight Sonata* puts her in 'seventh heaven'. She related a summary about Ludwig Van Beethoven. This was Piano Sonata No. 14. His most popular sonata; completed in 1801. It was dedicated to his pupil, Countess Giulietta Guicciandi. That Beethoven was a German composer and pianist, who became almost totally deaf for his last ten years of life.

They all returned to the fireplace setting and the reverend picked up where they had left off. Since Doris was in a good mood, everyone recovered and joined her in a good mood mode.]

Rev:
I'll jump in here. This is the old favorite. I think it will do you a lot of good. Elizabeth Barrett Browning wrote it in the early 1800s. As you may remember, Browning was an English poet of the Romantic Movement.

AMAZING FIRESIDE TALKS

How Do I Love Thee?
(Sonnet 43)

How do I love thee? Let me count the ways.
I love thee to the depth and breadth and height
My soul can reach, when feeling out of sight
For the ends of being and ideal grace.
I love thee to the level of every day's
Most quiet need, by sun and candle-light.
I love thee freely, as men strive for right.
I love thee purely, as they turn from praise.
I love thee with the passion put to use
In my old griefs, and with my childhood's faith.
I love thee with a love I seemed to lose
With my lost saints. I love thee with the breath,
Smiles, tears, of all my life; and, if God choose,
I shall but love thee better after death.

Lars:

Since I'm the professor philosopher sort of guy, I choose *Love's Philosophy* by Percy Bysshe Shelley, who was born in 1792 near Horsham, Sussex, England. Regarded as the finest of all the lyric poets in the English language. You'll see what I mean after you read it 2-3 times.

The fountains mingle with the river
And the rivers with the ocean,
The winds of heaven mix for ever
With a sweet emotion;
Nothing in the world is single,
All things by a law divine
In one another's being mingle—
Why not I with thine?

DR. CHARLES N. TOFTOY

See the mountains kiss high heaven,
And the waves clasp one another;
No sister-flower would be forgiven
If it disdain'd its brother;
And the sunlight clasps the earth,
And the moonbeams kiss the sea—
What is all this sweet work worth
If thou kiss not me?

Tiger:
   I guess I'm batting cleanup. Not real good at this 'love' stuff, but Beatrice helped me on this one. Even though I'm a rough and ready guy, I do like it a lot. I hope you do too. Since love is infinite, per Beatrice, this poem is very fitting. Written by John Donne. He was born in 1572 in London, England. Donne went to Oxford University and wrote many love poems. We think this is his best after researching about 83 poems.

Lovers' Infiniteness

If yet I have not all the love
Dear, I shall never have it all,
I cannot breathe one other sigh, to move,
Nor can entreat one other tear to fall.
All my treasure, which should purchase thee,
Sighs, tears, and oaths, and letters I have spent,
Yet no more can be due to me,
Than at the bargain made was meant.
If then thy gift of love were partial,
That some to me, some should to others fall,
Dear, I shall never have thee all.

AMAZING FIRESIDE TALKS

Or if then thou gavest me all,
All was but all, which thou hadst then;
But if in thy heart, since, there be or shall
New love created be, by other men,
Which have their stocks entire, and can in tears,
In sighs, in oaths, and letters outbid me,
This new love may beget new fears,
For, this love was not vowed by thee.
And yet it was, thy gift being general.
The ground, thy heart is mine; whatever shall
Grow there, dear, I should have it all.

Yet I would not have all yet,
He that hath all can have no more,
And since my love doth every day admit
New growth, thou shouldst have new rewards in store;
Thou canst not every day give me thy heart,
If thou canst give it, then thou never gav'st it;
Love's riddles are, that though thy heart depart,
It stays at home, and thou with losing sav'st it:
But we will have a way more liberal,
Than changing hearts, to join them, so we shall
Be one, and another's all.

Doris:
    Just out of interest, how many poems did everyone research before they selected the best one?

Tiger:
    83.

Brenda:
    110. All of Rumi's poems.

Lars:

46.

Rev:

One, because I knew the one I would want to share with you.

Doris:

Then, it's back to me—201. I guess that I win the prize, another one of my chocolate chip cookies. So that's a total of 441 poems. See there, we're all trying to do our best for **YOU**. I suggest you refer to these poems from time to time. Very meaningful and inspiring. These four love poems are 'keepers' for you. Enjoy.

Tiger:

I'm not really into this stuff, but I gotta admit these are moving, man…moving. I gar-ron-tee you dat'!

Doris:

New Orleans slang again, huh—Tiger?

Carl:

Knowing that LOVE was your topic, I looked up love in three dictionaries. Maybe this is a take off point for us:

- Merriam-Webster: *Strong affection for another arising out of kinship or personal ties.*
- Oxford dictionaries: *An intense feeling of deep affection.*
- The Free Online Dictionary: *An intense emotional attachment.*

These definitions seem very general and rhetorical. I know it's more than that.

Lars:

From sort of a cold academic point of view, I'll cover the five types of love. Then we can get into the nitty-gritty.

- Eros: passionate love for someone more than just love of friendship
- Phila: loyalty to friends, family, virtue and just plain friendship in Greek
- Agape: general affection for someone. Being content, love to all
- Storge: natural affection, relationships within your family
- Thelema: desire, to be prominent

Now that we have set the stage for love with definitions and the types of love, we are armed to dig further into the real stuff.

Brenda:

I think our best input for you tonight are the poems and quotes to come later. However, I'm going to jump ahead and give you a Buddha quote: *'Love is a gift of one's inner most soul to another so both can be whole.'*

But even Buddha can't answer key questions about love. After all, it's just a word. Love. Is it love, lust, infatuation, a crush or what? Whatever it is, will it last?

Lars:

Sorry, let me butt in. I had a close friend—got married—divorced within one year. Look at all the nice weddings. Everyone is happy. Love is in the air. And then…

Brenda:

Or is it?

Tiger:

Ritual before God…until death do us part. End up in court with an impersonal judge. What a way to go. The petals they threw at you outside the church have long died. So has the marriage. Maybe you feel love, but does the other person? Complex dance. I tell all my buddies to watch for warnings of your mind. Pay attention. Don't ignore telltale signs before you take the vow. It doesn't matter if people get hitched in a church, elope, or go before the Justice of the

Peace, if there are untruths floating around, love is not working.

Doris:
    Maybe it's just romance, not real love. So, love can be great at the beginning, but what happens when both people run out of gas?

Tiger:
    Better to love a pet. Don't give you any back talk...just unconditional love.

    [Just then, Sasha jumped into Lars lap...almost on cue! During the break, Lars and Tiger told the others about the *Mobility Assistance Service Dog Program*. A wounded warrior with the following results from combat injuries may be provided a Service Dog: post-traumatic stress disorder (PTSD), mobility issues, traumatic brain injury (TRI), or other severe difficulties.
    The working dog helps to calm the WW and assists in mitigating anger, rage, and impatience. The dog watches the WW's back. The dog turns on light switches, picks up items dropped, blocks out people who crowd in too close, and helps them return to places they use to frequent like grocery stores, movie theaters, sports events, restaurants.
    Tiger mentioned a Sergeant that he is mentoring now in the *Wounded Warrior Mentor Program*. The Sergeant showed Tiger what Babe does in action. He dropped his keys. Babe picked them up and gave the keys to the Sergeant. Since his leg was amputated above the knee due to a bomb incident in Iraq, he had some loss of equilibrium. As Babe saw him leaning to the left, he pushed against him...straightening him upright.
    Lars concluded saying that the service dog is the WW's best buddy. Sasha stretched up on Lars chest and gave him a bunch of kisses.]

Lars:
    As a sidebar here, Yorkies make great pets. Here are some of the points Doris and I make when we bring Sasha to perform pet therapy: nice and peaceful, accessible for petting, allergy proof, doesn't shed, and they do well around people.

Like in our first criminal case, William Crawford was never loved by anyone in his life. So he conjured an imaginary love with Goddess Kali. If you've never been truly loved...get a pet. A pet is a devoted friend and returns love faithfully. That's what Sasha does. The love is both ways. Unconditional, as mentioned by Tiger.

Doris:
Someone said that if you don't have love, honesty, selflessness, and compassion in your heart, then you are missing life completely.

Lars:
I think this is a lead-in to true love. Are you just in plain love or is it true love? There's a difference.

Dena:
I'm a good one to kick this off. Bottom line, my husband left me because I had my legs amputated due to the firefight in Iraq. He was a weak person. Of course, like Lars and Doris, Carl and I have only been married for one year. I think love is in your heart. For example, I want good things for Carl. No matter how much he gives, I want to give him more. It's a process. Intensity prevails. True love will endure via give-and-take. Carl?

Carl:
I think true love takes hard work and many people don't want to work hard at it. The reason that love is a complex dance is that when trust and confidence in the other person fades and is disrupted, the high voltage force of love goes south. Love is unconditional. You should love in simple terms. Keep it simple.

Lars:
I call true love deep-heart love. Lots of humility, which is a strength—not a weakness. Faithful, trustworthy, responsible, dedicated, ready to sacrifice, compromise...

Doris:
To me, true love is stronger than anything else in the world. These

true loves are the best of all time: Cleopatra and Mark Antony, Napoleon and Josephine de Beauharnais, Lancelot and Guinevere, Voltaire and Émilie du Chatelet, Czar Nicholas II and Alexandra Feodorovna. If you look up summaries of these romances, it will give you a warm, pleasurable feeling.

Brenda:
I would add Romeo and Juliet, and Juan and Evita Perón.

Tiger:
Hey—what about Bonnie and Clyde?

[Everyone looks at each other and shrugs their shoulders.]

Rev:
Younger generations think they're in love, but when things get tough, sometimes they quit. I think love is a lesson in life to experience. It's an energy that lives inside you. It's there. It comes and goes but the energy remains.

However, I do believe that love is a mystery. Love and God are mysteries because both are unexplainable. Corinthians 13:1-13: '...love is patient and kind.'

Tiger:
The real destroyer of marriage is selfishness—the worst trait of all. Greedy, arrogant, selfish, ego type of people don't fit into Doc's 'deep-heart love' concept. I've seen many of my self-centered buddies bungle up a marriage due to these traits.

Lars:
Before we get into a discussion about love being a mystery, or not, let me explain what I mean about deep-heart love. To keep a long story short, Doris loves waterfalls. I had Merrifield Garden Center build a nice cascading waterfall in the backyard. She had a full knee replacement and hurt her ankle skydiving. The doc said that a spa would do her a lot of good.

Now, we have an indoor spa. When I'm away at an academic

conference, I'm not lonely. Doris isn't lonely at home either. Our love is too heart-deep to be affected by necessary separations. I agree with the reverend that love is a mystery. It is elusive and an enigma.

Brenda:

Let's put the *rubber to the road*. Where did you meet your spouse or significant other? What would happen if you did not take that cruise, not attend that party or church function, not at the marathon race, not on vacation at that time, airline, the beach, yoga class…and so on?

If you hadn't been there, you never would have met. Frankly, you would never have seen that person, now your husband or wife, ever in your lifetime.

It's a riddle or puzzle—difficult to understand. The brain releases chemicals that blind you to reason logically. Mysterious.

Doris:

Another question for you: do you love your spouse or just like him or her? Mixed signals here. So, it is a puzzle.

Tiger:

My buddy met a Russian girl via an internet singles, dating site on the internet. Later, he married her. Like Brenda said, if he had never joined that internet singles group, he would never have known her. I might add that they are very happy and have been married for 12 years.

Lars:

It's the complex dance all right—complex chemistry. Being from The Business School, we always try to rationalize everything. But love can't be analyzed because rational thinking is overtaken by instinct. It is unpredictable.

Rev:

It is all tied up with emotions—the heart is calling out to you. The soul is urging you on and perhaps there is divine intervention, unknown to us.

Lars:

That's interesting because our next to last fireside talk will be a discussion of the indestructible SOUL. We're leaving our toughest topic as the finale—later on.

Tiger:

Since we were to talk about love as a mystery tonight, I brought the lyrics from *The Tubes*.

Brenda:

Who's that?

Tiger:

You're too young to know. They play Chicano Rock, east L.A., back to 1973, multiple Grammy award winners, lots of albums. I'm not singing it, just reading. Here's a copy for you:

Love's A Mystery
(I Don't Understand)

Real, almost real
I could feel the life flow into my veins
Done, now it's done
I have fallen for the final time
I can't get up again

Love's a mystery, I don't understand
Love's supposed to make you glad
Tell me why I feel so bad
Love's a mystery, I don't understand
I won't see you anymore
And that's what love is for
Then I don't understand

AMAZING FIRESIDE TALKS

Free, now you're free
You don't need me and you don't want what I give
Baby, here is my heart
Please, help me please
'Cause if life is made for hearts in love
then how am I to live

Love's a mystery, I don't understand
It's so hard to be alone
When the one you love is gone
Love's a mystery, I don't understand
You won't stay another day
And if that's all you can say
Then I don't understand

Love's a mystery, I don't understand
I won't see you anymore
And if that's what love is for
Then I don't understand

Doris:

I think if you feel your love is not strong enough with your partner, then try new things. Share interest in activities such as hobbies, travel, gardening, cooking, sports, theater, reading...

Rev:

You could be together as community volunteers. Lars and Doris bring their Yorkie to hospitals, rehab centers, senior adult centers. Sasha does tricks, they hold her—everyone is happy.

Pet therapy. I've seen couples get closer together by joining a bowling league. It could be anything, but try something if your love needs to be bucked up.

It does work.

Tiger:

I'm going to brag on Brenda, who I usually tease. Before we started tonight she spouted off *'I love you'* in several languages.

Brenda:

Oh well! Okay! I've got to do something about this, Tiger!

- French: je t'aime
- Irish: taim i'ngra leat
- Chinese: wo ie ni
- Spanish: te quiero
- Porteguese: eu amo-te
- Russian: ya lyublyu tebya
- Italian: ti amo
- Korean: tangsinul sarang ha yo
- Greek: s'agapo
- German: ich liebe dich
- Indian (India): moi tumak val pau
- Japanese: kimi o ai shiteru

Tiger:

See, she has a photographic memory! I know one from Brazil: 'eu te amo'. I know that because I spent 10 days in Rio. I had such a good time that I don't remember much.

Lars:

Like Tiger, I can add something to Brenda's list. Since I speak Vietnamese, I know that 'toi yeu em' is I love you. As a sidebar, I have to tell you all that the Vietnamese people are wonderful. And I love their food.

Rev:

What about Goddess Kali, Lars?

Lars:

Yup. She is revered and loved in India as the Goddess of Liberation. She is a destroyer of the ego. Kali was the imaginary girlfriend of Crawford, who was a killer we (the Alpha Team) pursued two criminal cases ago. Then in the last case, she helped us by visiting me from time to time. Long story, Rev. That's the short version.

Doris:

I agree with Lars' earlier comment. The best we can do for **YOU** is probably through poems, sayings, and quotes that are some of the best written about love, our most difficult topic so far.

Dena:

I'm not prepared, but I know this one by heart from Mother Teresa: *'The greatest science in the world; in heaven and on earth; is love.'* That quote helped me after my husband walked out on me. A fellow wounded warrior shared it with me.

Doris:

'If music be the master of love, play on.' That's my favorite from Shakespeare's *Twelfth Night, Act 1, Scene 1.*

Brenda:

Mother Teresa: *'Let us always meet each other with a smile, for the smile is the beginning of love.'*

Lars:

Aristotle wrote*: 'Love is composed of a single soul inhabiting two bodies.'*

Tiger:

Beatrice loves Pablo Neruda's works. So I brought a copy for you all, of his Sonnet XVII:

Sonnet XVII

I don't love you as if you were the salt-rose, topaz
Or arrow of carnations that propagate fire:
I love you as certain dark things are loved,
Secretly, between the shadow and the soul.

DR. CHARLES N. TOFTOY

I love you as the plant that doesn't bloom carries
Hidden within itself the light of those flowers,
And thanks to your love, darkly in my body
Lives the dense fragrance that rises from the earth.

I love you without knowing how,
or when, or from where,
I love you simply, without problems or pride:
I love you in this way because I don't know
any other way of loving

But this, in which there is no I or you,
So intimate that your hand upon my chest is my hand,
So intimate that when I fall asleep
it is your eyes that close.

Some of you know Neruda, a Chilean poet. Won the 1971 Nobel Prize; declared the greatest poet in the 20th century.

Rev:
I know you thought I'd have a Bible quote. But I decided that the famous quote by Rumi is better than anything I could come up with. Please read this one over a few times. It should help you.

A lifetime without love is
Of no account. Love is the
Water of life. Drink it down
With heart and soul.

But I will add on a Greek proverb: '*A heart that loves is always young.*'

Carl:
I'm like Dena in that I have a saying by Antoine de Saint- Exupéry

that is always taped to my refrigerator. *'Love is not just looking at each other, it's looking in the same direction.'* Dena and I are looking in the same direction. She is my best friend.

Doris:
Right on!

Lars:
Looks like we're wrapping up now.

Brenda:
Wait, before we close and I know we're already 2 hours into overtime, I have a beautiful closing to this tough topic. It's from Lady Bluerose, a wordpress.com site. I'll read it:

Love is Life's Greatest Mystery

Love is life's greatest mystery
An untapped continuous energy throughout history
Spoken of in soft gentle words
Or shouted from rooftops so it can be heard

Love is felt by touch and feel
Once touched you know the energy is very real
Love can be spoken and heard
Singing melodies of love or rhyming verses of words

Love can be seen even within the unseen
For the silver thread that connects
lights up through the moonbeams
Love can be tasted by a gentle kiss
Creating an energy of heavenly bliss

DR. CHARLES N. TOFTOY

Love whispers through the giant, majestic trees
One falls in love slowly like drifting Autumn leaves
One can fall rapidly as the rivers ever flowing into the ocean
Waves of the ebb and flow of tides create turbulent emotion

One falls for love or in and out of love
Always craving, seems no one can have enough
Promises are made to love forever and a day
Sometimes those promises have to be put aside,
but the love always stays

Each broken heart from a promise of love made
Will come back to haunt someone one day
Love is meant to grow and energize one's spirit
Bringing a small piece of the mystery,
it is meant for one to share it
Love's energy is there for anyone and everyone
Take a little of a lot, always remember to return some
For it is a give and take of this energy
that opens the heart of the soul
To hear a love calling to it from anywhere,
everywhere around the globe

Love is life's greatest and most challenging mystery
So tap into love and become part of making a glorious history
Share it, keep the promise you make
to love forever and a day
For the circle will go unbroken
as it is meant to be that way

[Everyone got up and applauded Brenda, requesting a copy of the very moving poem.]

AMAZING FIRESIDE TALKS

Lars:

Okay gang. Next week we'll discuss DENIAL. I hope you're not in denial because that's like living in darkness. If so, next week we'll give **YOU** thoughts to crawl out of denial for good.

***

The team rushed into the kitchen to fill up their mugs with hazelnut, white hot chocolate, and continued to chat about the wonder of pets. Sasha jumped into Lars's lap and Zoe, the younger Yorkie, hopped up into Doris's lap. Lars said that next week the doctor would implant a pacemaker to restore a normal heart rate.

Then he went on for 20 minutes about how people love their pets. He gave several examples. Lars told the team that it might be terrible to say, but he is more affected emotionally over the loss of a Yorkie than the death of a friend. The love lasts forever.

Sasha must have understood that comment because she proceeded to swarm all over Lars face with kisses. Zoe showed off, as usual, doing her favorite tricks, including jumping through a colorful hoop and hustling through an expandable tunnel. Everyone cheered, shook paws with both dogs and gave them treats.

The Rev could sense the love in the air amongst these professionals…the Alpha Team. A solid, trusting bond.

The high-5s ended the evening, which included high-5s from Sasha.

Mark Twain
-Samuel Langhorne Clemens-
(1835 – 1910)

American author and humorist. He wrote *The Adventures of Tom Sawyer* in 1876 and *The Adventures of Huckleberry Finn* in 1885. *Finn* was a sequel and often called the '*Great American Novel*'.

"Denial ain't just a river in Egypt."

- Mark Twain

Fireside Talk #13
The Defense Mechanism
of Choice: Denial

She stood next to the piano, waving her four arms with a sword in one hand, wearing a garland of 52 skulls. Goddess Kali zoomed in on Lars with her three eyes…looking beautiful, radiant black complexion, white teeth. Lars was stoking the fire…getting it ready for tonight's fireside talk. He was alone.

Kali said only one thing: *'Those who deny are liars.'* Then she danced away. Goddess Kali had helped Lars during the last cold case that the Alpha Team investigated for the local police. Her tips were insightful.

For the first time, Lars is wondering if this is an illusion…an unreal image. In his dreams, is Kali just a deceptive vision? Can it be a neurological disorder, like PTSD causing delusions…or an undetected brain injury?

In a criminal case, which preceded the Alpha Team's assigned cold case, Lars knew that the genius sociopath, William Crawford, was in love with Kali. Nobody ever loved Crawford, so his love for the Goddess was real...an illusion or delusion? Is Kali that powerful that she can draw you into her web?

Lars knows that there are thousands of devotees to Kali today that have an intimate bond with her in eastern India. They visit Kali Puja, a Bengali festival held every autumn in Kolkata, India.

Since Lars learned that Crawford wrote his thesis on Goddess Kali and the Thuggees at American University, he studied everything about her...trying to get a clue on what made Crawford tick.

He knew that the Thuggees, a Hindu and Muslim secret cult that was founded before 1356, were robbers and murderers. The Guinness Book of Records credits them with two million deaths, until the British eradicated them in the 1830s. The Thugs worshipped Kali. Thuggee means *'deceivers'*. Lars thought, *am I deceiving myself?*

From time to time, she reappears...in his dreams, too. Lars is asking himself a question tonight for the first time. *Am I illusional or delusional?* Right away, he thought of two firefights in Vietnam where he might have received brain damage even though undetected. Shot down in a helicopter and in another close encounter, he was blown off an Armored Personnel Carrier. Both affected his head, although the open wounds were to the body. The RPG that hit the APC caused both ears to bleed.

Was that it? Am I in denial about it? Maybe so, since I never talk about it. Are Kali's tips really my own tips I'm giving myself through her image?

***

Lars:

I'll be frank with you; I think denial is a deliberate masking of your feelings.

Brenda:

That sure gives us a kick-start to this fireside talk, Doc. It's actually better than Merriam-Webster: *'refusal to satisfy a request or desire; refusal to admit the truth or reality.'* I had a roommate in school who denied being on drugs. Later, she became an addict. It ruined her life.

Tiger:

I can't stand these drug-addicts and alcoholics who won't admit they have a problem. They lie to themselves. I've seen lots of guys in denial. Unfortunately, they end up abusing their spouse and family members. Nobody should have to take this kind of abuse.

Rev:

Now, we're looking at **YOU**. If you fit in this category—please get help. There's lots of help around. Don't live your life with anxiety or pain…just because you can't cope with it. Some people might seem to be beyond help. I have several tough examples that I've had to face as a reverend.

A mother's daughter was killed in Afghanistan. Ceremonies conducted; I presided at the funeral in Arlington Cemetery. Later at the reception at the Fort Myer Officer's Club, she said that her daughter was not in *'that coffin'*. She'll be home soon. This is a true story. She had to be sent to a mental institution in southern Virginia. I visited her out there. Didn't know who I was…no focus in her eyes.

There are people who refuse to admit that a traumatic event happened. Deny it. And for some, denial is very strong. When challenged, it can turn to serious anger. To wrap up my point here—I have to go back to the waste of energy thought again. Denial is a waste of energy. It takes energy to refuse to believe the truth. And you're just fooling yourself. Not a good way to live this life.

You are trying to lie to yourself when you are in denial. Deep inside, you know it to be true, so you make the agony of denial worse.

Doris:

I just thought of something. Denial protects the ego. The ego— what Lars's girlfriend, Goddess Kali, seeks to destroy.

[Everyone chuckles.]

DR. CHARLES N. TOFTOY

By the way, I was in denial about my husband's death on 9/11 in the World Trade Building. Think about it—he called me to tell me about the fire and that he was heading down from the 47th floor. I kept a tape of that loving message. Started drinking. Gave up my job. Turned into a recluse. Lars saved me—long story. But I was really in denial—picturing him walking through the door, playing the piano and so on. My advice is to face reality and eliminate denial. You'll feel so much better when the hurtful truth comes out. You'll be released from the anguish. You can dwell on things, but it's best to move on.

Tiger:

Yeah! Look at Lance Armstrong. He lied for many years about doping. The U.S. Anti-Doping Agency's investigation ruined his life. Your life can be ruined too if you hang onto denial.

My first wife carried on an affair for 3 years. She was acting weird. I hired a private detective. Photos of her and this newspaper boy in my bed. Dumped her the next day. Bad memory, but it's behind me. You always have to move forward. And be truthful to yourself.

Rev:

One thing you can do is to smile in the mirror at yourself. Do it once a day, like in the morning shaving or brushing your teeth, or putting on make-up. Look at yourself and smile—no matter how you feel. After a few weeks, for some reason, you'll feel better. It's osmosis at work. The smile makes you feel good about yourself. Be truthful and feel good about yourself. Don't accept denial. It builds up the baggage in your dark shadow that we talked about earlier.

Lars:

I think Leo Tolstoy wrote it best in *War and Peace*. Here, I'll read it to you:

> *At the approach of danger there are always two voices that speak with equal force in the heart of man: one very reasonably tells the man to consider the nature of the danger and the means to avoiding it; the other even more reasonable says that it is too painful and harassing to think of the danger,*

168

since it is not a man's power to provide for everything and escape from the general march of events; and that it is therefore better to turn aside from the painful subject till it has come, and to think of what is pleasant. In solitude a man generally yields to the first voice; in society to the second.

Lars:

My uncle had Alzheimer's. One day I saw the Chaplain walk by us. Stopped him and introduced him to my uncle, who was in a wheelchair. The Chaplain greeted him and held out his hand. My uncle said, 'Get lost.' Some people can't be helped even if they don't have a serious medical problem.

Brenda:

If you're trying to help someone who's in denial, do try talking to the person. Make it short—what you believe, so at least the person knows how you feel about whatever it is. After a while, it might sink in. After all, they are miserable inside. Consistent, repetitive short talks about how you feel might work.

Tiger:

One other thing may help you. Call in a professional to talk to the person. You're not a doctor so they don't want to listen to you, but they may listen to a pro. None of us on the Alpha Team is a doctor— we are just offering thoughts on all of these various matters to help **YOU**.

Rev:

Show empathy and that you are there to support him or her. One day, after you've stated your feelings you might see a positive reaction. This means he or she is asking for help. They have to want help. It can't be forced. If you are the one in denial, then please take our thoughts that are applicable.

Doris:

I would do it very simple. For example: *'I don't like it that you drink too much or do drugs.'* That's enough. Maybe it will get through and doing it that way avoids a certain confrontation resulting in zero results.

Tiger:

Yeah. Confrontations = zero results. That's for sure. Been there, done that.

Brenda:

I'd keep it very subtle, but mention whatever you plan to say in a consistent way. This may sound silly but play a game. Like, 'I'll write down my shortcomings on a sheet of paper. You do the same. We'll compare.' Maybe add a few good points. It's all worth a try.

Tiger:

I don't know if you want to come out of denial yourself, or pick up tips from us on how to get someone else out of denial. Either way, our ideas should *awaken you* or whomever you're helping. A person in denial can only lie to oneself for so long. It's got to be cured. Look at one of my favorite singers of the 1970's, Karen Carpenter. She died at the age of 32 due to heart failure resulting from anorexia nervosa. In denial, but couldn't someone have helped her? At least get her to a doctor and follow-up!

Lars:

That leads me to realize that denial can be a cover for anorexia, bipolar, ADHD, cancer, addiction, mental illness…almost any medical condition. My mother-in-law was diagnosed with colon cancer. She told her doctor off and walked out. Ignored it. Said it was heartburn or indigestion. Died a month ago. Deep denial. Deep.

Brenda:

The American Heart Association states that denial delays heart disease treatment. Some people put off a medical checkup, and then it's too late to cure whatever it is. Denial can be a killer. *Delay is the deadliest form of denial',* according to C. Northcote Parkinson. Parkinson was a British author and historian. He wrote *Parkinson's Law* in 1955.

Doris:

What Mark Twain meant was it's not just a river in Egypt; it's an ocean so big and deep that you can drown in it. Are you drowning in denial? Or is someone you want to help—drowning? If so, there's a lot of supportive help out there. You just need to research it out.

Lars:

Some of the experts in the sociology and psychological fields agree that there are several types of denial. Simple denial—denial of a painful fact; refuse to face facts. Minimisation denial—painful fact admitted but downplays seriousness. Transference denial—fact and seriousness admitted, but disowns any moral responsibility; even shifts culpability; avoids of harm to others as a result of his behavior.

Most of the simple denials are minor, such as: clearing throat, snuffing, shaking foot up and down with leg crossed, burping, whining, tapping fingers, passing gas. Temper tantrums. These continuous actions are irritating to others but are not dangerous denials. The person usually denies that he has this particular habit.

However, denials can move from simple ones to those that are dangerous. Examples are:

'The accident wasn't my fault...the roads were slippery' or 'the tires were bad.'

In fact, she was intoxicated while driving.

'My problem at work is due to my boss.'

Even though he was often late or abusing alcohol, leading to poor job performance.

'Sure, I'm a substance abuser but it's because of my work, family, insomnia, and a lousy relationship.'

Those in denial are extremely good at distractive and escapist tactics.

DR. CHARLES N. TOFTOY

Brenda:

A few other things drive me up the wall, like people who twiddle thumbs, chew gum, tap pencil, and crack knuckles over and over.

[Everyone nods in agreement. Then Tiger cracks his knuckles. Everyone laughs except Brenda. She rolls her eyes again and glares at Tiger.]

Rev:

When it's the dangerous type of denial, you should contact a professional interventionist. The interventionist can get the person in denial to the correct treatment center. I've done this for troops for many years. Intervention can assist in the treatment of many abuses: alcohol, crack cocaine, inhalants, crystal meth, sex, gambling, and others.

Tiger:

You can get free online assessments. I've had buddies who have looked up crisis centers on the internet. Some centers have 24-7 hotlines.

Rev:

There are a surprising number of people who are in denial about the condition of their heart. This delays treatment of their heart disease in some cases. Others deny a diagnosis of cancer.

Brenda:

The worst case of denial I've been faced with was my roommate, Laura. To make a long story short, she drank too much. It got worse over time. One time she went outside our apartment and danced naked along the sidewalk in full view of everybody nearby.

Laura blamed everybody—me, her boyfriend, doctor, mother and father, her boss—even her sweet aunt. She always told us: '*You would drink too if you had my problems.*' That was her cop-out, but we all suffered as a result of her hang-ups. Especially her mother and father. She hung herself, as you all know from what I told you two years ago.

[Suddenly Brenda burst out crying. Dug her head into Doris's tiny shoulder. Doris wrapped her arms around Brenda. All eyes filled to the brink. After a few moments, she slowly recovered.]

Brenda:

You have to realize that if you are in denial of some problem or truth, you are affecting the lives of those around you. You are hurting them. So you need to burst out of your cocoon and face reality. Otherwise, you are simply being self-centered. And that is not good.

Doris:

You've hit on something huge: self-centeredness. None of the articles I reviewed, some by experts on denial, ever mentioned self-centeredness. To me, self-centeredness is a form of insecurity and low self-esteem, which could be considered forms of denial.

Rev:

I can't stand self-centered people. They hurt those around them, as Brenda said. And denial causes others to carry your burden. It's not fair. Bill Kortenbach wrote a book, *Counterpredators,* which is about survival response conditioning. It's a 5-star rated book covering a modern solution to an ancient problem. He stated:

'Denial does not solve the problem. Denial does not make the problem go away. Denial does not give us peace of mind, which is what we are really seeking when we engage in it. Denial is a liar. It compounds the problem because it keeps us from seeing a solution and taking action to resolve it.'

Tiger:

Some people are in denial about their medical condition. My close friend said: 'I don't have to go to the doc. Not me!' So I ask 'how are you?' In an angry way he said, *'I'm okay. You okay?'* Three weeks later, he died of recurring prostate cancer. Knew it all the time, but kept it inside. *'I'm okay.'* Sure you are! True story, Bro. Denial. Denial. It's a killer, man. A killer when it runs deep. Don't let it run deep.

Lars:

Sometimes a person is so broken, you can't do anything. I've seen it in action, even at the VA hospital.

Doris:

Some support care groups, like tough love, might help. There is plenty of help easily available for you or the person you want to help.

Tiger:

I'm looking forward to next week's topic—PATIENCE. I'll be all ears because I've got an impatient person at home. Got what I mean?

Lars:

Yup! The roaring fire in our huge fireplace has turned to grey embers. So the fireplace might be trying to tell us something—wrap it up! By the way, this is a great setting for our discussions.

[Everybody nods in agreement.]

Doris:

I know we presented poems about love at our last session, but I'd like to end this fireside talk on denial with a poem by Helen Rosengren, published in 2009 by Beyond Prose (beyondprose.com). Her poem, coupled with Tolstoy's writings that Lars provided earlier tonight, really says it all about denial. I'll read it and give you all a copy:

Denial is a river
That flows through my veins
To my heart it delivers
A way to keep me sane
It just didn't happen
It just cannot be
That is the message
It brings home to me

Denial is a fence
Surrounding my soul
It is my only defense
To unbelieve what I am told

Block the pain from life
Try to set yourself free
Rid the suffering and strife
Trying to live inside me.

***

In bed that night, Doris expressed her strong denial after losing her husband on 9/11. That was the first time she admitted denial about it. She reminded Lars about her husband's telephone call from the 47th floor, saying that he was on the way to the lobby. He would call her from there. Lars kissed away her tears and gave her thoughtful words on encouragement as she fell fast asleep. Meanwhile Lars was visited by Goddess Kali in his dreams letting him know she is his strength and gives him courage.

Ralph Waldo Emerson
(1803 – 1882)

American essayist, lecturer, and poet, who led the
Transcendentalist movement of the mid-19th century.
He was a champion of individualism.

Fireside Talk #14
One Key to Self-Control: Patience

It was a Vietnam flashback. Lars' airborne unit was surrounded near An Khe. Lars took his time and at the right moment, called in napalm strikes from supporting aircraft on the Viet Cong, as they were moving in closer. The napalm strikes were so close that the heat burned Lars face. That put an end to that firefight. When the team arrived, Lars was sitting on the couch in a daze.

Tiger punched his shoulder, which snapped Lars out of his dream. After being questioned about it, Lars just said that he was daydreaming about a situation requiring patience.

After everyone settled down, Brenda opted to start the fireside talk. Before she started, Doris poured hot Caffé Latte in their mugs. A Martha Stewart favorite.

***

DR. CHARLES N. TOFTOY

Brenda:

The Dalai Lama said it best:

The practice of patience guards us against losing our presence of mind. It enables us to remain undisturbed, even when the situation is really difficult. It gives us a certain amount of inner peace, which allows us some self-control, so that we can choose to respond to situations in an appropriate and compassionate manner, rather than being driven by our disturbing emotions.

If you can take that message and absorb it internally, you're on the way to solving impatience. I think that learning patience is a lifelong *work in progress* with the outcome being emotional freedom.

Tiger:

I know a lot of guys that are 6 feet under because they were impatient.

Lars:

Me too, Tiger. Impatience causes you to make mistakes. A mistake multiplies until you are really in a heavy mess.

Brenda:

Been there, done that. I need to improve upon patience so I'm looking forward to this brainstorming discussion. Sometimes I get out of control. Christopher Reeve, Superman, said the most important thing he ever learned was patience.

Doris:

Think about what Ben Franklin said: '*He that can have patience can have what he will. It just means that you have to have forbearance and sometimes let Mother Nature rule.*' Remember, Ben Franklin was one of the Founding Fathers of the United States and called the 'First American'.

Rev:

I deal with impatient people every day. I know Tiger must face this too at Murphy Funeral Homes. I look at patience as a virtue. Being calm, controlling your emotions, tolerating delays without becoming upset. I like the saying by Phillips Brooks: '*Be patient and understanding. Life is too short to be vengeful or malicious.*' I'd appreciate it if you'd read this saying over 2-3 times, especially the last sentence. Please take it to heart or pass it on to someone you're trying to help. Put it on your refrigerator. It's under my desk glass cover in my home office. Very important that you keep things in perspective—that's what patience does for you. Brooks was an American clergyman and author. The lyricist of '*O Little Town of Bethlehem*'.

This is a sidebar for you. Mayor LaGuardia, in the 1930s, felt that patience and fortitude were important. That's what he named each of the huge marble, sculpted lions who stand guard at the New York Public Library—the Beaux-Arts building. He felt these two qualities, patience and fortitude, would be needed by New Yorkers to survive the depression. He felt patience was a strength. My take on patience is that it can help you ride out a tough time. By the way, my mother was a librarian at the NY Public Library.

Doris:

Let's not forget the fortitude and coming together of the New Yorkers during the 9/11 attacks. The crash of American airlines flight 11 into the North Tower and the United Airlines flight 175 into the South Tower resulted in 2,606 deaths in New York City. My husband was one of the victims. Four-hundred and eleven emergency workers died trying to rescue people and fight fires.

New Yorkers went into action and Major Giuliani stayed highly visible, keeping spirits up. During the chaos, New Yorkers kept their patience. On every anniversary of 9/11 in New York City, the names of victims are read. I can't get myself emotionally stable enough to partake in that respectful event.

My husband called me from the South Tower at 8:55am. He told me that there was a fire in the North Tower and that they had orders to evacuate. He was helping one of the disabled workers in his office to descend. At the end of the telephone conversation, he said, '*Love you—call you from the lobby.*' The plane hit the South Tower at

9:03am, just 8 minutes after his call. Naturally, I feel for the victims of the Pentagon crash and the Shanksville, Pennsylvania victims.

[Tears swelled in Doris's eyes. She bowed her head, as did the others. Clasping hands, silently in prayer, no words spoken.]

Tiger:

I think of all of those 2,977 people that died that day, often. I don't feel anything for the 19 hijackers. But I still don't think we've gotten payback for those deaths yet. I'd love to get a hold of some of those dudes. I'd…

Lars:

I'm off on a slight tangent here, but New York City represents the whole world. It never sleeps. It's alive all the time, dynamic and the people are resilient. Yet it's an intense place. Walt Whitman wrote: *'There is no place like it, no place with an atom of its glory, pride, and exultancy. It lays its hand upon a man's bowels; he grows drunk with ecstasy; he grows young and full of glory, he feels that he can never die.'* And they are patient people, having had to see their way through various hardships. I read a lot of Whitman in school. An American poet, essayist, and humanist; he has been labeled as the 'father of free verse'.

Brenda:

Reverend Whitcomb, this is the perfect time for Ralph Waldo Emerson's saying: *'Patience and Fortitude conquer all things.'* This supports LaGuardia's thought process. Emerson was a champion of individualism. A remarkable essayist, poet, and lecturer.

Lars:

Over the years, I've learned a few things on how patience can help you. Let me read my list: make better decisions, dissipates stress, cuts down irritability, reduces impulsiveness, minimizes your frustration, controls greed and self-centeredness. It also helps you to develop compassion.

In tough times, it helps you to persevere and be calm. My toughest times were close combat firefights. I learned to be calm or I wouldn't be here right now. My big tip for you is to change your attitude to one of calmness. Do work on it.

Doris:

This fits perfectly for me, Lars, because I have some tips for you on how to develop patience. Some of these are Brenda's based on our brainstorming chat before the session started tonight. I'll just read them off to you—apply any that **YOU** feel are applicable.

- Slow down—keep an open perspective, otherwise it's like wasteful energy—useless stress.
- Listen more rather than rattling on without thinking ahead of what you're about to say.
- Change your attitude. Put patience at the top of your 'to do' list.
- When you're in a jam, count to 10—then count backwards from 10 to 1. It works.
- This one may seem silly, but eat slowly. You may be eating too fast. Not good.
- Check yourself out on complaining. Stop—don't complain so much. I don't want to be around people that complain. Are you one of those?
- Accept it that you can't change certain things or people. And avoid negative people.
- Exercise. Yoga, tai chi, or even deep breathing. If you're not doing a little bit of deep breathing, you're missing out on a way to curtail stress.
- Sometimes laugh at yourself or breakout into a grin. You're chuckling inside. Sometimes when you grin, people wonder what you're up to.
- Don't rush around. Solution: better planning.
- Avoid all things and people that trigger your emotions. Totally.

Brian Adams wrote, **'*Patience is the greatest of all virtues.*'** Adams is a human dynamo having his hands in movies, theatre, writing, singing, producing.

Brenda:

Have any of you read *The Iliad*? Homer, 800 BC - 700 BC, wrote *'If I have ever made any valuable discoveries it has been owning more to patient attention, than to any other talent.'* He also wrote *The Odyssey.* Considered the greatest of all Greek epic poets.

To push the envelope a little further on BC guys, here's what Titus Maccius Plautus, 254 BC-184 BC, wrote in *Rudens: 'Patience is the best remedy for every trouble.'* Maccius was a Roman playwright whose comedies are the earliest surviving intact works in Latin literature.

Tiger:

I like the idea of all of us finding our triggers. For example, if waiting in line or someone cuts you off in traffic are triggers, then decide that now, as of today, you aren't going to react anymore. It's not worth it. Just move on—always forward, never backward. Road rage is for stupid people. I think Doris's idea of counting to 10, then backwards to one would help to avoid road rage and other situations that could get out of control. Snip it in the bud, I say!

Doris:

It seems that patience is all about tolerating delay and waiting, without having an outburst. Here's something we haven't told you yet. Patience assists us to be healthier. Because when we do get overly upset, what happens is our heart rate and blood pressure increase.

Let me introduce you to psychotherapy. You may want to get an appointment with a licensed professional for yourself or whomever you're helping. It's not counseling, but rather a relationship between you and the therapist. Takes about 6-8 weeks—can be longer. The benefits grow after treatment. You can check it out…there should be a psychotherapist in your area.

Tiger:

Doris should know; she has a Ph.D. in Psychology. It's worth a try for any of these disorders we've been talking about. We're just trying to give you several options.

Rev:

Sometimes it's painful; that is—whatever you are faced with, but patience coupled with fortitude is worth developing in order to endure. *'It is easier to find men who will volunteer to die, than to find those who are willing to endure pain with patience.'* Well said by Julius Caesar. A Roman general, statesman in Rome. He played a key role in the rise of the Roman Empire. Assassinated in 44BC at the Theatre of Pompey.

We've learned that there are seven emotions: adoration, joy, anxiety, anger, grief, fear, hate. If you're faced with any of the last five, then maybe take in seriously Doris's thought about psychotherapy. Everyone I've known that tried psychotherapy acknowledged improvement.

Tiger:

Prison didn't ruin Nelson Mandela. He said, *'Prison itself is a tremendous education in the need for patience and perseverance. It is above all a test of one's commitment.'*

Lars:

Next week we tackle DIGNITY, which is hardly ever discussed. We all want to be worthy of respect, so our session should be an eye-opener for **YOU**.

Tiger:

That's an important topic, Doc. Real important.

***

As the team was leaving, Lars and Tiger continued to chat about Mandela. Being black, Tiger told Lars how he and Beatrice admired Mandela for accomplishing so many things even though he was in prison for 27 years. Tiger mentioned that Mandela formed the African National Congress, led the non-violent defiance campaign against the Colonial government in 1952, organized the first law partnership in South Africa. Tiger was on a roll. Lars reminded Tiger that Nelson Mandela was the first black President in South Africa. And Tiger added that Mandela won the Nobel Prize in 1953 for ending the apartheid regime. They continued their discussion while Doris filled their mugs with hot Creole Coffee, which contains orange peel, lemon, cloves, and cinnamon. Tiger remarked how that was his favorite. It's a specialty served at Galatoire's in New Orleans.

Lars updated the team on his pacemaker implant surgery. He told the team how two leads were connected to the pacemaker and two leads to the right atrium and the right ventricle of the heart. It is set so his heart rate will not go below 70 beats per minute. A preventative measure. Simple surgery.

Nelson Rolihlahla Mandela
(1918 – 2013)

President of South Africa from 1994 to 1999.
President of the African National Congress (ANC) from 1991 to 1997.
Secretary General of the Non-Aligned Movement from 1998 to 1999.

*"Any man or institution that tries
to rob me of my dignity will lose."*

-Nelson Mandela

Fireside Talk #15
Live With Dignity

After gathering around the fireplace, Brenda explained a disaster that occurred three days ago. She was finishing up a cover story for *The Washington Post* with about two hours left until deadline.

It was a human-interest story about three Wounded Warriors; one lost his leg...the other two soldiers lost an arm in a firefight in Afghanistan. She interviewed them at Walter Reed National Military Medical Center in Bethesda, Maryland. Brenda had never seen such great spirit in anyone that she had ever met...until she met those three soldiers. Faced with months and even years of physical therapy, they held their heads high and were restless with spirit.

Brenda told the team, who are listening intently, that she asked them how they stayed in such good spirits. Sergeant Duncan, the one who lost his leg above the knee, said, *'The spirit is always in the heart. You can never let anything happen to take that away from you.'*

Did I ever choke up! That quote is in the article and I'll always remember it.

Now, the disaster. Suddenly, her computer locked up, crashed, or froze...she didn't know. Brenda got real hyper at this point, more like frantic to be honest. She thought that she had lost everything after hours of research and typing.

With a shaky voice, I called the Geeks at Best Buy in Falls Church. After settling me down, Amit told me to click on setting, then power. Under power, there are three choices: sleep, shut down, restart. Click on restart and give it a few minutes. I was so nervous that I spilled coffee on my nice rug. In orbit. When something goes wrong with my computer, I go ballistics.

After pacing around the room for several minutes, like a leopard, a miracle occurred. At least to me, a non-techy, it was a miracle. It became unfrozen. I was able to pick up where I left off and made the deadline.

I was so happy that I called Amit back to thank him. Amit explained what usually happens. It could be a computer memory problem, a corrupted program, an outdated device driver, or a virus. It's usually caused by applications or device drivers.

He said it disappears, but it's stored in the hard drive and is not visible to you. That's why CIA and FBI agents can find data on computers of suspects. Amit continued to say that if it makes me feel any better, all computers lock up or crash. No operating system is immune. Usually Windows encounters a load situation it can't handle.

Another way, Amit said, is to reboot by holding the power button down until the computer turns off. Wait a minute and turn it back on. He suggested that I restart my computer weekly. During the restart period, it gives the computer a chance to clear up temporary memory junk and allows updating. All news to me!

Anyhow, I went from an unhappy camper to a happy camper in about 15 minutes.

All the team members thanked Brenda because none of them knew about these troubleshooting methods. Actually, they put their hands together...clapping in appreciation for her sharing that information.

Lars told everyone: 'Now, let the games begin.'

***

Lars:

As the professor on our team, let me be frank about dignity. It's hardly ever talked about. Articles are rare. There's no academic course available. Yet, dignity is recognized worldwide as the most important quality because it really translates into self-respect.

To be excluded, discriminated against, or intimidated causes an erosion of our self-worth. This violates our dignity and we should fight against these things. What drives me 'up the wall' is when someone is being taken unfair advantage of and can't do anything about it.

Tiger:

Yeah, Doc, like our last two criminal cases, where the murderers took unfair advantage of their victims.

Lars:

Exactly, Tiger.

Brenda:

Those that are treated unfairly need to bring the issue out in the open. Don't let shame keep you from discussing whatever it is. Most of the perpetrators who are trying to rid you of self-respect are indifferent people. **YOU** need to stay away from those kinds of people. And frankly, stay away from heartless people. There are a lot of them in this world. Hardly dignified.

Doris:

To back you up, Brenda—here's what Dag Hammarskjöld, the second Secretary-General of the United States, from Sweden, said, *'The only kind of dignity that is genuine is that which is not diminished by the indifference of others.'* The people you are talking about get angry. But anger is only temporary. This is for you to remember— dignity is forever. It shows who **YOU** really are.

Rev:

At a recent Mass, Pope Francis talked about that it is work, not power or money that gives us a sense of dignity. He further added:

'Work gives us dignity! Those who work have dignity, a special dignity, a personal dignity: men and women who work are dignified. Instead, those who do not work do not have this dignity. But there are many who want to work and cannot. This is a burden on our conscience, because when society is organized in such a way that not everyone has the opportunity to work, to be anointed with the dignity of work, then there is something wrong with that society: it is not right! It goes against God himself, who wanted our dignity, starting from here.'

The best way to handle the heartless people Brenda and Doris mentioned is to calmly walk away. Do you want to know what dignity stands for? Kindness. Being kind, no matter what you're faced with, is dignity in action. The true dignity.

Brenda:
The way to show dignity is to treat everyone as you want to be treated. Regardless of whom they are, race, color, how they look— whether they're poor, rich, young, old. Just like the Pope said, everyone can live a dignified life. Volunteering at church, community, activities, hospital or doing what Lars and Doris do—pet therapy.

Tiger:
Also, Doc headed up the Homeless Program at GWU. And Doc doesn't look for credit. You should never take credit for doing good things.

Lars:
All Doris and I look for at Pet Therapy is for just one smile from those elders. It makes our day. Of course, they love Sasha, our Yorkie, so they're all happy. One thing we forgot in offering ways you can show dignity—being respectful to elders. Very important.

Doris:
Another way to grow your dignity is to be careful of your language.

DR. CHARLES N. TOFTOY

Tiger:

Yes. We shouldn't be using foul language. To me your dignity equals your reputation. You should never violate anyone's dignity—at the workplace, school, or anywhere for that matter. Each family member's dignity should be respected. It's not very dignified to yell or lay a hand on a family member. That's undignified and unnecessary. Not to pull out my black card but Booker T. Washington, the most influential black educator of the late 19th-early 20th centuries, said, *'No race can prosper till it learns that there is as much dignity in tilling a field as in writing a poem.'*

My poppa, down in the *Big Easy*, used to tell me that everyone counts. The janitor, garbage pick-up guys, blue-collar workers, white-collar workers; they're all important. The guy that cleans and waxes the floors at night knows more about how to do that job than you do. You'll learn that when you talk to the janitor. That's an example of what my pop meant. He drilled that into me. Good advice for **YOU**.

Brenda:

Let me go back to an earlier point. If you are being put down, you should get outside help. If you broke your leg, you would get help, right? So similarly, if you or the person you're helping is being mistreated, then you need to get help. As a caregiver, you need to respect the person you are caring for, in terms of understanding their decisions, wants, and needs. Sometimes it's tough, but they need their space, too. You may try to be too protective. Anyway, food for thought.

Rev:

Washington Irving, 1783-1859, wrote: *'There is a healthful hardiness about real dignity that never dreads contact and communication with others, however humble.'*

Not to beat you up on religion but Proverbs 31:25 states, *'Strength and dignity are her clothing. And she smiles at the future.'* Irving was a famous American author and diplomat. He wrote: *'The Legend of Sleepy Hollow'* and *'Rip Van Winkle'*.

And I'll add one more for you. It's a Malagasy Proverb: *'Poverty won't allow him to lift up his head; dignity won't allow him to bow it down.'*

By the way, Malagasy is an Austronesian language. It is the national language of Madagascar. I remember well about people working in a huge landfill in Brazil. Generation after generation of families has worked there. They have self-pride. My message is that whatever you do—live with dignity. If you fail to treat yourself with self-respect, then you are letting yourself down…and others around you.

Brenda:

In my earlier years I was a Certified Nursing Assistant (CNA), I worked in a nursing home for 5 years. We learned to treat residents with dignity and to respect their privacy. Actually, residents have legal rights to protect their dignity. Countries that are strong advocates for residents' quality of care are Canada, Australia, New Zealand, and the UK. Specific rights differ by jurisdiction, but dignity always tops the list of protected rights.

In the US, residents' rights are protected at the State and Federal levels. There are other rights protected to include freedom from restraint.

Lars:

I remember visiting Nana, my grandmother, in a Florida nursing home. I was shocked when I went into her room and saw her spread-eagled with her arms and legs tied down. Her husband was a highly respected minister for 60 active years. And here she was with a dignity quotient of zero. I've never forgotten that visit.

Brenda:

That's terrible, Lars. I learned that some of the staff aides are more interested in their paychecks than the care of the residents.

Doris:

On an unscheduled visit, I found my uncle wallowing in urine…naked. The nursing home provided an attention device close by but nobody responded to his rings. One day, a nurse on a routine visit, found him dead. He had pulled out his breathing tube during the night.

Brenda:

There have been many studies on nursing home care, particularly a qualitative descriptive interview study done in the Netherlands. The findings were that maintaining the residents' dignity-conserving aspects was the number one concern. They found that physical impairment and being dependent on others threatened the residents' dignity.

There are many ways to conserve the residents' dignity. No need to go into those approaches. My main point in bring this to your attention, was to show the importance of maintaining our dignity.

The reason I'm making this point is that many of us are faced with the decision to put a loved one in an assisted living facility or a nursing home. It's tough. Maybe you are faced with that situation now. If so, please remember that, no matter what, the person's dignity must be respected. This is my strongest and most meaningful point that I can make tonight.

[Brenda wipes away tears.]

Tiger:

I've worked in funeral homes for 21 years. I helped my father run the family-operated funeral home in New Orleans. Now I'm the associate Director of *Murphy Funeral Homes* here in Arlington, Virginia. Our funeral home is *A Dignified Memorial Provider*, which is comprised of 1,800 licensed providers in North America.

Funeral Directors have a code of ethics to strictly adhere to, set forth by the *National Funeral Directors Association.* There are several aspects of the code to include *dignified personal services and confidentiality*.

We always treat a deceased person with dignity and respect. They are covered in the preparation room and dignity is tantamount in our work. I prepare the departed as if I'm the last person to care for him or her. I'm the last friend before they are ushered off into the funeral services. I close their eyes for the last time.

[Tiger chokes. Doris holds his hand.]

AMAZING FIRESIDE TALKS

Lars:

Let's make something clear right now. The Alpha Team is not looking at dignity as it pertains to: the upper strata of people, a dignitary, one holding high office, grandeur, or snobbish people. No, we are passing on thoughts to you at the 'grass roots' level because dignity pertains to ALL of us. You want your self-respect with a sense of self-worth.

Do you feel that **YOU** have dignity? Or, based on our thoughts so far, you need to work on it? Do work on it. We all need to do that because dignity is renowned for being the top personal characteristic a person can attain. It is the umbrella, over all your other qualities. Think about it.

Tiger:

That's true, Doc.

Doris:

I studied Immanuel Kant, a philosopher in the 17th and 18th centuries—the Age of Enlightenment. He believed that '*Mortality, and humanity as capable of it, is that which alone has dignity.*' Kant stressed that free will is the essential human dignity giving humans to choose their own actions. See, that's important for you…to choose your own actions.

Brenda:

I like that a lot, Doris. We haven't touched on free will, but it does apply to dignity. You have the free will to take actions as you see fit. Dignity helps you to make better choices and gives you enough depth to avoid making a fool out of yourself.

Tiger:

Since I'm Catholic, I know the Catholic Church and Kant's view on human dignity are similar in that free will is a big part of dignity.

Rev:

To bring out dignity in another way, there was a 1967 movie, '*Cool Hand Luke*', starring Paul Newman and George Kennedy. Luke refused to submit to the prison system. He was treated unfairly by the warden and tortured. But Luke influenced his prison mates to maintain their dignity. The movie is a classic. You should see it. Kennedy won an Oscar for best supporting actor. Newman was nominated for best actor.

Doris:

I read an article by Luo Haocai in the Guangming Daily about respecting human dignity in different cultures. So it's not just us, but on a grandiose scale—the whole world needs to pay attention to improving the dignity of the entire human race.

When I looked at dignity from a worldwide perspective, I discovered two interesting things that might be of interest to you— more like sidebars to our discussion. The Constitution of Switzerland states that '*Swiss citizens must respect the dignity of animals, plants, and other organisms.*' The German Constitution says that '*human dignity shall be inviolable. To respect and protect it shall be the duty of all state authority.*'

I'm sure other Constitutions refer to dignity too, but these are just two examples. By the way, Luo Haocai was the Vice Chairman of the 10th CPPC National Committee and taught law at Beijing University.

Tiger:

Not meaning to play my black card, but Jackie Robinson held his head up high and certainly displayed dignified courage in the face of virulent racism. It was dignity that carried Robinson through his ordeal. What a super baseball player.

Doris:

If we're talking about famous people, I've chosen 3 women that fit into the dignity role: Jacqueline Kennedy—especially during the hours after John's assassination where she displayed poise and dignity, Princess Di—most dignified of the UK Royalty, and Dolley Madison—most loved of all first ladies.

Lars:

Being Norwegian, I've got to add Crown Prince Haakon of

Norway—developed the Global Dignity Initiative with emphasis on the youth.

Rev:

We've got to include Nelson Mandela. A real freedom fighter, politician, activist, and lawyer. He was called the Father of South Africa. Some called him Tata, or father. A notable work of his was *Long Walk To Freedom.* A website can be referred to, to learn more about him: www.nelsonmandela.org. As most of you know, he won the Nobel Peace Prize and the Presidential Medal of Freedom amongst 250 other awards.

Tiger:

I've got to tell you all about Treme. You talk about people with dignity and having a high regard for where they live! Treme, historically called Faubourg Treme, residents have a lot of pride. It's where I grew up. It's one of the oldest Creole and African American districts in the US.

My dad was proud of having a Treme address. And I'm proud to have been born in the *Big Easy.*

The people are rebuilding after the Katrina disaster. Their dignity is at stake because Treme has such a worthy history. They want to continue the honor of the past. It is compose of 19th Century Creole cottages and Spanish mansions. Slaves and blacks mingled together in Congo Square to play music, dance the Bamboula—a traditional African dance, and sell their crafts.

Jazz began here. For example, the Treme Brass Band plays at the Candlelight Lounge, and there are lots of other places that play music such as Joe's Cozy Corner and Kermit's Treme Speakeasy. The Saint Augustine Church—1842 vintage—was the most integrated church in the country just after it started. Notables and 19th Century Voodoo Queen Marie Laveau are buried in the Saint Louis Cemetery.

So you see there is a lot of history to protect. The eminence of Treme is at stake. There's even a movement for dignity and rights in post-Katrina. It's conducted by the New Orleans Workers' Center for Racial Justice. The Center organizes day laborers and homeless residents to build this dignity movement. HBO has a TV series named

Treme, which depicts post-Katrina in New Orleans.

My aunt drowned during Katrina. She was like a Mom to me. She died as a result of levees having been built incorrectly and poorly maintained.

[Tiger wiped his eyes. Doris whimpered quietly. Others eyes filled.]

Lars:

We can close this important session with a quote from Real Live Preacher: *'Dignity comes not from control, but from understanding who you are and taking your rightful place in the world.'* Gordon Atkinson set up this blog site, *Real Live Preacher*, where he posted stories and essays. A complex site with a massive database.

Now, everybody, I have a special homework assignment for you.

Doris:

The professor again. What's up, Lars?

Lars:

Well, a little over a month from now we'll have a fireside talk on the SOUL. We need to read *'Care of the Soul'* by Thomas Moore. I've read it before, years ago, but I'm going to read it again. It is rich, invigorating and inspiring, has depth, a look at reality, and it makes you think about your own soul.

You can get it at the local library, Amazon, or via Kindle. This gives you a heads-up. Don't forget next week's fireside talk is on INTEGRITY.

***

Reverend Whitcomb sauntered into the kitchen to join the others. The spacious kitchen is the final spot the team visits before leaving for home each week. The Rev thoroughly enjoys Doris's French country style kitchen. Sitting on one of the stools, with a wicker cover, he admired the long rectangular worktable with a large colorful, ceramic rooster placed on one end…in an action pose…head up, ready to crow.

The table had six stools around it with open shelves underneath. Cabinets galore.

Flagstone floor, rustic iron light fixtures, rusted metal furniture, exposed ceiling beam, low hanging light fixtures, shiny copper pots hanging on the wall, and green plants everywhere.

Whitcomb adored the colors, reminding him of Provence: burnt orange, yellow soft gold, cobalt blue, bright green, fire engine red. Walls were made of rough stained plaster. One wall was in blue tile, each tile with a different design. Large prints of L'Arc de Triumph, Le Louve, and the Eiffel Tower. In summary, a kitchen of natural, rustic elegance.

After the discussions, each Thursday evening, the kitchen was a great place to relax and chitchat. Being a gourmet cook, Doris always had pastries or a special hot drink to cap off the evening. The weather was so cold that the hot drinks were welcome. They all crowded around Doris as she poured them a Minty Hot Cocoa Float. Her recipe was cocoa with a small scoop of mint chocolate chip ice cream with a sprig of mint.

Everyone was getting excited about the upcoming fireside talk on the Soul next month. Doris's hot drink sparked them even more as they began to express different initial views about the Soul.

Lars reminded them that the Moore book is at most local libraries or it can be purchased at Amazon.com or via Kindle.

He added that *'If we don't believe in the soul. Then we may pay for that in some personal outgoing way, like anger leading to violence.'* He passed on a statement by Thomas Moore, *'A genuine odyssey is not about piling up experiences. It is a deeply felt, risky, unpredictable tour of the soul.'* Lars supports Plato and Socrates in the belief that the soul is immortal.

Tiger, being a Catholic, told the others that many Catholics believe in Purgatory for your final purification before going to Heaven. They believe in Hell too.

Doris isn't so sure if there's a soul or not. She's not sure if there is life after death either. Doris gave another differing viewpoint using the Muslims as an example. Most Muslims believe that the soul comes into existence the same time as the body. Then, it has a life of its own with the body having been a temporary carrier.

The reverend ended this informal discussion by recognizing that the Bible doesn't define the Soul concept. *And, as long as you are alive, those who have died, remain alive. Their memories live on in your heart.* Everyone gave the Rev a hearty 'Amen', plus high-5s.

Lars said that it looks like we'll have some interesting thoughts to share, when we tackle the Soul in more detail. Then, he and Tiger started to talk about the Washington Redskins, with the Rev listening on intently. Doris and Brenda planned a lunch together at Coastal Flats restaurant at Tyson's Corner. That will give them a chance to check out two new boutiques.

The team polished off the rest of the Minty Hot Cocoa Float and departed.

Part III

Additional Life Changing Thoughts

A Pause in the Action
Integrity
Character
Ego
Compassion
Humility

"It always seems impossible until it's done."
– Nelson Mandela

Mark Twain
-Samuel Langhorne Clemens-
(1835 – 1910)

American author and humorist

"The right word may be effective, but no word was ever as effective as a rightly timed pause."

- Mark Twain

Fireside Talk #16
A Pause in the Action

The team wanted to hear about Brenda's visit to the Washington National Zoo on its 125th anniversary. Of course, the main event was Bao Bao, the new baby female cub of Mei Xiang. Brenda was able to see Bao Bao pounce on Mei's head and saw her sleeping on her back. Brenda saw Mei Xiang's enlarged wrist, which helps Giant Pandas grasp bamboo.

Brenda passed on information she learned from Ellen Childs, the Zoo's Giant Panda Keeper. Pandas: eat 20-45 pounds of bamboo daily, sleep 10-12 hours per day, and play a lot. In addition to bamboo, Bao Bao eats sugar cane, rice gruel, carrots, apples, and cooked sweet potatoes. Bao Bao likes apple juice, too.

Ellen said that Giant Pandas have lived in bamboo forests for several million years. There are about 2,000 in the wild, mostly located in the mountains of central China.

Brenda mentioned that she visited the Giant Panda Research Base in Chengdu, China three years ago. She saw 30 pandas, which are free to roam around the huge protected refuge park. And baby pandas in incubators. The babies were the size of a golf ball. One funny thing she saw were Giant Pandas sleeping in the bottom of trees under stumps...their favorite sleeping abode. Everyone gave Brenda a thumbs up as they sipped their peppermint hot chocolate a' la Doris.

***

Lars:

This is really not a fireside talk session tonight. Rather, it's a time for reflection. We hope you have already read parts of this book twice or even three times. This is the kind of book to keep on hand for reference when you're down in the dumps or you have a big challenge. The point is that you should gain something that will improve the way you look at things.

This book is written *to* **YOU** and *for* **YOU**, the reader. I am very proud of the Alpha Team. The last two criminal cases we worked on are documented in two books. All of our backgrounds were covered in those two books.

But just to remind you: Tiger is a Vietnam Vet, former police officer in New Orleans, and now an Associate Funeral Director here in Arlington. I'm also a Vietnam Vet, did the Corporate World and Academia. Doris is a former FBI profiler, into astrology, psychology, and medium-ship. Brenda is our *Washington Post* journalist, photographic memory, on the street crime reporter.

We bring a lot of experience to the table, yet I must state that the thoughts rendered in these fireside talks are our suggestions and ideas. No one here is an expert on any of these topical areas. Most of our thoughts are meant to be startlingly open and revealing.

Tiger:

Yeah, and Doc, Brenda takes notes just the way we talk—not perfect grammar or gooey stuff. I think our practical thoughts will help anyone. I'm glad we're meeting tonight more as a break in the action...for **YOU**, the reader—sort of a breather.

AMAZING FIRESIDE TALKS

Doris:

If we have set **YOU** out to change for the better, then we are happy. The Alpha Team wants you to shake off the shadow that lurks behind you. Actually, a shadow lurks behind all of us. We just need to lighten up the dark shadow and turn it into a golden shadow.

We're trying to be *'just us'* and tell it like it is, with no fluff or rhetoric. You have to decide what to absorb or dismiss from our fireside talks, or modify in order to help **YOU** through a particular situation.

Brenda:

And to wrap up this part, we do lots of research to include: interviews with people who will remain anonymous, books, hundreds of journal articles and internet articles, quotes and poems.

Lars:

Thank **YOU** for pausing with us here. We just want to make sure all of our oars are in the water moving forward in a nice rhythm. It's a time to recharge our minds and keep a good perspective on the big picture. Sort of a pause in the action to refocus.

Next week our topic is INTEGRITY, followed by character, ego, humility, suicide, inspiration, soul and life's a paradox.

***

In the kitchen, Doris dished out a plate of crème caramel to everyone. A French dessert of caramel custard with a layer of soft caramel on top, which is Lars favorite. He calls it *'flan'*.

Tiger had been bugging Doris for weeks to talk about being an FBI profiler. She chose this opportunity to relate her views about profiling. She was an FBI agent for 7 years, after majoring in Behavioral Science at the University of Virginia. Then, she became a profiler or Special Agent with the *National Center for the Analysis of Violent Crime,* located in Quantico, Virginia.

We try to determine personality traits and behavioral characteristics of an unknown offender. Doris told the team that her experience dealt mostly with homicides, child abductions, and rapes.

Doris was able to track down one killer based on where and when he usually made his strikes. In this particular case, she told the team, the police had little evidence or clues. She was to narrow the suspect pool. Doris watched and listened, two important ingredients for a profiler. She outlined his crime zone. Criminals usually commit crimes near where they live...maybe only ½ mile from their home.

When they moved in on this killer, Doris was there and actually shot him as he tried to escape. He was DOA...dead on arrival at the hospital.

Team members listened intently. They knew that Doris was recognized as the best FBI profiler in the country. She was awarded the FBI Medal of Valor, the FBI's highest award.

After finishing up their latte coffee, they went outside to face a snowy drive home.

Confucius
(551–479 BC)

Chinese teacher, editor, politician, and philosopher
of the Spring and Autumn period of Chinese history. His main
interests were moral and social philosophy and ethics.

"To see what is right and not to do it is cowardice."

- Confucius

Fireside Talk #17
Integrity—A Solid Force

A few days ago, Tiger's wife, Beatrice, called Doris to tell her that Tiger has been having terrible dreams for the past month. Most are nightmares involving Vietnam battles and death. She wondered if Doris could bring it up at a meeting, so that Tiger might get some relief.

Doris decided to try it and surprisingly achieved satisfactory results. You must remember that the team has a tight bond with one another. They've been through a lot together...life and near death situations. They share personal information, know the names of their pets, go to lunch, dinners at each other's homes, email, telephone conference calls, and call each other often. It is the pinnacle of camaraderie...even more than a well-oiled athletic team.

Tiger told them that the dead he cares for at Murphy Funeral Homes remind him of the deaths in Vietnam that he witnessed first-hand. One time his unit came across a South Vietnamese battalion that had been totally eliminated. Bodies were stacked neatly in a pile along a road. Tiger helped to carry the bloated bodies to load on helicopters. Bodies would blow up on him. He told them about two other horrific battles he was in and that he could have been killed over 20 times while engaged in close combat situations.

This is the first time Tiger has ever related any Vietnam war stories. Most hard-core soldiers do not talk about war. They keep it inside. When Tiger finished, his hands were shaking. *"So, I dealt with the dead in Vietnam, as I am dealing with the dead now."*

Tiger started out helping his Dad as a youngster with his family business, *The Greene Funeral Home*, in New Orleans. During high school years, he would help out as an attendant during the summers. Tiger handled basic tasks like setting up caskets, and assisting mourners. Later, when he left the Army as a Sergeant E-6, Tiger returned to help the family business. Then, he got the job offer in Arlington, Virginia with Murphy Funeral Homes. Tiger told the team that he earned an Associate Degree in Mortuary Science at Strayer University. That degree enabled him to be promoted to an Associate Funeral Director.

Tiger helps the Funeral Director prepare the dead bodies and coordinate funeral services. Tiger supervises attendants who place the casket in the parlor, arrange floral and lights around the casket, closes casket, escorts mourners, greets visitors, and plans for limousines.

Tiger was on a roll. More relaxed. He was proud to tell the team that it takes a special person to join this career field. You have to be compassionate, have empathy, provide emotional support. You need to recognize cultural differences, have a responsible attitude, sensitivity, and good communication skills.

Many funeral homes are adding other services to their business. Usually, they have many rooms and large parking areas. Some now handle weddings, birthdays, Rotary Club luncheons, outdoor barbeques, and business conferences.

In about 2 weeks, Doris will learn from Beatrice that Tiger's bad dreams have subsided. Also, that there is a significant improvement in his PTSD situation.

Doris realized that Tiger felt secure in relating a few of his many war stories to a small group of people, the Alpha Team, who he respects for having solid integrity. It showed Doris the importance of relieving yourself of dark baggage, which affects your daily living. To her, Tiger seemed to be much more at ease.

***

Brenda:

Let me read this poem to you all. It's entitled *'Integrity'* by Gary Dodd, who is a passionate Australian poet. It's my best shot about integrity.

Integrity
is standing up
for what
you believe in.

It is treating everyone
equally and fairly,
acting independent
of others that do otherwise.

It is being
open and honest,
responsible for
all of your actions.

It is speaking out
when others
are treated poorly.

It is refusing
to participate
in actions
detrimental to others.

It is admitting
and apologizing
for your errors,
when mistakes
are made.

It is respecting
your environment,
your fellow humans,
and yourself.

Integrity
is not a characteristic,
it is
a way of life.

It is
what you do,
and what you say,
always.

It sets you
apart from others;
it defines
you as a person.

Treat others
as you would want
to be treated.

Be upstanding,
be forthright,

be conscious
of your actions.
Remember
to always
act
with integrity.

Tiger:

Does that say it all, or what?

Lars:

Many public officials, high ranking military officers and corporate executives have failed their integrity. It's amazing to see some of these leaders being guilty of one or more of the following inexcusable behavior flaws: scams, forgery, sexting, explicit photos and text messages, bigamy, fraud, extramarital affairs, forcible sodomy, sexual misconduct...

These people may show phony integrity on the outside but inside themselves, they suffer from greed, lust, selfishness, and from being self-centered.

Tiger:

They forget, Doc that their personal honor is at stake. They need to hold on to their integrity. It's like running your car on empty most of the time.

Brenda:

Especially the politicians who flip-flop all the time. Zero integrity. Zero. It has a serious and tragic impact for all of us—not just their families.

Doris:

I don't see how wives of these selfish liars, who show no empathy for others, can stay with them. They let down womanhood by sticking it out because of money and because they're weak. My God, look what these guys have done to them. Where's their personal integrity?

Lars:

Looks like we're bringing these thoughts to you because you can see how you can fall into a trap. The big point is that you can't recover your reputation. Integrity is like a precious diamond—now it's just a piece of dirt.

Brenda:

And the guilty ones always come up with the usual apologies: 'I'm deeply sorry for the embarrassment because of my actions', or something like that. We know it's all baloney. They make me sick to my stomach.

Lars:

Recently there have been several general officers found guilty of irregularities. That really bothers me because we have a Uniform Code of Military Justice. It's a court martial offense, in some cases, for conduct unbecoming an officer and a gentleman. It covers any commissioned officer, cadet, or midshipman. These guys were caught misusing government dollars for travel, lodging, and other expenses. Misuse of campaign funds by politicians for the same activities to include buying clothes for their spouse. How crummy can you get?

Tiger:

Yeah, Doc you have to draw your integrity line in the sand. That's what we'd like **YOU** to do. Please don't fall into these traps. If you're assisting someone, lead them out of these temptations.

Lars:

It all comes back to fairness. *Choosing the harder right instead of the easier wrong.* When you take the easy way, you undermine others.

Brenda:

All of these scumbags have to live with their guilt. Do they have a conscience?

Rev:

They are faced with *'boomerang integrity'*, where after committing these wrongful acts, integrity flies right back at them in the name of an upset God. A failure in integrity returns after they are found out.

Tiger:

Like Doc said, I think we're telling you that developing integrity will help you sleep easily at night without a guilty complex about anything. None of these sorry people can sleep at night. They are haunted by fear of being found out. Hypocrites don't do what they say. We want **YOU** to walk the talk.. The Alpha Team does. That's it in a nutshell. Sleep well; I do.

Brenda:

Ralph Waldo Emerson wrote, *'Guard your integrity as a sacred thing.'* If you do, I think you'll sleep good at night per Tiger's comments. No self-doubts, guilty feelings or regrets. I think integrity will make you feel good about yourself. We all need to work on it— it's an odyssey—a journey of learning.

Lars:

What is your integrity quotient? That's a new term—my term. What I mean is how do you rate on a 1-10 rating scale in regards to integrity? Is it a 10, a 7, or 2? To determine how you stand just ask yourself these questions:

- Do I do what I say I'm going to do?
- Do I keep my promises?

You should develop <u>zero tolerance</u> for keeping your word. I believe you can improve your integrity quotient and we'll give you thoughts to help build a solid integrity base. You've got to have it because people know when you don't. They may not say anything to you but silently they know you are not a person of your word. Wow! This is really important, gang.

Brenda:

It seems that you have to be honest with yourself in order to have integrity at the 10-quotient level. You have to defeat any demons

212

inside your mind and body. Like Buddha wrote, '*It is better to conquer yourself than to win a thousand battles. Then the victory is yours. It cannot be taken from you, not by angels or by demons, heaven or hell.*'

You just can't be a fake and try to show exterior integrity, when on the inside you are cheating on the real integrity. This is superficial integrity. You can't sleep soundly at night when you know that you are a fool. And that's what you are—A fool.

Tiger:

Or a phony. I hate phonies. Too many of them. To them, greed and selfishness come before goodness. My mother told me to watch out for these kinds of people. My mother was like a saint to me. My N'Awlins' Momma Saint!

Lars:

Since I'm our Aristotle, Socrates, Plato guy, let me follow the Buddha quote of Brenda's with Plato: '*For a man to conquer himself is the first and noblest of all victories.*'

Rev:

To me you've got to have a clear conscience. You should try to stick to Luke 6:31: '*And as you wish that others would do to you, do so to them.*' Wouldn't you be better off if you stuck to the Golden Rule? What Lars, Tiger, and Brenda covered about the conduct of higher level people is appalling. Not accepted by God, I assure you.

A good Proverb that supports this is 10:9, '*Whoever walks in integrity walks securely, but he who makes his ways crooked will be found out.*' And Proverbs 28:6 follows these thoughts nicely, '*Better is a poor man who walks in his integrity than a rich man who is crooked in his ways.*'

All of these Biblical passages support what we're talking about. I'm acting like a reverend again, but I did my homework for this session. The bottom line is that you need to set up your own code of values.

As you live your life, try hard to stick with your code. Again, those people out there that are committing these personal irregularities are not in good stead with God. I can assure you of that. They need to change their ways if it isn't too late.

Tiger:

Beatrice and I were talking about integrity the other day. She insisted that I give you all a copy of a poem, *'My Life'* by Temitope Popoola, a Nigerian author and writer, which is really moving. It means a lot to us since we're black. By the way, Ytmitope Popoola also wrote the play entitled *'Love'*. Take a look at the poem. I'll read it to everybody.

I'm black and proud,
My skin is rich and has veins of integrity!
My heart is soft, beautiful and not gritty.
My eyes are intent, yet filled with warmth.
My lips are full and give out smiles that melts the heart.
I might have had challenges,
Might have seen things worthy of pushing one to the edge,
But I won't lose my head over those things!
Standing tall and overcoming is the best option,
But indeed, life could be so cruel
The one you expect so much from could disappoint you in a flash.
What is this world that the material things have gained priority?
Mscheeeew, vanity upon vanity, all is vanity.
And if you hate me because I'm rigid, then so be it!
My principles will not change, they'll remain the same.
That is what makes me.
Some things are logical, and it is only normal for one to do them!
I would not sell my birthright over a plate of porridge!
I will not let down my guard over things that are not worth it!
I am me! And I am black and beautiful!
And the blood of modesty flow through me!

Rev:

I'm going to hit this hard. *Your life is a waste if you don't have integrity.* In life, we breathe in and out. Is that all there is to it? No. Integrity is your solid, sacred force. It's yours, nobody else's. You

214

have to grow it over time. It grows by overcoming struggles and fighting through tough situations—facing them head-on.

A person who has lost his or her integrity, like those mentioned by Lars, have to be suffering inside. Without integrity, you cannot have a truly happy life. There is no other way.

Integrity comes from the Latin word, *'integri'* meaning 'wholeness'. So to be a whole person you need integrity. Then yes— you can sleep good at night.

For those of you who believe in God, Psalm 25:20-21 is a nice Godly plea:

'Guard my life and rescue me; let me not be put to shame, for I take refuge in you. May integrity and uprightness protect me, because my hope is in you.'

As a reverend, I can tell you that if you are upright, like we're discussing here, He will take care of you. To add on to this, Proverbs 11:3 *'The integrity of the upright will guide them...'*

For me there are some upsetting things going on. Some of the findings about Americans by Patterson and Kim in their book, *'The Day America Told the Truth'*, a *New York Times* bestseller, were:

- only 13% believe in the Ten Commandments
- 91% of Americans lie regularly
- 30% are not sure if they love their spouse
- More than 20% goof off at work

Do you lie regularly? Do you really love your spouse? Do you believe in the Ten Commandments? Perhaps when Doris covers ways to improve your integrity, you'll come to grips with these questions if they are appropriate to you. I'll leave you now with the idea of having your own moral code so you have peace of mind. However, it should be based on the Ten Commandments. Don't forget, I'm the reverend in this group. Just remember, **YOU** can't expect to be respected if you don't have integrity.

Brenda:
Rev, this fits right in with what I uncovered in *'Golden Nuggets'*

by Sir John Templeton, a pioneer global investor, businessman, and philanthropist:

'Probably the greatest secret to peace of mind is living the life of personal integrity—not what people think of you, but what you know of yourself. If you remain true to your ethical principles, your personal integrity can become an attractive beacon for success on every level. Listen carefully to the inner promptings of conscience and live peacefully.'

To back you up Rev, a whole person is the only way to have peace of mind. Personal integrity gives you that true wholeness.

Lars:

I played a lot of racquetball especially when I was assigned to the Pentagon. This is a quote from an unknown author about Ruben Gonzalez. Gonzalez had the kind of integrity we're discussing here tonight. True, genuine integrity. Doing what's right regardless of the outcome.

Ruben Gonzalez was in the final match of a professional racquetball tournament. It was his first shot at a victory on the pro circuit, and he was playing the perennial champion. In the fourth and final game, at match point, Gonzalez made a super kill shot into the front wall to win it all. The referee called it good. One of the two linesmen affirmed that the shot was in. But Gonzalez, after a moment's hesitation, turned around, shook his opponent's hand, and declared that his shot had hit the floor first. As a result, he lost the match. He walked off the court. Everybody was stunned. Who could ever imagine it in any sport or endeavor? A player, with everything officially in his favor, with victory in his hand, disqualified himself at match point and lost!

When asked why he did it, Reuben said, 'It was the

*only thing I could do to maintain my INTEGRITY.'
Reuben Gonzalez realized that he could always win
another match, but he could never regain his lost
INTEGRITY.*

Brenda:

Doris, before you give our readers ways to grow their integrity, I'd like to cover a few points on why you should take on the challenge of growing your integrity. A low quotient level of integrity, per Doc's rating system, will cause you to have poor health, anxiety, depression, stress, and personal relationships will suffer. It's really 'bad news bears' to walk around with a lack of integrity.

To me it means honesty. Integrity = honesty. Faith in yourself, like the Rev says. It's an odyssey—a tough walk—a journey over time to build your integrity up to a quotient of 10.

Who are **YOU?** Ever ask that question? Do it now, please. Whatever your integrity is—is you! The real you. It could take your entire life to discover who you are.

The puppy wants to grow up and be bigger like its momma; the tadpole wants to be a frog, and so on. So, what about you? Stick to building your integrity because that can be your legacy. Nobody can beat that as a legacy. While you're doing this, you'll feel your self-confidence building up.

Sorry, Doris I just wanted to inject these thoughts before you give us good advice on improving our integrity.

Doris:

First of all, you need to answer these questions for yourself. Do you:

- Keep your promises?
- Cover up mistakes?
- Lie or cheat? Example: cheat on a test.
- Do what you say.
- Tell the truth?
- Cut corners?

- Exaggerate, like on resumes?
- Do the right thing, regardless of outcomes?

As Brenda stated, it takes years to build integrity as your solid force; yet it can be completely shattered in a few minutes. Here's some thoughts on building your integrity:

- Keep promises, always
- Walk the talk. J.D. Messinger said it best about people with integrity: *'Says what they mean, means what they say, and does what they say.'* Messinger was a Naval Academy graduate and former CEO of Ernst & Young, Singapore. He's the Exxon executive who supervised the Valdez Oil spill cleanup.
- Keep in touch with what's inside you. Don't get too filled up with external information
- Always do what you think is right, steer with your gut
- Repair relationships if there is something wrong
- Keep good friends. Drop losers
- Be humble—it's a strength
- Support others. Compliment them, recognize contributions
- Listen to elders; they have wise advice
- Stand up for your core values and beliefs
- Trust yourself, which enables you to trust others
- Work on worthy projects

You can change the person you are regardless of the way you were brought up or taught. Actually, you are born with integrity. It's yours, but it's up to you to grow it. You don't need to be rich and famous. To live with integrity is more important. And your integrity lifestyle will spill off to others, which will help them on their integrity journey.

A number of people say *you should do the right thing for the right reason, whether someone is watching or not.* That's my bottom line for you. Think about what I just said. It's my best advice. And remember, we're here to help you or have you to apply some of these thoughts to someone in need. Modify them to fit your cause.

AMAZING FIRESIDE TALKS

Tiger:

I guess I'm the Alpha Team's blunt guy, but I hate these feeble-minded hypocrites and people who fake personalities. Again, Congress is so dysfunctional and set in paralysis that it makes me sick. Don't be like this. Please follow Doris's thoughts. Remember, if someone is dishonest with other people, he will be dishonest with you, even though you think they won't be. I guar-ron-tee you 'dat. These guys have little compassion.

I agree with the Rev about the strength of will power. Drop your guard and there goes your integrity—right down the toilet.

Rev:

Integrity is a puzzle because some people think they have high integrity, yet they act immorally or have immoral views. I like the wholeness thought, whereby you integrate parts of your personality into a whole. Can you do that? Try it. Again, your will power is the core of integrity—the foundation on which it stands.

Tiger:

I think you can tell little white lies now and then.

[Everyone shakes their heads and shrugs.]

Okay, I know you don't like that, but let me give you two examples. And we all could think of hundreds of examples in regards to white lies. These two examples are true.

I was visiting my wounded warrior at Walter Reed—Bethesda. I'm his mentor. Lost one arm and one leg. His 21 year-old wife was sitting in his room next to the bed. I sat on the bed talking to him for a while and he asked how he looked. I said, 'Hey man, you look fine for what you've been through.' He smiled. In reality, he looked like death warmed over. A little white lie. What am I supposed to do, say 'Hank, you look pale'?

My wife and I were shopping at Macy's, Ballston Mall. She tried on a blouse. Opinion? Well, I said it wasn't her color and it's so-so. No problem, she tried on others. Not a white lie. The truth. We walked out of Macy's with a full shopping bag as usual.

Now, another white lie. In Starbuck's at Lyon Village, with a small group. Susie said that she just bought a new blouse. Do you like it? It's nice, Susie—nice. Actually, she looked terrible in it. Wrong color, terrible design. A needed white lie. It made her feel good. However, Doc, it doesn't result in a drop of my integrity quotient of 10. I just don't want our reader to feel that he or she has to walk around, like a block of wood, with this idealistic integrity thing. No, I like the realistic integrity viewpoint. However your 10 slips quickly to zero when you make one of those major errors in judgments like we talked about earlier: the public officials, generals, corporate executives.

Doris:

Everyone seems to feel okay with your little white lie thought, Tiger…but these 'little white lies' can splinter your integrity. It can mess up the other person so you have to be careful with the little lies. On the other hand, if a very frank, honest response will hurt the person's feelings, then maybe a little white lie is okay, I guess I'm talking out of both sides of my mouth. It just depends on the circumstances in real time. In Miguel Ruiz book, '*The Four Agreements*' he states, '*Speak with integrity.*' That also means to not gossip. A Mexican writer, Ruiz's teachings focus on Ancient Toltec to achieve happiness, peace, and love.

Tiger:

I agree. Hey! If you're gossiping—knock it off right now. It's wasted energy, per the Rev, and it is trouble. You lose friends, too. Gossipers are betrayers of trust.

Lars:

Those that gossip are trying to take the spotlight off themselves and put it on another person. It's a form of bullying.

Brenda:

Samuel Johnson wrote, '*There can be no friendship without confidence, and no confidence without integrity.*' Johnson was an English writer and poet. He's considered the most distinguished man of letters in English history.

Rev:

Jesus Christ has integrity.

Lars:

Right off the bat I'd say, Socrates—when facing certain execution he stated the truth.

Tiger:

Nelson Mandela, Gandhi. Both were for freedom of the peoples everywhere.

Brenda:

Joan of Arc and Helen Keller. Strong leaders with immense willpower and perseverance.

Rev:

Don't forget Honest Abe Lincoln. A caring President of the people.

Lars:

All the Alpha Team members are a 10. I think you need to listen to your gut or inner voice. It will tell you what's right or wrong. Without integrity, you suffer pain inside yourself. Do try Doris's ideas on improving integrity. It's a virtue that defines your character. Which, by the way, is our next fireside talk topic.

Doris:

I'd like to close this session with a quote from a talk given by the great designer, author, futurist, and inventor: Richard Buckminster Fuller. It's called '*On Integrity.*'

I want you to think about this as individuals. An individual will say this to me: What can I do? What can I do? I am just a little tiny guy.

And, I say, what you can do—I'm repeating something I said to you earlier—that we are really in the final examination—I did get, last night, to you that we are a function of the universe. We're here for local universe information gathering, local problem solving in support of the integrity of eternally regenerative universe.

But integrity is the essence. In an invisible world, there are no visible aesthetics. In an invisible world, the only aesthetic is integrity. It's our great computer world we're going into.

So, I simply say, I am really confronting you with the way— I've lived through all that—because I am a comprehensiveist, I've kept the records; that's the only reason I'm able to say these things to you I am up to. I am giving you a very faithful record of what's going on economically.

So, I simply say, what you can do personally is commit yourself to what is truth. That's all.

You have to remember that we didn't invent-design the universe, and we're not running the universe.

I'm absolutely willing to give credit to what the Indians say 'The Great Spirit.' The word God tends to infer a human being's form, so I say 'The Great Spirit' so you realize that I don't mean in anthropomorphic when I say God.

But, if you operate with integrity, God wants you to know right now whether human beings have the courage to go along with their own minds, or do you have to go with the crowd? Do you have to go evenly with the game or are you going to dare?

If we really dare to go with our minds, we'll stay here. We'll go into an entirely new era of humanity.

It will not be a matter of earning a living. You'll be doing what you see needs to be done because you'll feel you'll want to do it—you'll want to qualify to be able to serve one another. There will be nothing—you will have no question at all about earning a living.

At any rate, personally then—we've got two minutes to this session—it comes back to each one of you, as the numbers multiply of individuals who are willing to commit themselves to integrity—whatever the truth may be—and really commit themselves to making all of humanity a success.

You have to ask yourself the question: Are my reflexes so conditioned that I resent someone else enjoying themselves? Am I really telling to really love my humanity, my fellow?

If you do that, we will win. If you can do it, if it is spontaneously arousable in you to operate with integrity and really go along to love—to love comprehensively. That's it.

By the way, anthropomorphic might be a word that throws you. It threw me. According to Merriam-Webster, it means *ascribing human characteristics to nonhuman things; considering animals as having human qualities.*

Also, Fuller published more than 30 books.

***

In the kitchen, some team members asked Tiger a few general questions about the funeral business. They could tell that Tiger was passionate about his profession.

He told them that cremations are on the rise. Over 40% are cremated in the US as compared to 3.56% in 1960. Over 95% are cremated in Japan—72.44% in the UK. Cremations are the choice by people living in large, old cities because cemeteries are filled up…there's a lack of space. And cremations are cheaper, about $3,725 compared to a burial average of $8,565.

Tiger explained his personal view that when he is preparing a body that he is their last friend who cares. Thus, Tiger makes sure he treats them with dignity and respect. *"I talk to them, God rest their souls."*

All eyes filled with tears. Team members put their hands together in the air…like a sports team. They yelled, TIGER-TIGER-TIGER! Everyone took another macaroon for the road. They know Doris's macaroons are the best and that she uses a 200-year-old recipe.

William Franklin "Billy" Graham, Jr.
(Born November 7, 1918)

American evangelical Christian evangelist,
ordained as a Southern Baptist minister

*"When wealth is lost, nothing is lost;
when health is lost, something is lost;
when character is lost, all is lost."*

- Billy Graham

Fireside Talk #18
Character—The Glue
That Seals Your Fate

Reverend Whitcomb arrived early. Lars was setting up the logs in the fireplace. The Rev asked Lars how he stayed in such good physical condition. Lars told him that it was due to getting ready for the challenges of the Senior Olympics. This stirred up the Rev's interest since Whitcomb was an athlete in high school and college. He asked Lars to tell him more about it. Just then, the rest of the team showed up and wanted to hear about it too.

Lars explained that the Northern Virginia Senior Olympics (NVSO) has all the track & field events of the regular Olympics. Except, there are an additional 30 events. It's for seniors who are 50+ in age. The purpose is to provide seniors an opportunity to compete and enjoy fellowship.

Lars said that he competes in about 10 events...the 800m, 1600m, long jump, javelin throw, and shot put. Other events that he participates in are: basketball free throws, softball hit and throw, football throw, tennis, and miniature golf.

Usually the NVSO are conducted in September. Many NVSO competitors participate in the Senior Virginia Games and the National Senior Games. Senior Games are conducted annually in each state in the US. Gold, silver and, bronze medals are awarded after each event.

It's fun and you meet wonderful people. It makes you have something to look forward to and keeps you in shape. Tiger chimed in saying that he competes in the 60-yard dash. The Rev said he'd like to play tennis. Lars mentioned that he hadn't thought of this until now, but participating in some of these sporting events builds character. And character is our fireside talk for tonight. Everyone gave Lars a high-5.

***

Brenda:

Let's start out with definitions. Here are two definitions of character:

1) *One of the attributes or features that make up and distinguish an individual* (Merriam-Webster)
2) *The mental and moral qualities distinctive to an individual* (Oxford Dictionary).

Rev:

It's really up to you to form your own character. Since it's your most important lifetime asset, do take it seriously and start working on it now. It really is what's inside you—your habits—how you act with friends. Plutarch, the Greek biographer (47-120 AD) said it best, *'Character is simply habit long continued.' People* know your true worth from your character—not reputation.

Brenda:

What you just said, Rev, fits perfectly into what Buddha says about character:

DR. CHARLES N. TOFTOY

The thought manifests as the word;
The word manifests as the deed;
The deed develops into habit;
And habit hardens into character;
So watch the thought and its ways with care,
And let it spring from love,
Born out of concern for all beings...
As the shadow follows the body,
As we think, so we become.

I've got to get this point in here before we finish tonight. And that is, people who are prejudice are people with low character. So frankly, if you have prejudices, I suggest you give them up. You'll be a stronger person by doing so. Try it. I did. And remember Reverend Whitcomb's comments about wasted energy? Well, getting yourself worked up over being prejudiced against a person because of race, religion, or color, or sexual preference is wasted energy. And it's in poor taste. Plus, it shows you have a low character index. Outwardly, you may fake it, appearing not to be prejudiced. Saying the right thing. Inside there's resentment or even hate.

Rev:
God didn't create us as all men or as all women. Instead according to Genesis 1:27—*So God created man in His own image, in the image of God He created him; male and female He created them.*

Tiger:
I think these people of low quality have a deep dark shadow following them. It adds to the pile of baggage already there. I've had people sway me to agree with their opinion. I should have never veered off from my gut instinct. I learned. For you, I say stick to your gut instinct and defend the right cause.

Let me get Abraham Lincoln in here on this one: *'Character is like a tree and reputation like a shadow. The shadow is what we think of it; the tree is the real thing.'* As our 16th President, Lincoln had a gift for getting to the point in a few words. After all, the Gettysburg Address was 272 words. Anyhow, this is my favorite saying about character.

Brenda:

I think character is how you treat others, even though they can't do anything for you. You don't care one way or the other. Also, not taking credit for things; rather, pass the credit on to others. You should make this your top aim.

Rev:

I'm not bringing God into this, but you've got to be self-motivated to do the right thing. It's inside you. We all need to focus on our individual character. Or refocus, if we've let it slide for a while and maybe fallen to a temptation or two.

Lars:

The Alpha Team thoughts are designed to give **YOU** new purposes in life. Or a new purpose for someone you are trying to help.

An unknown writer provided a saying that provides more insight to what I'm talking about: *'Thoughts lead to purpose; purposes go forth in action; actions form habits; habits decide character; and character fixes our destiny.'*

Let me follow this with a Portuguese proverb: *Good habits result from resisting temptation.* The temptations route chosen by the high-ranking officials, that we discussed last week, ruined their character standing. It can never be recovered. Ever.

Doris:

I think those public officials and others were more concerned with their thinking on their reputations, but your character is who you are— inside. Dwight L. Moody said, *'If I take care of my character, my reputation will take care of me.'* Moody was an American evangelist and publisher. He founded the Moody Church. Died in 1899. As Lars said, those high public officials were weak in mind because they chose temptation over character.

Thomas Paine, the famous American political activist and author, wrote: *Character is much easier kept than recovered.* A sidebar here...Paine inspired the Patriots in 1776 to declare independence from Great Britain. Also, you may remember that Thomas Paine wrote *Common Sense,* a pro-independence monograph and he was considered the Father of the American Revolution. To continue, when caught, these people always apologize and provide the usual phony excuses, but their character is gone forever, which reinforces Lars's viewpoint.

I found the most beautiful and profound list of character traits that I've ever seen.

It was a post by Larry on the website: character.training.com. The working definitions are from Character First ™. I made a copy of it for each of you.

Character Traits

Alertness
Being aware of what is taking place around me so I can have the right responses

Attentiveness
Showing the worth of a person or task by giving my undivided concentration

Availability
Making my schedule and priorities secondary to the wishes of those I serve

Benevolence
Giving to others' basic needs without having as my motive personal reward

Boldness
Confidence to say or do what is true, right, and just

Cautiousness
Knowing the importance of right timing in accomplishing right actions

AMAZING FIRESIDE TALKS

Compassion
Investing whatever is necessary to heal the hurts of others

Contentment
Realizing that true happiness does not depend on material conditions

Creativity
Approaching a need, a task, or an idea from a new perspective

Decisiveness
The ability to recognize key factors and finalize difficult decisions

Deference
Limiting my freedom so I do not offend the tastes of those around me

Dependability
Fulfilling what I consented to do, even if it means unexpected sacrifice

Determination
Purposing to accomplish right goals at the right time, regardless of the opposition

Diligence
Investing all my energy to complete the tasks assigned to me

Discernment
Understanding the deeper reasons why things happen

Discretion
Recognizing and avoiding words, actions, and attitudes that could bring undesirable consequences

DR. CHARLES N. TOFTOY

Endurance
The inward strength to withstand stress and do my best

Enthusiasm
Expressing joy in each task as I give it my best effort

Faith
Confidence that actions rooted in good character will yield the best outcome, even when I cannot see how

Flexibility
Willingness to change plans or ideas without getting upset

Forgiveness
Clearing the record of those who have wronged me and not holding a grudge

Generosity
Carefully managing my resources so I can freely give to those in need

Gentleness
Showing consideration and personal concern for others

Gratefulness
Letting others know by my words and actions how they have benefited my life

Honor
Respecting others because of their worth as human beings

Hospitality
Cheerfully sharing food, shelter, and friendship with others

Humility
Acknowledging that achievement results from the investment of others in my life

Initiative
Recognizing and doing what needs to be done before I am asked to do it

Joyfulness
Maintaining a good attitude, even when faced with unpleasant conditions

Justice
Taking personal responsibility to uphold what is pure, right, and true

Loyalty
Using difficult times to demonstrate my commitment to those I serve

Meekness
Yielding my personal rights and expectations with a desire to serve

Obedience
Quickly and cheerfully carrying out the direction of those who are responsible for me

Orderliness
Arranging myself and my surroundings to achieve greater efficiency

Patience
Accepting a difficult situation without giving a deadline to remove it

Persuasiveness
Guiding vital truths around another's mental roadblocks

Punctuality
Showing esteem for others by doing the right thing at the

right time

Resourcefulness
Making wise use of what others might overlook or discard

Responsibility
Knowing and doing what is expected of me

Security
Structuring my life around that which cannot be destroyed or taken away

Self-Control
Rejecting wrong desires and doing what is right

Sensitivity
Using my senses to perceive the true attitudes and emotions of others

Sincerity
Eagerly doing what is right with transparent motives

Thoroughness
Knowing what factors will diminish the effectiveness of my work or words, if neglected

Thriftiness
Allowing myself and others to spend only what is necessary

Tolerance
Accepting others at different levels of maturity

Truthfulness
Earning future trust by accurately reporting past facts

Virtue
The moral excellence evident in my life as I consistently do

what is right

Wisdom
Making practical applications of truth in daily decisions

Brenda:
 It's ***great!*** Everything you need in order to work on these traits or qualities of character. This should be very helpful to **YOU.**

Rev:
 I like the list, but we need to add integrity and holiness. It is a very good guidepost for **YOU.** Absolutely the best.

Lars:
 We all need to work on these traits to build character. Your genuine character is based on the integration of all of these qualities, or the aggregate of them.

Tiger:
 Beatrice gave me a poem to read to you. She loves it and near the end it reads, *It's character that seals our fate.* The author is unknown.

My Mother Says

My mother says she doesn't care
About the color of my hair,
Or if my eyes are blue or brown,
Or if my nose turns up or down.
My mother says these things don't matter.

My mother says she doesn't care
If I'm dark or if I'm fair,
If I'm thin or if I'm fat.
She doesn't fret o'er things like that.
My mother says these things don't matter.

DR. CHARLES N. TOFTOY

But if I cheat or tell a lie,
Or do mean things to make folks cry,
Or if I'm rude or impolite,
And do not try to do what's right...
My mother says that these things matter.

It isn't looks that makes us great;
It's character that seals our fate.
It's what's within our hearts, you see,
That makes or mars our destiny.
And that's what really matters.

Rev:

I'm looking forward to next week, everybody—when we discuss EGO.

***

Doris herded them to the hallway where several classic paintings were hanging on the walls in a row. Doris's home art gallery. She told them that her favorite painting was Van Gogh's '*Vase with Twelve Sunflowers*'; completed in 1889. His purpose was to brighten up the walls of his work studio.

Van Gogh adored the yellow color, which represented happiness to him. Incidentally, the Dutch feel that sunflowers are a symbol of loyalty and devotion. It is the picture that Van Gogh was most proud of. He became known throughout the world for his series of sunflower pictures.

A bit of trivia...there are more than 30 species of sunflowers. Doris continued, saying that Van Gogh's sunflowers are of the Teddy Bear variety with a large puffball look. It is housed in Munich.

Tiger gaped at the picture with admiration. He was fancied with the 3" gold gabled frame, which set the picture off in a splendorous manner.

Now, Doris steered them to the kitchen.

She surprised them with hot coconut eggnog. Everyone gives Doris a rousing cheer. The hot eggnog would hit the spot as they faced a wintry drive home.

They continued to chat about tonight's thoughts. They all agreed that Doris's list was something special. Brenda was saying how she liked the line in Tiger's poem about *character sealing our fate.*

Deepak Chopra
(Born October 22, 1947)

Indian-American author and
alternative medicine / New Age guru.

"The Ego is not who you really are. The ego is your self-image; it is your social mask; it is the role you are playing. Your social mask thrives on approval. It wants control, and it is sustained by power, because it lives in fear."

- Deepak Chopra

Fireside Talk #19
Beware of the Ego

All of a sudden, there she was…Goddess Kali dressed in her usual garb. Necklace of a string of skulls, girdle of human hands, garland of 50 human heads, sword in one hand, demon head in another. Black complexion, white teeth, long red tongue, three red eyes, two dead heads for earrings.

Lars was alone, sitting next to the fireplace in which a raging, crackling fire was underway. Beautiful fire in the huge fireplace. Waiting for the others to show up for the discussion about the ego.

"My God, Kali you've returned!"

"Yes, I only came to have you tell the Alpha Team how I feel about ego."

"I know you are the *Destroyer of Ego.*"

"Let me direct my points to your reader. Your ego is like putting yourself in prison. The ego prison. Ego blocks the path of spiritual growth. Reverend Whitcomb will like that thought. It really is a delusional, selfish view of reality. So discard your ego—your masks, and remove the illusion of the ego. It *is* an illusion. Not real. I put the ego to death. Free yourself; a new path without the ego—go beyond yourself—the ego holds you back. Kill it."

"I'll pass this on, Goddess Kali."

She dances out of sight. Lars scratches his head wondering if he is dreaming or just plain illusional. He hears noises alerting him to the arrival of team members. Everyone is now seated around the fireplace.

***

Lars:

Before we start, I must tell you that I just had a visitation by Goddess Kali.

[He covers Kali's comments.]

Tiger:

Too bad she can't be with us.

Lars:

She is; don't kid yourself. She knew we were covering ego tonight, so she wanted to get her viewpoint across to us.

Doris:

This is sure a different start for us. But I agree with her.

Lars:

Remember…Crawford, the murderer, was in love with her.

Tiger:

That Crawford case was a tough one. A genius sociopath.

Brenda:

Here's how to destroy your ego. Follow the words of Kabir's poem:

AMAZING FIRESIDE TALKS

If you want the truth,
I'll tell you the truth:
Listen to the secret sound,
The real sound,
Which is inside you.

Brenda:

Kabir, or Kabira, was a poet and Saint of India. His legacy continues with a membership of 9.6 million members of the Kabir Panthis sect. Most of them are located in North and Central India. He wrote some wonderful poems. This is one of them, which is fitting for tonight since we are discussing ego. This means we need to look inside ourselves to rid ourselves of the *holier than thou* type of behavior.

Lars:

We agreed that we'd start with the worst form of ego; then discuss the ego in general.

Doris:

And the worst form is the egotist.

Brenda:

As defined by Collins English Dictionary: *A conceited boastful person; a self-interested person. Ego maniac—boaster, swaggerer, self-seeker, narcissist—bighead, blowhard, self-admirer.*

Doris:

I made a list of egotist's traits: arrogant; impulsive; insensitive; no empathy; inflated view of ME, SELF and I; want of power; swollen head; extremely angry when frustrated; boastful; critical attitude; above other people; no concern for others; loving one's self; self-promoting.

Rev:

That all gives us a good frame of reference for our discussion. Thomas Carlyle wrote: *Egotism is the source and summary of all faults and miseries.* Carlyle was a Scottish philosopher during the Victorian era. He believed in heroic leadership. As a reverend, I must say that an egotist distances himself from God—there's no human dignity.

Tiger:
Yeah! And Rev, it means he or she just stays in the dark shadows.

Rev:
It's an ugly trait.

Tiger:
I got fired twice by narcissistic idiots. I can't stand them. They ain't worth your time. Again, as the Rev has stated, a waste of your energy.

Doris:
In regards to helping somebody with an incredible ego, all you can do is tell them how you feel over and over again. Tell the person that you feel ignored and want to be part of the conversation. But be ready for criticism. Just hope that over time osmosis will seep in.

Lars:
Since my undergraduate degree is in engineering, let me define osmosis for you guys. It's a type of diffusion. A simple example is through osmosis, plant roots draw water from the soil. From my West Point days, I remember it being the passage of a solvent through a semi-permeable membrane from a less concentrated to a more concentrated solution until both solutions are of the same concentration.
Do you notice how a drop of water spreads on a paper towel? That is a form of osmosis. Tiger's hand is flying in the air!

Tiger:
Better yet, cut bait on an egotist or narcissist. That's my best advice to you.

AMAZING FIRESIDE TALKS

Lars:

I've seen it in the military, corporate and academic worlds, and I've worked in all three of those sectors. Like Tiger, I've been upended by several of these types of people. Can't stand them. If it's happened to you, then you know what I mean.

Doris:

If you have any of the traits I listed, be honest with yourself and try to shed them quickly. Or if another person you care about demonstrates some of these traits, read on—our thoughts are designed to help **YOU**.

Brenda:

Judge Michael Russo called Ariel Castro an *extreme narcissist.* Remember, he got life plus 1,000 years for kidnapping and abusing three women for over 10 years.

Tiger:

Should have gotten the death penalty. Sorry sucker!

Brenda:

Well, he did commit suicide in prison.

Lars:

We'll be talking about *inner presence* and that's what Michelle Knight, one of Castro's victims, has developed. She's dedicating her life to helping abused victims—a real Joan of Arc. So see, you can become better after having undergone a traumatic experience. Again, think of our quadriplegic soldier. Brave guy. And brave Michelle.

Brenda:

Narcissism was named for a mythological character, Narcissus, who fell in love with his own reflection in a pool. Do you look in the mirror and fall in love with yourself? I hope not. A smile is okay however!

You guys may not know it, but there is a term, grandiosity, which is a person on a higher level of the egotist. Distorts reality, superior to others and over-reacts to criticism. Gets extremely angry and very defensive. I wrote an article for *The Washington Post* a few years ago on a fugitive who was a grandiosity type.

Lars:
When thinking of historical people with usually large egos, I include: Hitler, Stalin, Churchill, Benedict Arnold, and John Wilkes Booth.

Tiger:
Mine are rather tough guys: Billy the Kid, 'Pretty Boy' Floyd, Jesses James, and Jack the Ripper.

Doris:
We've got to add Marie Antoinette to the mix.

Brenda:
And Elizabeth Bathory. She probably had the biggest ego in history. She was called the Blood Countess of Hungary. She brutally murdered girls from 1590-1610 and bathed in their blood to rejuvenate her skin and lengthen her life. Known as the most prolific woman serial killer in history.

Doris:
A little trivia here, but Tom Draper, played by Jon Hamm, in the TV series, *Mad Men*, has an ego a mile high. I like the series because it is set in the 1960s when society was changing so much. And we have to realize that we're faced with constant change.

Tiger:
Can you tolerate people that adore themselves and act like they're better than you?

Lars:
Nope. Good lead in, Tiger, for our general coverage of the ego. Some people argue, in the literature, that there is good to the ego. We realize that if the ego translates to self-confidence and improved self-

esteem, then that's okay.

But we're now talking about those who have an ego that irritates you. They are an annoyance. People that you want to avoid.

Brenda:

Along with Buddhism, I studied Taoism. I've uncovered some remarkable pieces by Lao Tzu in the *Tao Te Ching*. Remember these works go back 2,500 years. Real wisdom to help you annihilate your ego. I'll read them now.

To serve your ego is to worship
a false identity created by
yourself. It is like someone suffering
from amnesia reinventing herself
because she has forgotten who she is.

After the ego has perished, the true self
rises from its dustlike desert flowers
after spring showers have swept
across arid plains.

And my last piece is from Hua Hu Ching, the ancient Taoist book:

The ego is a monkey catapulting through the jungle: totally fascinated by the realm of the senses, it swings from one desire to the next, one conflict to the next, one self-centered idea to the next. If you threaten it, it actually fears for its life. Let this monkey go. Let the senses go. Let desires go. Let conflicts go. Let ideas go. Let the fiction of life and death go. Just remain in the center, watching. And then forget that you are there.

There's so much wisdom here. The idea is to live your life without having the ego in control.

Lars:

I've come up with an amazing, original thought about ego for you. It's not in any ego research literature that I'm aware of. I'm excited about passing it on to you.

Tiger:

Let's have the scoop, Doc.

Lars:

The ego is the culprit that controls your actions. It shields or protects the issues in the baggage found in your dark shadow that we discussed earlier. So when you snap at someone, act impulsive or arrogant, it is the ego protecting your hang-ups and deep issues. It is, therefore, controlling your personality. The probability is high that you don't even realize it. Thus, you have to be honest: look inside yourself, face the items in your dark shadow and dump them. When you do that, you will be enlightened, feel light-headed, because you've removed some of these burdens you've been living with. We all have to do this.

Tiger:

Leave it up to the professor to come up with an original clinching thought for us.

Doris:

By doing what Lars said, you could reset your life or at least improve it. It makes a lot of sense.

Brenda:

It may have to be done gradually. You can't just turn around, face the dark shadow following you, and dump everything that's in your bag. We've already covered what could be in your baggage like anxiety, denial, depression, a sour relationship, something in your past, traumatic event, etc.

Doris:

Here's one problem with ego. Your insides project your outside, which is how people perceive you. So, if your ego controls your inside, then people see the outside only, which displays to them a flaw in your character. It's a stumbling block and you have to do something about it—now. Otherwise, you may not know it, but people size you up as being a phony person.

Tiger:

Yeah! Having a false, meaningless personality. I've seen friends of mine make bad decisions because they hid behind the ego shield. Two of my Vietnam buddies committed suicide, so the ego can lead to self-destruction. In their cases, the ego was a powerful force that controlled those two guys. For them, and many others, the ego was a social mask. It distracted them from the real world. They hid in their inner darkness. Sad. Don't let this happen to you or to someone you're trying to help.

Lars:

I've run into people in all the working sectors, where their ego led to their demise. They loved power—overdid it. Close minded, obsessed with themselves, full of excuses. None of them were respected. The ego was their master. It's really a monster living inside of you. And the monster is not you—the real you—it's an image you've created, as we discussed before, about the dark shadow that follows us wherever we go. Well, part of our dark side is our ego.

Brenda:

The ego has to be in control. It may be controlling you or your friend right now. You may not even know it. But soon in this discussion, we're going to provide thoughts to help you starve the ego.

Lars:

Before we provide guidelines to annihilate your ego per Kali, once and for all, let's discuss the results of the ego. How it plays out. By doing this type of brainstorming, we will set you up to take in our suggestions to give the ego a good stiff-arm!

DR. CHARLES N. TOFTOY

Rev:

In our religious circles, we consider the ego as a source of evil. The bloated ego causes distress. There is a Proverb, not sure which one, that reads: *It is the nature of the ego to take, and the nature of the spirit to share.* In talking to hundreds of troops, I've found that their ego is a defense mechanism against feelings of failure or shame. Covering up something in their past. It reduces them to be like a wooden block. Nothing left inside. The ego is in control. It is ugly and blocks all the spirit in your heart. It covers up everything good about you.

For a lot of these combat-tested soldiers, some wounded warriors, the ego plays back the past to haunt them. It's a haunting, especially as a result of a traumatic event. Or a call in the night about the death of a loved one. That's terrible, but the ego plays on it and keeps playing back that situation in your mind indefinitely, unless you do something about it.

You become a slave to your ego. Unable to shake the memory—causing you to live a shallow life. No matter what has happened to you or your friend, the ego is the invisible enemy that needs to be defeated.

Lars:

Rev, perfect stepping-stone for us to provide tips on destroying the ego. I think this part of our discussion may change your life. Of course, for the better.

Okay, my first thought is for you to stop using I, me, myself, or mine in talking, emails, letters, and any other communications. As a matter of fact, eliminate the use of these self-oriented words, or at least minimize them.

Doris:

I looked up the definitions of ego and self- esteem. Some of it comes from the *World English Dictionary*. It's a fine line. Self-esteem is more positive, showing confidence even though it is an exaggeratedly favorable impression of oneself. Whereas, ego is more negative and counter-productive—the person feeling superior to others and conceited.

AMAZING FIRESIDE TALKS

Brenda:

As we proceed to provide ways to shrink your ego, let me start with a writing from the Dalai Lama:

> Be a good human being, a warm-hearted affectionate person. That is my fundamental belief. Having a sense of caring, a feeling of compassion will bring happiness of peace of mind to oneself and automatically create a positive atmosphere.

Some points about the Dalai Lama to refresh you. He's lived in exile from Tibet since 1952. Tenzin Gyatso is the 14th Dalai Lama. He wrote the *Little Book of Inner Peace*. It covers how to live a peaceful life when faced with the conflicts of modern life.

Doris:

We all have an ego. Yes. You have one, but **YOU** can manage it. Think about this. Does your inside match your outside? If not, you may have an enlarged ego which out-sizes your inside feelings.

Tiger:

When you look in the mirror, do you see a fake person? I hope not. If you do, it's the ego at work. You need to escape the prison of your ego. Tell me, are you full of yourself? Whoops! That's not good. Be more realistic about everything. This will drown your ego, which is an illusion anyway.

Brenda:

If you do certain things, you'll make the ego suffer and you'll feel better. Here are a few:

- Feel the way you want to feel
- See the big picture
- Stay away from abusive and negative people
- Be compassionate and generous. Volunteer more, such as Meals on Wheels or at a hospital, whatever.

- Stop worrying about winning; just do your best
- Stop complaining. The ego feeds off this.
- Try to do good deeds. Help others
- Don't pretend to others
- Be a good listener
- Simplify your life. Ego loves complexities
- Be more humble; it's a strength
- Be your authentic self. The real you

Doris:

Like Lars said about I, me, mine, myself—try to change that to we, us, ourselves. Don't be offended and as Brenda said, you can't win all the time. So don't get hung-up on it. Here's one thing that I think is important. Don't be afraid to say 'I don't know'. Don't pretend to know. It's okay. Try to develop a sense of caring. The problem is that the ego lives inside you, but it radiates outward which shows the dark, distasteful side of you. You have to shed your ego. You'll never be happy if you let the ego run your life.

Rev:

I thought of another one for you. It's easy to do. Make someone feel good every day. Love your spouse, your pet—*something*. Birds, butterflies, whatever. This kills the ego. Drains it of power. You're becoming your true self. Being at peace and understanding yourself is important. I say, let your instincts guide you. You'll start feeling serenity inside yourself.

Of course, you could meditate. If that's not for you, okay; but it does give you inner peace. Just don't let people bother you. It's a waste of energy. Also, meditation will help to control your thoughts and desires. This causes the ego to go out of control, making you the master of yourself, rather than the ego being your master. Much better situation.

Lars:

At this point, I could ask you a few questions:

- Do you know who you really are?

- What do you fear or dread the most?

To answer the above questions, meet with a friend. Ask the friend what your hang-ups are. That's real introspection. It will alert you to your triggers which you need to avoid. Avoid the situations that will make you tense. Stay clear of them. For example, if speaking in front of a group of people stresses you out, then don't do it. Period!

My point is when you give your ego a right hook punch and knock it out, it's like starting your life all over again.

Brenda:

I'd like to add a couple more points. Stick with today, like *CARPE DIEM*. Follow your heart. Again, as mentioned …go by instinct and intuition. That's what I do.

I've learned a lot from karate. Mainly awareness. It teaches you to build a strong inner fortitude. Sometimes you're down, frustrated like I was. When I started, everyone kicked my butt. I got tired of that. My ego was in play, letting me be frustrated by failure. But in the end, I kicked the instructors' butts. And achieved my black belt. Anything can be overcome. You've got to kick you ego's butt! Just like Gautama Buddha said, *'Wear your ego like a loose fitting garment.'*

Doris:

Before we're done here tonight, let's put more emphasis on minimizing the use of: I, I've, my, me, myself, mine. The ego wants you to over-use these words. It's hungry. The ego gets its belly full the more you use—I, I, I.

To those listening to you or reading your emails, messages or letters, it comes off as if the world revolves around you. In reality, you revolve around the world. You are a speck in the universe. We all are just specks. For example, off the top, let's pretend that you're saying or writing this: *'I hope to see you soon. I've really missed you. I'm busy at my work.'* Wow! Is that ever wrong. Much better to do it this way, *'Hope to see you soon. Miss you. Been busy at work.'*

Our advice is to take yourself out of the limelight. Put your emphasis on others. When you minimize the use of these *ego words*, your personality changes for the better. It's osmosis at work, which

Lars described for us earlier. It cuts back on all the ego bad traits we've covered tonight. I got an email last week. It was a paragraph about 3 inches long. There were six I's, two my's and two I've s. Start cutting back on them.

Deepak Chopra, the American-Indian author and holistic New Age guru, said it best. Also, Chopra is known for being an alternative medicine practitioner.

'If you want to reach a state of bliss, then go beyond your ego and the internal dialogue.

Make a decision to relinquish the need to control, the need to be approved, and the need to judge. Those are the three things the ego is doing all the time. It's very important to be aware of them every time they come up.'

Tiger:

It's like *The Washington Post* saying, *'If you don't get it, you don't get it.'*

Rev:

We've been talking about getting inside yourself so you learn whom you really are. We want you to be calm, at peace with yourself, and be happier than you presently are. Our thoughts should help. Just remember, the ego complicates your life. Rumi made a wonderful statement: *'The ego is a veil between humans and God.'* Also, another Rumi quote is appropriate:

'Sever the chains of the ego. Set yourself free and witness the bright essence of your inner being. Discover within your heart the wisdom of a prophet without books, without teachers, and without prudence.'

I have to say again, that mediation does help. If it's not a Godly mediation—that's okay. It can be about what you want to do. Go on a picture-taking safari, make a butterfly garden, hike the trails…but something natural that makes you feel good. What you can do to help others—that's something good to meditate about.

Doris:

This is from the Dalai Lama's *Little Book of Inner Peace*:

> *The common enemy of all religious disciplines is selfishness of mind. For it is just this which causes ignorance, anger and passion, which are at the root of all the troubles of the world.*

> *Desires can be either negative or positive. If I desire to acquire something for myself—let's say I desire good health when I am ill or a bowl of rice when I am hungry—such a desire is perfectly justified. The same applies to selfishness, which can be either negative or positive.*

> *In most cases, asserting oneself only leads to disappointment, or to conflict with other egos that feel as exclusively about their existence as we do about our own.*

> *This is especially true when a strongly developed ego indulges in capricious or demanding behavior.*

> *The illusion of having a permanent self is a secret danger that stalks us all: I want this, I want that. It can even lead us to kill. Excessive selfishness leads to uncontrollable perversions, which always end badly. But on the other hand, a firm confident sense of self can be a very positive element.*

> *Without a strong sense of self, that is, of one's skills, potential, and convictions, nobody can take on significant responsibilities. Responsibility requires true self-confidence. How could a mother without hands save her child from the river?*

Doris:

I read it five times. What a gem of wisdom. Amazing thinking by the Dalai Lama. Here's a copy of it for everybody. My advice is to read it over a few times, not just once. Take your time.

[Everyone talked amongst each other about reading the Dalai Lama's book in the near future. That wisdom to be able to live a fulfilling life in today's world is the type of inspiration we all need.]

Tiger:

Let's go back to the mirror again. Truthfully, when you look in the mirror, do you see an imposter who knows that you feel inadequate compared to others. Yet, you put on a front to mask your real self—the *inside you*. The *inner you* is more important than the *outer you*. As you improve the *inner you*, hopefully using some of the Alpha Team's thoughts, the *outside you* will take care of itself. I sound like a philosopher.

Brenda:

Tenzin Gyatso, the 14th Dalai Lama said: *'The foundation of the Buddha's teachings lies in compassion, and the reason for practicing the teachings is to wipe out the persistence of ego, the number-one enemy of compassion.'*

I always tell people that compassion is a personal strength. We need more compassion.

Lars:

A good way to end tonight's fireside talk, Brenda. Because next week, we trade our thoughts about COMPASSION.

***

Brenda got up—walked back and forth in front of the fireplace. Did some quick stretches and sat back down to sip her decaf coffee. During the fireside talks, about every 30 minutes, she gets up to stretch.

A few minutes later, the traditional rendezvous took place in the kitchen. Above the kitchen entrance is a sign: *'La Cuisine de Doris.'* The kitchen of Doris.

Doris served lemon soufflés. Everyone had a dreamy look as they smacked their lips over this special dessert. Doris told them that this dessert was developed in France in the 1700s. The team expressed ideas about compassion and switched to current events before they left.

Plato
427 B.C.-347 B.C.

Philosopher and mathematician

"Be kind, for everyone you meet is fighting a hard battle."

- Plato

Fireside Talk #20
Cultivate Compassion in your Life

Brenda limped into the living room. She looked as if she had been mugged. Her left arm was in a sling; black and blue bruises on the left side of her neck, extending down from her jawbone.

Doris rushed to her and gave a big bear hug. Others hugged her too, including Tiger who made her wince when he bumped her left shoulder.

Brenda calmed everyone down, telling them that it was an injury while being tested for her 3rd degree black belt rank two days ago. The instructor got in a lucky kick to her shoulder. Two other instructors wanted to help her off the mat. Brenda waved them off and continued. In severe pain, she charged the instructor, kicked him in the chest, which knocked him to the mat.

His eyeglasses flew 20 feet and smashed against the wall. She passed her test, which enabled her to maintain her 3rd degree status.

She has to wait 3 years to attempt 4th degree black belt rank, after having achieved the 3rd degree.

The team asked more questions about karate so Brenda did her best to respond. Yes, there are nine belt ranks: white, orange, yellow, camouflage, green, purple, blue, brown, and red. Black is the final rank, being special by having 9 degrees. The number 9 is an important number to Koreans. Each belt rank requires testing of a certain number of moves…kicks, blocks, dodging, parrying, strikes, sparing, and other forms.

For example, the white belt requires 18 moves; her 3rd degree black belt is 83 moves. All promotional rank tests are judged by a panel with ratings of 'full pass', 'half pass', and 'no change'. Included is a written test with questions on terminology. You have to pass a test within 6 months of achieving current rank, or you're diverted back to next lowest rank. Brenda said that if she hadn't passed the recent test, she would return to 2nd degree. That's why she got up and gave a desperation charge at the instructor.

Alpha Team members remember how Brenda's karate skills played an important role in their last two criminal cases. She added that high kicking and fast hand punches are key elements of taekwondo. Lots of emphasis on kicks, since the leg is the longest, strongest limb with a lesser chance of retaliation.

In competitive sparing, you get one point for a punch to the body or head, two points for a kick to body, and three points for a kick to the head.

Sometimes you are required to break boards or bricks. She mentioned that she has broken a lot of boards. Tiger shouted *'Oorah'*.

Brenda massaged her shoulder and told them that an MRI indicated some injury to her rotator cup, the deltoid and trapezius muscles, and various tendons and ligaments. The doctor gave her ten exercises to do and that she should expect a full recovery in 3 months.

Everyone thanked Brenda and patted her on the right shoulder.

Doris poured hot winter lemonade in their 'Alpha Team' mugs. It was so delicious that Brenda asked for the recipe. Proudly, Doris said: 'You slice a lemon and skewer it into a cinnamon stick. Stir in honey and microwave until hot.'

***

AMAZING FIRESIDE TALKS

Lars:

Big surprise tonight. As you can see, Cory Swink, Arlington County Police Chief, is here with us.

[Everyone gives Cory a welcome wave.]

Lars:

For the reverend's benefit, Cory is my brother-in-law. Our Alpha Team has worked two cases with the ACPD. When his officers are clueless on a case, sometimes he calls us in to help. Although it's a parallel investigation, we operate in a clandestine way—in private coordination with Cory and certain homicide detectives. Also, Cory knows the drill about our fireside talks, so let's get started!

Cory:

Let me say something quickly, Lars. I'm here tonight because I've learned compassion. Not only through police work, but because my heart was broken a few years ago when my 16-year-old son was killed in an auto accident. I felt like 80% of me was gone. Compassion brought Marlene and I back to our old selves.

I know the Alpha Team is going to give **YOU** suggestions as to how to improve your compassion. I must say that your life is hollow and just plain shallow without compassion.

[Cory choked out most of his message after mentioning the death of his only son.]

Tiger:

Having been a cop in the Big Easy and working in funeral homes, I really value compassion. I agree with the Chief that without compassion, your life is really nothing. Nothing at all!

Lars:

Let me butt in to make something clear to Cory. After we finish our fireside talk topic discussion for the evening, we cover our approach to the next week's topic. Several weeks ago, we agreed on all 25 important life topics before we started these talk discussions. The topics are random—with no real priority of order because they are all important. And certainly, our list is not all-inclusive. It's a brainstorming session, Cory, so feel free to pop in with your thoughts anytime.

[Cory nods.]

Brenda:

We need to be clear on what compassion is and isn't. My main task tonight is to explain what it is. Merriam-Webster's definition is: *A sympathetic consciousness of others' distress together with a desire to alleviate it.* In other words, you have sympathetic feelings rather than being callous. It really lives in your heart. As you grow it, you become who you truly are. So, compassion is your way of being. As a compassionate person, you try to alleviate those who suffer. It is different from sympathy, because compassion is the focal point of many traits, the interdependence of many things. It's a strength—not a weakness. It's the only way to become a better person—by practicing compassion.

Compassion is like an 'unsung hero'—it is an unsung, or rather unheralded, trait. It rolls up many virtues we have talked about to include being fair, respectful and kind. It is a powerful tool. Gives you inner strength, which is needed in these times of complexity.

Rev:

I don't see how anyone can survive without compassion because it robs your dark shadow of some of its hideous baggage. And when you display compassion, it will then spill off unto others who will subsequently pass it on. It's sort of like creating a wonderful cycle.

As stated in Luke 6:31: *Do unto others as you would have them do unto you.* It really is our moral duty to develop compassion, especially these days where some people feel that we're living in a 'me' generation.

Tiger:

Ten-4 on that, Rev. Yeah, you right! Many people are glued to their cell phones and care more about their latte than real important issues. I see them in Starbucks. Yeah! Man! Sad.

Be honest. Do you have compassion for your family members, relatives, close friends and frankly—everyone? When's the last time you showed real concern? I mean caring, kindness, a genuine desire to help…just plain warmth. Even a soft tap on the shoulder.

Doris:
Just a soft touch goes a long way. No words have to be spoken.

Lars:
An example of a lack of compassion on display was when General George S. Patton slapped two US Army soldiers and berated them at an evacuation hospital during the Sicily Campaign of WWII. Patton was a hard charging commander of the Seventh Army. He was flashy, boots highly polished, pearl handle pistol, and indispensable to General Eisenhower's war efforts. Eisenhower knew that Patton was brash, impulsive, and lacked self-restraint. Patton sent a directive to his Seventh Army commanders, as follows:

'It has come to my attention that a very small number of soldiers are going to the hospital on the pretext that they are nervously incapable of combat. Such men are cowards and bring discredit on the army and disgrace to their comrades, whom they heartlessly leave to endure the dangers of battle while they, themselves, use the hospital as a means of escape. You will take measures to see that such cases are not sent to the hospital, but dealt with in their units. Those who are not willing to fight will be tried by court-martial for cowardice in the face of the enemy.'

Both soldiers he slapped were in the First Infantry Division. The first one he slapped across the chin with his gloves. He dragged the private out of the tent and yelled, '*You hear me, you gutless %#&*? You're going back to the front*'.

A week later, he confronted another soldier in the hospital. Slapped the private twice, knocking off his helmet liner. Patton screamed, *'Your nerves—#*&@$!, you are just a #@&%* coward. Shut up that #@&% crying. I won't have these brave men who have been shot at seeing this yellow #*&#@ sitting here crying'.*

Patton returned to command, but his career was over.

Tiger:

I didn't know it was two soldiers!

Lars:

Yup. Two. Roosevelt and Congress wanted Patton to be sent home. Ike saved him, but took away his combat command for nearly one year. This is what we don't want you to do—act impulsively against another person. Impulsive acts often lead to regret later on. Sometimes the damage it causes cannot be undone. Put your personal feelings in check.

Tiger:

On a special operations mission, I parachuted in at night to make a kill of a terrible, ruthless enemy leader. Caught him and while I held my .45 pistol against his head, he asked for a drink of water. I gave him a drink out of my canteen. A compassionate gesture.

I'll wrap my part up by reading a quote by Leo Buscaglia, an American author known as 'Dr. Love':

> *'Too often we underestimate the power of a touch, a smile, a kind word, a listening ear, an honest compliment, or the smallest act of caring, all of which have the potential to turn a life around.'*

Leo hit the mark—just a word or a touch. We've got to do more of that in our daily lives.

Doris:

I'll tackle the way to grow **YOUR** compassion. Got to do it. It will change your life. No doubt. You should practice it daily. Here's a few thoughts:

- Stop being negative. No more of this. Period.
- Be your genuine self, your authentic you.
- Express a caring attitude.
- Give words of encouragement each day.
- Be nice, but don't let people walk all over you.
- Help others. Talk to the sufferer about things you have in common.
- Help the community—homeless kitchens, donate clothes, etc.
- Be a model person that doesn't criticize or put people down. Think of the quadriplegic soldier—a true role model. Very compassionate.
- Take the focus off yourself; instead focus on someone in need. This is powerful.
- Don't let yourself get angry. Anger is no longer in your make-up. Gone forever. Please.
- Help someone in your neighborhood who's sick or lonely. Alleviate some of the burden by being kind.
- Put other's needs first, yours second.

If you really want to set compassion growth as a goal for yourself, at bedtime review how you were compassionate during that day.

Cory:
All of these compassionate actions will make you happier. Tenzin Gyatso, the 14th Dalai Lama said, *'If you want others to be happy, practice compassion. If you want to be happy, practice compassion'*.

See Lars, I did my homework. As I said earlier, after the sudden, tragic loss of our son, we discovered compassion. It renewed our lives. It does give you inner peace. You do become happier—long-term. I feel like a real human being again. Pretty downtrodden for a while there.

Brenda:
I found an interesting medical discovery. People who practice compassion produce 100% more DHEA, a hormone that slows the aging process. It's a stress hormone.

Lars:

That's enough for me—let's all start practicing it ASAP!

Tiger:

Yeah dudes, next week we'll look younger!

[Everyone chuckles. Brenda grins and rolls her eyes.]

Lars:

I'd say we should all work on it. Don't let what compassion you have, collapse. Keep cranking it up. A commitment to yourself.

Brenda:

I had a girlfriend who got depressed to the point where she didn't even want to get out of bed. Long story, but I was able to get compassion in her life by listening and being there for her. She became a new person. Now she's a CEO of a large construction company—which has traditionally been a man's world. I kept telling her that you can't give up. Spent time with her doing a lot of active listening until she slowly came out of her cocoon.

Rev:

A little tidbit, but since it was brought up tonight about Germans rescuing Jews from the Nazis it might be interesting to note that in Judaism, God is the compassionate, the Father of Compassion. Those under-cover Germans never gave up. What compassion they displayed! Never even considering rewards for what they did, or consequences if they got caught either.

I want to read you a wonderful poem about compassion, written by Sri Chinmoy. Chinmoy was an Indian spiritual master, born in Bangladeash.

Write down how many things you want.
Meditate on how many things you need.
When you write them down
You will see
That you want millions of things.

AMAZING FIRESIDE TALKS

When you meditate
You will notice
That you need only one thing
And that is God the Compassion.
God the eternal Compassion.

Like I said before, take time to meditate...alone. Brenda pushes *deep breathing*. Do that while you're meditating. In all my dealings with young couples, I've found that compassion is the most important trait in attracting a mate. Surveys prove this point.

Tiger:
I think compassion is an instinct. If someone is a victim of violence, you should want to help that person. It's very instinctive in combat situations—to help your buddies no matter what. And in the police and funeral home business it has a big play. We all have compassion inside us; you just need to work on it more. It is life changing. You will feel it and others will recognize it. In combat, we are wired to help anyone suffering. It's automatic or you're a poor soldier. If you don't have this feeling inside you, I suggest you work on it. You will become a new you.

When grieving people come to us at the funeral home, we need to help them work through their distress. We should all be doing that in our everyday life.

Doris:
I visited the Holocaust Museum in DC last month. My key thought for our topic tonight is this: it's one thing to think you have compassion, but what do you do with it? How do you put it into play?

Here's where I'm going with this. Put your compassion into action every day. It will make your life better and other people's lives better. All of this could lead to a more compassionate country. That's the bigger picture.

Rev:
Amen. That's exactly what we need more of in this country.

DR. CHARLES N. TOFTOY

Lars:

Let me make one thing perfectly clear.

[Lars uses Nixon's voice… giggles galore.]

Compassion is not a weakness. It is not a feminine trait. In the literature, some people peg it this way because women are more sympathetic than men. But as we have told you, compassion is a far cry from sympathy.

Again, it is many of the wonderful virtues rolled up into one trait. The best trait a person can develop. Please work on it. You'll see a remarkable change in yourself. Don't just read our thoughts; put in action some of them that you are comfortable with. Compassion in action is the key.

Brenda:

I agree with you Doc. Please follow Doris's ways to grow compassion. Make it **YOUR** strongest character trait. Stick with people that deeply display compassion. They are real people. They've found themselves. You can tell. Just look for it. Albert Schweitzer wrote: *The purpose of human life is to serve, and to show compassion and the will to help others.* Schweitzer was a German theologian and philosopher. He won the Nobel Peace Prize in 1952, for his philosophy of *'Reverence for Life'*. **YOU** need to show compassion. When you work on it, per Doris's tips, you will feel better inside. That's where it counts—**YOUR** inner feelings.

Tiger:

Beatrice, my ever-loving wife, has a favorite saying by Gary Snyder. She wanted me to pass it on to you all tonight. *'O, ah! The awareness of emptiness brings forth a heart of compassion!'* Snyder is an American poet and essayist. He is called the 'Poet Laureate of Deep Ecology.' He received the Pulitzer Prize for Poetry. Also, he was the inspiration for Japhy Ryder in Jack Kerouac's novel, *The Dharma Bums.* Beatrice has it taped to our refrigerator.

AMAZING FIRESIDE TALKS

Rev:

John Wesley, a Theologian back in the 1900's hit the nail on the head, by saying, *'Do all the good you can, by all the means you can, in all the ways you can, in all the places you can, at all the times you can, to all the people you can, as long as ever you can'.*

It's important to reach out. Gosh, I feel so good when I do it. You should start doing it, even if in a small way. Then you're following Schweitzer's advice. We need to lose the 'me' syndrome.

Doris:

This is my favorite poem about compassion. It's on my refrigerator via a magnet. I read it often.

It's by Aleasa from www.poemslovers.com:

My Heart Full of Compassion

I cannot ease your aching heart,
Nor take the pain away.
But let me stay and take your hand
And walk with you today.
I'll listen when you need to talk,
I'll wipe your tears away.
I'll share your worries when they come,
I'll help you face your fears.
I'm here and I will stand by you,
Each hill you have to climb.
So take my hand lets face the world,
You're not alone for I'm still here,
I'll go that extra mile,
And when your grief is easier,
I'll help you learn to smile.

[Everyone cheers and claps their hands for Doris. They nod their heads in approval. Brenda brushes a tear aside. Tiger clears his throat. An emotional moment for the team. Lars pulls out a Kleenex from his pocket and hands it to Brenda.]

Lars:
Well, the fire is still roaring, so we can stay to talk over our approach to next week's fireside talk on HUMILITY.

[Tiger scoots to the kitchen to get a bold decaf!]

Cory:
It's been good being here. I wasn't going to do this, but based on the thoughts presented tonight, I'll give everyone a copy of *Dare to Be* by Steve Maraboli from *Life, the Truth, and Being Free*. The reason it fits is that what you all have said is true: you've got to put compassion in action. You have to *Dare to Be*. You only live once. Maraboli's comment was presented at a grieving group session that Marlene and I attended. It helps a lot. Also, Maraboli is considered a life-changing speaker.

Dare to Be

When a new day begins,
dare to smile gratefully.
When there is darkness,
dare to be the first to shine a light.
When there is injustice,
dare to be the first to condemn it.
When something seems difficult,
dare to do it anyway.
When life seems to beat you down,
dare to fight back.
When there seems to be no hope,
dare to find some.
When you're feeling tired,
dare to keep going.
When times are tough,

dare to be tougher.
When love hurts you,
dare to love again.
When someone is hurting,
dare to help them heal.
When another is lost,
dare to help them find the way.
When a friend falls,
dare to be the first to extend a hand.
When you cross paths with another,
dare to make them smile.
When you feel great,
dare to help someone else feel great too.
When the day has ended,
dare to feel as you've done your best.
Dare to be the best you can—
At all times, Dare to be!

Lars:

The bottom line on this evening's fireside talk is that since compassion is the umbrella hovering over many virtuous traits...we need to grow the seed that lies inside all of us. That reminds me of a Henry Wadsworth Longfellow's saying: *Kind hearts are the gardens, Kind thoughts are the roots, Kind words are the flowers, Kind deeds are the fruits, Take care of your garden And keep out the weeds, Fill it with sunshine, Kind words, and Kind deeds.*

Let me remind you about Henry W. Longfellow. American poet and author who wrote *Paul Revere's Ride,* and *Evangeline.* He wrote for the common people. Longfellow was one of the famous five *'Fireside Poets'*, including William Cullen Bryant, John Greenleaf Whittier, James Russell Lowell, and Oliver Wendell Holmes.

You can grow the seed into a compassionate garden, which is the real you—the inner self, not the outside shell.

***

DR. CHARLES N. TOFTOY

Everyone gathered around the piano, mug of hot winter lemonade in hand. Doris played Joseph Haydn's *'Piano Concert in D Major'* with gusto. As she played, Doris would give little tidbits about Haydn. Austrian composer, called the 'Father of the Symphony', most celebrated composer in Europe. Other famous works were Symphony No. 94 and Symphony No. 99, amongst many others.

She told them that Haydn was a catholic and when he had a tough time with a composition, he would take out his rosary, which seemed to be an effective practice for him. Haydn died in Vienna in 1809.

The team adjourned to the kitchen to chitchat, after giving Doris a roaring applause.

C.S. Lewis
-Clive Staples Lewis-
(1898 – 1963)

Known to his friends and family as "Jack",
a novelist, poet, academic, medievalist, literary critic,
essayist, lay theologian, and Christian apologist.

"Humility is not thinking less of yourself,
it's thinking of yourself less."

- C.S. Lewis

Fireside Talk #21
Humility Makes You An Angel

Lars, Tiger, and Reverend Whitcomb were standing by the fireplace. There were four charred logs in the hearth, and Lars added 3 new ones. He started a roaring fire within a few minutes. They talked about what units they were in while serving in Vietnam, and where they were located. The Rev mentioned that he served with the First Infantry Division...the Big Red One, the same unit as Lars on his second one-year tour, but at different times.

Tiger asked a few questions about what it is like to be a military chaplain. Just then, Doris and Brenda joined them, having been in the kitchen preparing the surprise.

Whitcomb told them that he started out at Princeton's Theological Seminary. After a conflict of beliefs with the lead instructor, he transferred to Duke University's Divinity School. He graduated with a Master of Divinity, which took 3 years. The Divinity School was founded in 1926, and was the first graduate school at Duke.

The team wanted to know about the type of courses the Rev studied. Some of the courses covered: American Christianity, Social Organization of American Religion, Old and New testaments, Church History and others.

The final exams are thorough and each one is 3 hours long. The Divinity School is known worldwide for its strength of faculty and academic rigor.

The Rev popped his chest up proudly. Team members were surprised at the educational requirements for many reverends. They talked about how some people call themselves reverends, but their backgrounds are not solid.

The principal competency of chaplains is counseling. Chaplains work with soldiers of all faiths. The Army, Navy, and Air Force have Chaplain Corps. They are designated as non-combatants., and are not supposed to participate in hostilities. Even so, the Army and Marines had 100 chaplains killed in action in World War II.

There are Roman Catholic chaplains and military Rabbis. All chaplains work closely together. There was always a shortage of Catholic chaplains at Ft. Myer where the Rev was the head garrison chaplain. He spent a lot of time in meetings and counseling garrison soldiers, who had personal difficulties.

Counseling includes families. The Protestant church services are at 7:45am and 10:30am. Whitcomb usually presided at the later service. The congregation has always been unusual. It's composed of mostly older parishioners. Young families have found it too expensive to live close in. And Ft. Myer is close in to DC. Many retirees bought homes nearby during World War II and the Korean War at low prices, so Ft. Myer is easy for them to visit.

Six Army chaplains have won the Medal of Honor…four in WWII and two in the Vietnam War. Most of these were awarded for rescuing wounded, and under fire, carrying them back to the rear. Even though chaplains are required to be unarmed, over the years 26 chaplains have received the Distinguished Service Cross, 45 the Silver Star, 719 the Bronze Star, and 109 were awarded the Purple Heart.

Reverend Whitcomb bowed and everyone gave an '*Amen*'.

***

Tiger:

We've got hot apple cider and pralines tonight - 'laissaz les bon temps rouler.' Let the good times roll. A N'awlins treat. Later, Doris has a surprise for us.

Brenda:

What are pralines, Tiger?

Tiger:

You haven't lived girl! A candy patty made with brown sugar and filled with pecans. A must in New Orleans.

Brenda:

Hey, that sounds good, Tiger. Now, since our topic tonight is humility…let's get rolling.

[She rubs her shoulder and moves it back and forth.]

According to Merriam-Webster, humility is *the quality of state of not thinking you are better than other people.* It does not mean you are weak or indecisive. The ordeals we go through teach us humility, which is a life-long journey.

Rev:

I know Doris is coming up with 50 ways you can enhance the quality of your humility. I'm looking forward to that. Here is my short list: don't try to be better than others all of the time; confess your errors; ignore applause—it should not be self-serving or you are naïve; be gracious to others; don't think too highly of yourself—instead, work on your self-respect, which is far more important.

Humility makes you a real person with depth. Peter Marshall wrote: '*Lord where we are wrong, make us willing to change; where we are right, make us easy to live with.*' What I meant about ignoring applause was that you should redirect praise to others. Like when Lars won the Ernst & Young 'Entrepreneur of the Year' award a few years ago. He accepted the award, but quickly stated that it was his students that earned it by helping companies in the local business community.

Lars:

I brought up last time about Patton slapping two soldiers. Impulsive. No compassion or humility shown on his part. We want you to learn about *how* humility is so important. We don't want you to lash out at anybody.

Think of people that are role models, who display humility. The generals of yesteryear: Ike, MacArthur, Bradley and Marshall were like Gods in those days. They had dignity and respect. Other than Alexander Haig and Creighton Abrams, we haven't had leaders with the depth of those guys. They all told it like it is—some of the others are more interested in their rank and promotion, so they'll kiss boots in a heartbeat. Many are merely 'yes men'!

Tiger:

Sometimes I feel as if our country is run by weak and shallow people, in comparison to the statesmen of many years ago. The Alpha Team wants you to be humble, which gives **YOU** depth and joy. And it is a strength…not a weakness. All my airborne-ranger buddies are tough, but humble. They would give their life for you.

Rev:

Amen, my dear man. Amen.

[The Rev scratches at a rash on his right cheek.]

Doris:

There's a ton of value in Mike King's list about ways to be more humble and to act humbly. King is an electrical engineer in Calgary. He created *Learn This* to help others cope with life. He's big into self-learning and did an exhaustive search about humility, narrowing it down to 50 points to remember. I showed the list to my FBI trainees and they all said: *Simply outstanding. We're going to share it with everyone we know*. It gives you a lot to think about. A list for you to keep handy. These are unique ideas that put my original short list to shame. Let's read through them together.

1. Use the response It's My Pleasure when someone thanks you

    for doing something

2. Use the response I'd be honored when someone asks you to help them or do something with them
3. <u>Listen</u> more than you talk
4. Count to 3 before adding to a conversation to ensure the other person is done
5. Be willing to follow another person in conversation even if you don't get to talk about your idea
6. Always offer to improve someone else's idea and give them credit
7. Give credit for <u>other's ideas</u> that you are carrying through on
8. Ask others for the opinion of others
9. Ask others to join conversations and contribute
10. It's OKAY to be wrong and so admit it
11. Admit when you don't understand or know something
12. Appreciate others who learn something quickly and say so
13. Be quick to apologize when you do something wrong
14. Study moral principles
15. Use <u>moral principles</u> to guide you
16. You are God's creation, not your own
17. Recognize your talents as gifts, not your own ability
18. Know how your skills can be developed by the help of others
19. Share your own knowledge to pass on what you have learned
20. Pass on thanks when you receive it to those who helped you achieve what was thanked
21. Value other people's time as much as your own
22. Never equate time spent with people to a dollar value
23. Don't boast about your achievements, let others recognize them instead
24. Keep your goals to yourself
25. Help other people with their goals
26. Realize the potential in others
27. Know that timing is everything and everyone excels at different times in life
28. Being the 1st follower is often the best way to lead
29. Since winning isn't everything, you don't have to win
30. Recognize that you have faults

31. Remember you are a sinner (in other words, you are no better or worse than anyone else)
32. Ignore first impressions of people
33. Give others the benefit of the doubt
34. Provide positive and encouraging feedback instead of criticism
35. Make a choice to act more humbly
36. Practice at least one humble act each day
37. Be grateful for successes without boasting about them
38. Know how to accept praise with a simple thank you, don't elaborate on it or talk more about it
39. Recognize the individualism of others and yourself, there is no need to conform
40. Share your core values and live them accordingly regardless of the circumstances
41. Prioritize things in your life and rate your actions on whether to follow that priority or not
42. Rate other people as first, be less significant
43. Forgive those who wrong you and move on without revenge or lashing back
44. Serve others and not yourself first
45. Seek wisdom, which is knowledge of what is true coupled with just judgment of action
46. Recognize and know that you know little and there is always more to learn
47. Avoid explosive reactions, and subside any aggression
48. Accept new ideas and change, not being stuck on what you knew before
49. Teach all that you can for the benefit of others
50. Learn from and model the life of the most humble teachers in history (Jesus, Gandhi, Mother Teresa, Buddha, etc.)

Doris:
Which is your favorite one of the 50?

Tiger:
#3—*Listen more than you talk.*
Brenda:

#44—*Serve others and not yourself first.*

Rev:
#16—*You are God's creation, not your own.*

Lars:
#26—*Realize the potential in others.*

Doris:
And mine is #36—*Practice at least one humble act each day.* And I'm going to do it.

Lars:
All of these are wonderful thoughts by King. The Alpha Team would like you to read through them a few times and apply the ones that you need to work on. You might want to keep this list handy. It's very helpful.

Tiger:
Recently, Michelle Obama said it well: *'We learned about gratitude and humility—that so many people had a hand in our success, from the teachers who inspired us to the janitors who kept our school clean...and we were taught to value everyone's contribution and treat everyone with respect.'*

Rev:
It's rewarding to practice humility. I do it every day in my role as a reverend. It promotes spirit, loyalty and teamwork. It makes you feel like an angel from above.

Brenda:
I've found that people who are secure with themselves and have self-esteem are the most humble. You can be like this, too. These two quotes may help: *'It is always the secure who are humble'*, by Gilbert Keith Chesterton, a British writer in the early 1900's. He was called the prince of paradox, and *'Few are humble, for it takes a self-esteem few possess'*, by Robert Brault, who has been a freelance writer for 40

years. His main contributions are to magazines and newspapers.

Rev:

When you practice humility, you'll never feel empty again.

Tiger:

Yeah! You know…accomplish stuff, but it doesn't matter who gets the credit. When I scored a touchdown in high school, I didn't feel like I was *the man* because my teammates got me there. I let them know it, too.

Lars:

In short, if you find yourself guilty of any of these following points, then please work on your humility: try to take credit, bragging, you are better than others, got to be right no matter what, and you can do everything by yourself—don't need help. These are terrible traits.

Doris:

Sorry, let me butt out with this saying by George Arliss: *'Humility is the only true wisdom by which we prepare our minds for all the possible changes of life.'* Arliss was the first British actor to win an *Academy Award.* He won the *Best Actor Academy Award* for *'Disraeli'* in 1929. He was also an author and playwright.

Lars:

Next week we share our thoughts and experience in regards to SUICIDE. I just learned that 22 veterans commit suicide every day in our country.

***

They were all settled, on stools, at the long rectangular kitchen worktable. They talked about several of Mike King's points. All of them agreed that King's list could be life changing. After about 30 minutes, Lars said that he'd like to piggyback the Rev's comments about chaplains.

Lars was in the 24th Infantry Division in Germany, so that's why he knows about the massacre that took place during the Korean War…the Battle of Taejon.

Thirty critically wounded soldiers of the 24th Infantry Division's 19th Infantry regiment were stranded, all alone, on the top of a mountain. Herman G. Felhoelter, a US Army chaplain, was praying over the wounded. The North Korean Army troops discovered their position. They executed Felhoelter as he was praying and they killed all 30 of the wounded soldiers who could not defend themselves.

Lars told the team that Reverend Whitcomb is a very humble and compassionate man…like Pope Francis. He failed to tell you that he was awarded the Silver Star for carrying a seriously wounded soldier through a minefield during a battle near Lai Khe in Vietnam. So, he's one of those 45 chaplains who have been awarded the Silver Star and one of the 109 who received the Purple Heart.

The Alpha team knocked 3 times on the wooden table. Brenda wiped away a tear. Doris's eyes were so full that she had to go to the bathroom to wash her face with cold water.

As planned, Doris brought out a huge tray of three cheeses: Muenster, Chevre (goat), and Babybeh. Garnished with beautiful slices of strawberries and apples. Rice crackers too. Doris filled their Alpha Team mugs with café au lait. Tiger bellowed out: '*Oh la la.*'

Later, Doris gave Brenda an Aleve since her shoulder was acting up. Brenda told everyone that she got a cortisone injection in her left shoulder yesterday but sometimes it takes 48-72 hours to take effect. It does reduce the inflammation and pain. Sometimes relief can last for months or years according to her doctor. Brenda opted to depart, leaving Lars, Tiger, and the Rev to talk about sports. Doris went to bed.

Part IV

Wrapping Up With Four More Topics

Suicide
Soul
Inspiration
Life is a Paradox

"There is no passion to be found playing small—in settling for a life that is less than the one you are capable of living."

– Nelson Mandela

Jonathan Swift
(1667 –1745)

Anglo-Irish satirist, essayist, political
pamphleteer, poet and cleric who became
Dean of St Patrick's Cathedral, Dublin.

"May you live all the days of your life."

- Jonathan Swift

Fireside Talk #22
Never, Ever Attempt Suicide

As Alpha Team leader, Lars decided to start tonight's session in the kitchen. It would give the team an opportunity to reflect on someone they know about who committed suicide... a close and personal suicide episode. They could get this off their chests prior to starting the fireside talk in the living room. All agreed that this was a good idea. As planned together, Doris had prepared croissants and butterscotch coffee, made with butterscotch chips, honey, whipped cream, and half and half.

They were all sitting around the kitchen worktable, nibbling on Doris's croissants and sipping the fantastic, tasty coffee.

Lars led off, saying that his West Point roommate's father committed suicide when Jim was 14. He found his father in their garage, a victim of carbon monoxide. Jim related to Lars that he had never told anyone about it. Lars said that Jim was the most wonderful roommate a guy could have. Lars realized that the suicide caused Jim to be withdrawn and an introvert. The impact of suicide on loved ones is gigantic.

Brenda reminded the team about her girlfriend, who shared an apartment with her while they were going to graduate school at the University of Maryland. As Brenda entered the apartment, she was confronted with Betsy hanging from the chandelier. Her Chihuahua was going around in circles beneath her feet, which were 3 feet above the floor. Brenda still has nightmares about it. Betsy's entire family was devastated.

Brenda added that her sister's husband, of 25 years, and father of her 3 children, Iraq vet, killed himself about one year after their divorce. The effects of 4-5 deployments in Iraq and Afghanistan, plus the divorce caused him to go downhill fast. My sister had to identify his body…wasn't pretty. The two sons don't acknowledge him, whereas the daughter keeps his picture bedside, and displays the flag from the funeral in her room.

One of Tiger's buddies, a former Marine, lived on the streets of San Francisco, beneath bridges and in canyons. Some in that group were 22 years old to include female vets who witnessed combat. One night, Tiger told the team, his buddy hung himself under a bridge.

Doris's aunt knows a woman vet, paratrooper, with a three -year - old son who slept in a car for 10 weeks. Later, she lived in a garage, bathing in a utility sink used to wash auto parts and other machine tools. She left her son with her mother. She lived with family members, friends, or anyone who could put her up for 2-3 weeks. She was found dead in her father's car as the result of rat poison. Her aunt told Doris that the woman had been a pretty cheerleader in high school, but four tours to Afghanistan ruined her…severe PTSD.

The reverend told them that he has been involved with many suicides. Twenty-two veterans commit suicide per day. Even though he is retired, the Rev helps as much as he can for families of vets.

Whitcomb's main point was that suicide leaves a grueling trail for others…spouses, children, brothers, sisters, grandparents, aunts, uncles, In many cases it adversely affects their life journey. He mentioned that right now he's helping with a woman vet whose 16-year-old son jumped from the top floor of the Holiday Inn in

Springfield, Virginia 2 weeks ago. Only three months ago, my neighbor's daughter was killed by a man she met on Craigslist. He committed suicide 2 hours later.

Lars said that these true, personal stories, close to our hearts, are stepping-stones to our constructive discussions about suicide. Everyone adjourned to the living room.

Brenda got up and stood near the fireplace, ready to kick-off the fireside talk.

***

Brenda:

My five-part series on suicide that I wrote for *The Washington Post* over a year ago, gives me a head start on this topic. Let me share some of my pencil notes that I made after reviewing my articles. This will give us a broad perspective before we discuss symptoms and ways to prevent suicide.

Lars:

Before you start, Brenda, I want to let **YOU** know that we decided to include suicide as one of our fireside talks because it is so prevalent today. When you finish this discussion of ours, we feel that **YOU** will dismiss the idea of suicide completely, or it will help you to handle a prospective suicidal person that you are aware of. Though a repeat from earlier, if this book helps one person, then it's been worth it.

Brenda:

There's a suicide every 2 minutes in China. They have 250,000 to 300,000 suicides each year—1/4 of the total of global suicides. Greenland is high in suicides, too. About 30,000 commit suicide in America annually. The American Association of Suicidology states that there are 91 suicides every day in America. The Association's goal is to prevent suicide by being the national clearinghouse for suicide information.

I covered the entire Veterans scene, which indicated that 349 veterans committed suicide in 2012. About 22 veterans commit suicide each day' as previously mentioned. In 2010 and 2011, more soldiers died from suicide than those that died in combat. This gives you the big picture. About 70% of those who commit suicide tell someone that they are thinking about taking their own life, or there are telltale-warning signs.

Lars:

Having studied WWII in depth, I remember that during April and May of 1945, there were 5,000 suicides in Berlin. That included Hitler. While I was serving in Berlin as a 2nd lieutenant, I guarded Spandau Prison with my rifle platoon. Rudolph Hess, Albert Speer, and Baldur Schirach were the inmates. Rudolph Hess committed suicide at Spandau in 1987. This all shows that we've got to do something about suppressing suicides.

As a sidebar, I might remind you all about these three Nazis. Hess was the Deputy Fuhrer, Speer was Hitler's chief architect and Minister of Armaments and War Production. Baldur Schirach was the Nazi Youth Leader. He and Speer were the only two who denounced Hitler at the Nuremburg trials.

Tiger:

To me, suicide is the devil in disguise. It's the ultimate act of desperation, which can be avoided.

For example, I think the two tragedies at Ft. Hood could have been avoided. Army Specialist Ivan Lopez committed suicide after killing 3 and wounding 16. He was being treated for depression and anxiety. Sure wish he had read our thoughts on those two areas. He left four children. Major Hasan killed 13 and wounded over 30 in the other Ft. Hood incident in 2009. Although he didn't commit suicide, he's on death row…nearly the same thing.

Lars:

That's the dark side, Tiger. Most Army guys rebound quickly and move on in their military or civilian career. But those with a severe physical and emotional impairment are the ones that can suddenly flip out.

Rev:

I conducted a funeral service, two weeks ago, for a wonderful female Sergeant who was killed in Afghanistan. Her parents wanted me to read from Wisdom 3:1-5, 9, which is in line with our topic tonight, so I'll read it to you all now.

> *'But the Souls of the righteous are in the hand of God, and no torment will ever touch them. In the eyes of the foolish they seemed to have died, and their departure was thought to be a disaster, and their going from us to be their destruction: but they are at peace. For though in the sight of others they were punished, their hope is full of immortality. Having been disciplined a little, they will receive great good, because God tested them and found them worthy of himself, Those who trust in him will understand truth, and the faithful will abide with him in love, because grace and mercy are upon his holy ones, and he watches over his elect.'*

That was from *The Old Testament*. The verse meant a lot to the suffering family. We printed it in the funeral service bulletin entitled: The Burial of the Dead.

Brenda:
I know you all are going to ask me about Buddhist beliefs in regards to suicide. Buddha says little about it; however, it is given that suicide should be avoided because your rebirth will be affected. It's bad karma. The self-immolation by Buddhists in Vietnam was considered by them as a noble act. Not so—by most Buddhists, because the bad karma is that you leave family and friends to suffer for the rest of their lives.

A few more stats. Nearly one million people commit suicide each year worldwide. Males are four times more likely to do it than females. What people don't know is that about 10-20 million people attempt suicide every year and fail. Let me wrap up some other points that were covered in my five articles. Those that committed suicide in ancient Athens were buried alone without a headstone. Louis XIV in 1670 had them dragged face down through the streets and thrown in a garbage heap. In 1978, 918 members of the peoples Temple cult in Jonestown, drank grape Flavor Aid laced with cyanide. During the last days of the Battle of Saipan in 1944, over 10,000 Japanese civilians committed suicide by jumping off 'suicide cliff' and 'Banzai' cliff.

Doris:
    Now, we want to provide you with telltale signs to look for, that you might spot in an acquaintance or friend, family member—anybody, including yourself. Watch out for these!
    Depression is easy to mask. It may be triggered by a traumatic event. Also, bi-polar, mood swings, Schizophrenia, unable to sleep, domestic violence, physical abuse—even rape. If someone talks about suicide—be careful—they're liable to do it. I know you all have other signs to look for.

Lars:
    Yup! I knew a vet who lost his job and home. Committed suicide. He felt that he was taken advantage of. He slipped into seclusion. Drugs, alcohol followed. He felt expendable. Another sad truth is that some soldiers commit suicide deliberately because they feel the insurance payout is worth more to their family than their life.

Tiger:
    Also, a serious illness or accident can trigger suicidal feelings. Or a divorce. The day after my buddy was divorced, he shot himself. He lost interest in everything.

Doris:
    You all made me think of a few other symptoms, such as being violent, impulsive, and basically bored—having a dull, sluggish feeling.

Brenda:
    These are good points that **YOU** should remember. I think the big

ones are mental disorders and substance abuse. Other rather broad causative factors could be poverty, being homeless, unemployed or having a serious medical condition. Hanging is the most used method in most countries. Also, pesticide poisoning and firearms are close behind. Actually the current surveys indicate that the most popular methods of suicide are gunshot, followed by these: drug overdose, hanging, poisoning, inhaling carbon monoxide, suffocation, jumping, slitting wrist, electrocution, drowning.

Let's get into steps you can take to help yourself or someone that appears to have these signs.

But first, let me mention euthanasia, which I covered in my *Post* articles. It's mercy killing. If you watched Dexter, the TV show—you saw Dexter pull the tube on his sister, Debbie. Personally, I have a statement in my medical files not to resuscitate.

I recommend everyone have that taken care of unless you want to live longer in a vegetable state. Takes a lot of stress off your family members. Your position on this matter should be in your medical file.

Rev:

Really wonderful, helpful thoughts here tonight. Those thoughts will make you aware of those that might have suicidal tendencies. In Exodus 20:13, The Bible states: *Thou shalt not kill.* In Ecclesiastes 7:17 it states: *...why shouldest thou die before thy time?*

What I get out of the Bible is that we shouldn't commit murder; that if you kill yourself, you've murdered yourself. It's tough to ask for forgiveness if you've committed suicide and since sin cannot enter heaven, you go to hell. That is the viewpoint of many Christians. The Conservative Protestants feel that it is a sin, self-murder—like murdering someone else. It's a criminal offense in many Islamic countries.

In my opinion, suicide won't solve your problems or difficulties, which are temporary in nature. But suicide is permanent. Even being sad or bored is temporary. Life swings back and forth like a pendulum.

Tiger:

Yeah Rev—life is like the stock market. Hey! We've got everyone doing the *Gumbo Ya-Ya!*

Brenda:
Meaning?

Tiger:
Everyone talking at once.

Lars:
Yup! Let's let Reverend Whitcomb continue. He's on a roll.

[But first, they took a quick stretch break. Doris brought in more croissants and everyone filled their Alpha Team mugs with butterscotch coffee.]

Rev:
The Catholic Church views suicide as a sin, but they have lightened up their views somewhat. Islam states that it is one of the greatest sins. *'And do not kill yourselves...'* comes from the Quran. Muslim scholars and clerics view suicide as forbidden, denouncing suicide to include suicide bombing.

The answer to William Shakespeare's *'To be, or not to be'* is easy. The answer is *to be*. You've got to keep on living. I explain this to soldiers: that Hamlet, in Act 3 Scene 1, questions whether it's worthwhile to keep living when facing many hardships. We all face hardships, but they come and go. We have to work through them and never give up.

Brenda:
In my articles that I wrote for *The Washington Post*, I included contact points. Here's a good summary for you.

• National Suicide Prevention Lifeline, which is 24/7:
1-800-273-8255
(TTY: 1-800-7004TTY)
www.suicidepreventionlifeline.org

• Suicide Certified Crisis Hotline
1-800-784-2433

AMAZING FIRESIDE TALKS

www.hopeline.com

• Every state has a suicide hotline, for example for Virginia and the Washington, D.C. Metro Area it is:
703-527-4077

• Most countries have a 24-hour nationwide service too. You may be reading this book from your own country. Try Befrienders Worldwide, which is located in London at:
    44(0) 7528595113
    info@befrienders.org
This is from Helpguide.com. You can find a helpline by country and language too.

• You can find a therapist online who will provide services over the internet at: HelpHorizons.com, Find-a-therapist.com, and onlineclinics.com. These are E-Therapy clinics from www.metanoia.org/suicide/. You can check them out. By citing these does not mean that we recommend them. But probably, it's worth a try. Makes it easier to get started by having initial therapy online. Some may be free.

• And of course don't forget 9-1-1 if urgent.

Tiger:
    There are laundry lists of warning signs and prevention tips in books, journal articles, newspapers, internet articles. Many just go on and on. Blah, blah, blah. Some are good, but others might not give you the appropriate advice. You just have to take away what fits best for you. Like our amazing thoughts…put into play our ideas that fit your situation.

Lars:
    The Alpha Team met last week on how to handle this sensitive topic. All of us have had at least one suicide close to home. In my case, it was my brother. Doris's aunt. Tiger's best soldier friend. And Brenda's roommate. So we've all been close to it.

We've decided to give you our frank thoughts that you can apply. Not cookie cutter types, but actions you can use in the real world. Nothing lame.

Doris:

This might surprise you but we've all agreed that you, or whomever you are trying to help, should get a dog. You're probably thinking, 'What?' Suggest that the person adopt a dog from your local refuge. You will be saving the dog. An admirable act. It takes the focus off the suicidal feelings. You have something to love and care for. Your best friend. Ditto for cat lovers. The answers to helping someone out of suicide don't have to be cold, clinical methods. There's an *Animal Welfare League* in every state. The contact in Arlington, Virginia is 703-931-9241, mail@anla.org. When Lars and I bring our Yorkie to places for pet therapy, it makes everyone happy. It makes their day. This can be your newly created world. It rotates around your dog. Put your dog first in your life instead of yourself. Dogs have souls, as you will learn next week. Again, this applies to other pets...not just dogs.

Brenda:

Other simple points are: play your favorite music throughout the house or apartment continuously, take up writing poems, walk outside—see the trees, birds, flowers, squirrels, chipmunks. Really see them. Take it all in. Go to parks. Hang out. There are lots of reasons to stick around in this world.

Watch ducks. Go where there are geese flyways. In our area, it's the Blackwater Refuge in Easton, Maryland. It's euphoric to see 40,000 geese all at once, honking and carrying on. Go to a waterfall. Do whatever you like—that makes **YOU** feel significant. Your rebirth.

Rev:

Another *common sense* idea is to affix important names and telephone numbers on your refrigerator. In very clear print, easy to read, such as: doctor, family members, friends, counselor, others that you may need to call quickly. Even post 9-1-1. It will give you a secure feeling to know that you have people to call at your fingertips.

Those who really care. Like Brenda said, if you can develop a cause you believe in and put your faith in it, then do it. To piggyback Doris's comment, you might want to be a dog walker. The dogs will love you for it. You could volunteer at your local vet or dog shelter. I was in Buenos Aires two years ago and discovered that dog walkers were paid as a full-time job…a career field. We have many of them here too. That's something worth following up on. Do what you love to do.

Lars:

Believe me—*YOU can't help someone all by yourself.* The primary care doctor is first in my book. The suicidal person probably doesn't want to be referred to a professional therapist at first. But he/she knows the primary care doctor who they've known from the past having been treated for colds, and had physicals, blood tests—routine stuff. There's more of a comfort zone there.

Situational depression is common. We've all had it, but if it continues then counseling and medication are needed. Again, you can't do it alone is my point. Some involvement may be necessary by any of the following: psychotherapist, psychologist, psychiatrist, friend, reverend, rabbi, priest—you have to decide. But others need to help out in severe cases. I'll give you two real-life examples later on. Some of the simple, common sense thoughts we've provided here can turn people around who have had suicidal thoughts for years.

Tiger:

Veterans have to take care of themselves, too. There are a lot of benefits. They need to read the VA guidelines and use organizations like the Disabled American Veterans, Paralyzed Veterans of America and other organizations. Visit and talk to fellow veterans at the Veterans of Foreign Wars and the American Legion. All of them will take you under their wing and make you a part of their group. Frankly, I'd have a tough time living with myself, knowing I had killed myself. Sometimes it's a struggle to survive, but you can do it. Time heals.

Rev:

To add to some of the common sense points made by you guys, let me say that watching the stars at night is enlightening. Don't just look at them, but relax and take it all in—all the movements—the wonder. Shift your TV focus to neat things like Discovery, National Geographic, Animal Planet, History channels. Lastly, don't forget Doris's idea about deep breathing. It works.

Lars:

I think you need to get a counselor for the person. Bring him or her to the counselor yourself, or have the counselor come to the person's home or apartment. You just need to have faith and make this break-through.

My big point is **LISTEN-LISTEN-LISTEN**. The suicidal person should talk 80% of the time, you—20%. It can go like this: 'Hey! I'm concerned about you lately.' 'What's up?' 'How are you doing?' 'You're not your old self.' 'I'll play good listener.' Be very patient—that's the real key. Be frank in your comments.

Tiger:

You know, Doc, that shows the person or Wounded Warrior that you care. To be frank, do you know what is really important in helping yourself or someone else to get out of a rut? Make something with your own hands. It doesn't matter what it is. Something you have an interest in. If you like to fly fish, then make your own flies. My father did. Build birdhouses, draw, any craft, make things. It's yours and you can be proud of it. Are you proud of something you buy? Not often. But if you make it...Yes, pride rises to the top. I've seen this in action. It works.

Doris:

And your voice and concerned manner will show the person that you are trying to help in a sincere manner. Need to follow-up, 'Call if you need anything.' 'I'm here for you.' They need to hear this. And, as mentioned before, attach your telephone number to their refrigerator. When they see that number exposed...right in front...it gives them a comfort feeling.

Tiger:

Yeah! If the person, or you, is into drugs and alcohol, tell him or her to knock it off. I would ask what is pushing you over the cliff to even consider suicide? Chronic back pain, revenge, bullying, and many other situations may cause the 'down in the dumps' feeling.

Brenda:

Like Lars said, be a good listener. For goodness sake, don't give advice, avoid arguing and don't say thoughtless things. What I mean by that, is don't tell them how super life is. You've got a lot to live for. No. No. No. And don't tell them about the starving children in Africa or the victims of shootings. Not about the soldier with no limbs, who we mentioned earlier. Again, no. no. no.

A person might feel suicidal when pain and problems exceed the resources for coping. But we're providing you with resources tonight, which should help. Just pick out our thoughts that might work for your situation. Just remember with help, most people work through all of this.

Here's a good example. Montel Medley is not a disabled veteran and he does not have a physical disability. He was diagnosed as having autism at age 3. He went through special-education classes in elementary school and fought through numerous obstacles. Guess what? Last week, he graduated from Surrattsville High School in Prince George's County, Maryland with a 4.0 grade-point average. He was the school's valedictorian. In his speech at graduation Montel said, *'Having a disability doesn't mean you have a disadvantage.'* He continued, *'Sometimes it can be an advantage.'*

My point for relating this story is that no matter what disadvantage you are faced with, there are ways to move forward.

Tiger:

Excellent example for all of us, Brenda. Like someone said earlier, the person may need counseling and medication. I know Wounded Warriors and others that take Trazodone for depression and schizophrenia. With counseling, they are doing fine. Not suicidal anymore.

But as Doc has said before, we aren't medical experts, so you have to check in with your doctor. It seems to help to keep a mental balance. That's what we're all after—mental balance.

Lars:

I'm the Socrates and Plato guy. Socrates said that suicide is always wrong. Plato wrote that suicide is disgraceful, bury them in unmarked graves. It's an act of cowardice or laziness. That's what they said.

Marcus Cicero got it right when he said, *'Where there is life, there is hope.'* Cicero was born in Rome, 106BC. Philosopher, orator, lawyer, politician. Considered Rome's greatest orator. Suicide has far-reaching repercussions. Others live with the grief and pain throughout their life. Family members: mother, father, aunts, uncles, sisters, brothers, grandparents, friends… may feel shame, guilt, and certainly heartaches. Plus, they remain confused somewhat.

Rev:

A little faith and a hug go a long way. This was copied by me from a headstone in a cemetery in Ireland:

> *Death leaves a heartache*
> *no one can heal, love leaves*
> *a memory no one can steal.*

Brenda:

In one of my articles, I wrote that you leave a 'scorched earth' remembrance behind you. Everyone is in misery. It is a selfish move. My roommate hung herself. I came on the scene first. It sticks with me. In college one of our cheerleaders over-dosed on Xanax. Absolutely shocking. I'll never forget that one either. It just sticks with you.   Duffy Laudick, an American musician and poet who has written over 70 poems, wrote:

> *Some use death to flee,*
> *But suicide lacks honor.*
> *Living takes courage.*

I know we've mentioned a lot of things here tonight, but I think telling the person to 'call if you need anything' is important. And have those important names and telephone numbers front and center.

AMAZING FIRESIDE TALKS

Here's a handout that I copied for everyone. It's from www.helpguide.org. We don't know who's reading this book. I mean, you could be a teenager, parent of teens, or teen guardian…that's why I included warning signs in teenagers. These two lists piggyback our points and may help to tackle this sensitive issue.

Talking about suicide	Any talk about suicide, dying, or self-harm, such as I wish I hadn't been born, If I see you again… and I'd be better off dead.
Seeking out lethal means	Seeking access to guns, pills, knives, or other objects that could be used in a suicide attempt.
Preoccupation with death	Unusual focus on death, dying, or violence. Writing poems or stories about death.
No hope for the future	Feelings of helplessness, hopelessness, and being trapped (There's no way out). Belief that things will never get better or change.
Self-loathing, self-hatred	Feelings of worthlessness, guilt, shame, and self-hatred. Feeling like a burden (Everyone would be better off without me).
Getting affairs in order	Making out a will. Giving away prized possessions. Making arrangements for family members.
Saying goodbye	Unusual or unexpected visits or calls to family and friends. Saying goodbye to people as if they won't be seen again.
Withdrawing from others	Withdrawing from friends and family. Increasing social isolation. Desire to be left alone.
Self-destructive behavior	Increased alcohol or drug use, reckless driving, unsafe sex. Taking unnecessary risks as if they have a death wish.
Sudden sense of calm	A sudden sense of calm and happiness after being extremely depressed can mean that the person has made a decision to commit suicide.

DR. CHARLES N. TOFTOY

Suicide Warning Signs in Teens

Additional warning signs that a teen may be considering suicide:
- Change in eating and sleeping habits
- Withdrawal from friends, family, and regular activities
- Violent or rebellious behavior, running away
- Drug and alcohol use
- Unusual neglect of personal appearance
- Persistent boredom, difficulty concentrating, or a decline in the quality of schoolwork
- Frequent complaints about physical symptoms, often related to emotions, such as stomachaches, headaches, fatigue, etc.
- Not tolerating praise or rewards
- *Source: American Academy of Child & Adolescent Psychiatry*

Lars:

Now my professor side comes out. If you're helping a suicidal-prone person, have that person draw up a '24 hour plan' with your help. In that plan goes stuff like spending more time with a certain family member, counseling help, construct a telephone list of important contacts, new things to do…nothing negative. One hundred percent of the focus is on the person.

Then the plan can continue out to 72 hours and more. As the plan keeps being embellished, before long the person is playing ping-pong, pickleball, shooting pool, swimming, and some of the other things we've suggested. These activities can be done at your local community center or high school. The first time I was wounded badly in Vietnam, everyone at the field hospital was trying to heal me. That's what you and all of us need to do—heal others.

As Brenda noted, in 2010 and 2011 more soldiers died from suicide than died in combat. Something's wrong about that picture! We can change it with careful thoughts.

Doris:

I like what Mother Theresa said: '*Yesterday is gone. Tomorrow has not yet come. We have only today. Let us begin.*'

And Eleanor Roosevelt wrote: '*Life was meant to be lived, and curiosity must be kept alive. One must never, for whatever reason, turn his back on life.'*

To me, these are stimulating and are encouraging to *hang in there*, as Lars says.

Lars:

Here are my two true stories, I promised. Long stories, but I'll give you the short versions.

Got a call one night about midnight from a fellow officer. We were at the same military post. Sounded depressed. Got up, dressed—went to see him. I played good listener. I left at 4am. Never told anyone until right now.

Three years later, I was walking in the Pentagon Concourse and out of the blue, he grabbed me. Told me that he was planning to commit suicide that night. It even gives me a chill thinking about it now. But I did let him do the talking. My point: we've all got to LISTEN more.

I mentioned a soldier with PTSD who was on a suicide watch. No physical wound from Iraq or Afghanistan, but 100% PTSD. It worried me. I told him to call anytime. He did. I'd be on vacation and think of him, like 9pm at night and so on.

We met several times and when I finally got out of him what his main interest was, things reversed 180°. He wanted to help kids at risk. Had him make up a business plan.

Now he's CEO of his own company that helps kids in distress. He's excited and happy. Even his wife returned to him.

Brenda:

I like what Doc said about the fact that a hug now and then can do the trick. And to **listen, listen, listen.**

It reminded me of what Leo Buscaglia said: *'Too often we underestimate the power of a touch, a smile, a kind word, a listening ear, an honest compliment, or the smallest act of caring, all of which have the potential to turn a life around.'*

Buscaglia, an American poet, was a professor at the University of California. He was moved by one of his students who committed suicide, which led him to write lovely messages.

His students called him, *Dr. Love.*

We have to admit that it's a mental health issue. A normal, mentally balanced person doesn't commit suicide.

As we pass on these thoughts, just remember you can't tackle it alone. Get help. As we've shown, plenty of help is available.

Lars:
Next week we discuss the SOUL.

Tiger:
That's a tough one, Doc…

Rev:
Oh, I can't wait for that one.

***

Lars, Tiger, and the Rev continued their ongoing sports discussions, giving their views on the Washington, D.C. based pro teams: baseball, football, basketball, ice hockey, soccer, and tennis.

After the Rev and Brenda departed, Lars and Tiger expanded on their opinions of the pro teams.

Doris went to bed.

By midnight, they agreed that their favorite teams were the Nationals, Redskins, and Capitals…in that order.

Baltimore is located nearby, so they included the Orioles as number 4.

They don't really follow any of the others: Wizards and Mystics (basketball), DC United (soccer), Washington Freedom (women's soccer), or the Kastles (team tennis).

Lars and Tiger smacked their chests together, gave each other hip bumps, and Lars guided Tiger to the front door.

On his way to the bedroom, Lars looked back and saw Goddess Kali standing by the fireplace.

She was smiling.

GODDESS KALI

Rumi
(1207 - 1273)

Medieval era Persian poet. Major work was the *Spiritual* Couplets, *a 6-volume poem containing 27,000 lines of Persian poetry.*

*"When you do something from your soul,
you feel a river moving in you, a joy..."*

- Rumi

Fireside Talk #23
The Indestructible Soul

Lars had just finished stoking the fire. He sat down, gazing into the fire, contemplating whether to share his dream from last night. He and Goddess Kali were sitting in the living room having an in-depth conversation. He was mesmerized by the fire.

Doris joined him and saw Lars in a trance-like state. She's coped with his Vietnam nightmare flashbacks and sudden states of mind, when Lars slips into a trance, eyes not focused. Doris snapped Lars out of the trance. After hearing what transpired the night before, she encouraged Lars to share his Kali dream encounter with the team.

When everyone was seated around the fireplace, Lars stood up and told them that he would like to relate his dream. They gave Lars an enthusiastic thumbs-up. Tiger raised up two thumbs.

Lars began, reminding them about the Alpha Team's first criminal case, involving the sociopath genius, William Crawford. He was in love with Goddess Kali. To get to know Crawford's mindset better, Lars did an in-depth study of her. And, Goddess Kali helped Lars on their last case by giving tips on how to track down Taurus, the serial killer. Deep in thought, Lars covers some of Kali's background.

It is really Hindu mythology. Millions of Hindus revere her as their *Mother Goddess*. She is especially worshipped in Kashmir Kerala, South India, Bengal, and Assam. Bengalis believe '*She Is Our Mother*'. That Kali rages against injustice and inflated egos...things that block self-realization. Kali is celebrated as the Goddess that liberates inspiration, as exemplified by the beautiful Dakshineswar Kali Temple in Kolkata, India.

In the dream Kali's main points were:

- Eradicate negative thoughts.
- Take a no-nonsense approach to things and dispel bad habits.
- Free yourself from illusions, falsehoods.
- You achieve wholeness when you face your fears and reclaim the pieces of your dark shadow.
- To fulfill life, you must accept change.
- Be strong and fearless. Some fears are hidden in social masks.

We talked back and forth, but these 6 points summarize her advice to pass on to the team.

At the conclusion, she looked into my eyes and said: '*Remember, my black color has significance. All colors merge with black...it absorbs and dissolves them. People should be proud to be black.*' In a gentle, loving way, she said: '*I am your protector. I remove the dreadful ego and liberate the soul from the cycle of birth and death. So Doc, you should act fully and freely because I reveal to you your mortality.*'

She danced towards the door and disappeared. Then I woke up. It was 3:10am.

To Lars, the team and the Rev looked like his students...taking in every word. Brenda brought up a follow-on point about Hinduism being the most diverse religion in the world. Afterlife is transmigration where you take rebirth as another human being. In other words, we recycle into a new life. The Soul takes on limitless births. Also, Brenda added that 20% of the world's religious population is Hindu or Buddhist; both believe in reincarnation. Twenty-five per cent of

Americans believe in reincarnation.

Doris piped in saying that she and Lars have been taking Yoga lessons twice weekly. We befriended a woman, Karen Haynes, who told us about a Yoga class she used to take several years ago. It was called *Kali's Yoga*. Karen said that Goddess Kali is considered as the primary Goddess of Yoga. Doris told the team that Karen's Yoga classmates had a Kali primary mantra…KRIM (Kreen) which signifies the power of action. Later, they advanced to Kali's higher-level mantra…KRIM HUM HRIM, which builds on the power of KRIM. According to Karen, all of this charged her with adrenaline, which enhanced her spiritual energy.

Karen suggested that Lars and I should find our Kali side. To her group, Goddess Kali is a warrior who represents enlightenment. She symbolizes spiritual and psychological liberation

Lars concluded saying that once you let Goddess Kali inside yourself, you seem to feel liberated and a new sense of energy evolves. Lars glanced at the window and saw Goddess Kali giving him an on-target smile.

The team sipped their white spiced coffee, laced with cinnamon and cardamom. They readied themselves for a challenging topic of discussion…the soul and afterlife.

***

Rev:

YOU have to believe in something. I won't play the religious card here. Some of your beliefs are clear. Just one example. You believe the sun exists. Lo and behold you look upward to the sky and there it is, in its shining glory. Almost everything depends on it. So you believe it because it is true. The sun exists and you accept that fact.

However, some of our beliefs are not conclusive. You may have friends that believe a certain way about something that you feel is absurd. Probably vice-versa is in play too.

Dictionary.com has a respectful definition of belief—*confidence in the truth or existence of something not immediately susceptible to rigorous proof.* Some people believe in God, others in Allah, Buddha, or other higher powers. Some people still think the world is flat. Is it really round? Unbelievable but true. All kinds of folks make up this world! My point is we have to believe or accept some things without positive knowledge. A lot of this is psychological—that we have trust and faith in something.

Maybe you don't have faith in God, but you have faith in yourself because you know that you're a good person. That's fine. Is there an afterlife? Do we have a soul? That's the purpose of this fireside talk—to give you our best shot. As we roll along here during our discussion, please keep in mind that you do need to believe and have faith or you'll lead an empty life. And not everything has such a high degree of certainty as the existence of the sun. Let's be frank, we have to believe in things we can't necessarily see, yet we believe they exist; therefore we have faith in our belief.

Since we're trying to cover many aspects of the soul, I'll mention a few points about atheists. I know you're thinking—'Oh! I know about them—they don't believe in God and are going to hell'! On the contrary, most atheists choose logic to determine their beliefs. Life has a lot of meaning to them. Contrary to popular opinion, most atheists appreciate the world. They like music, science, the ocean...they just feel that they don't owe anything to a higher power.

In my line of work, I've dealt with many atheists. They feel that there is no evidence and the soul is a mystical entity—not a type of matter that exits the body upon death. In short, atheists don't believe in a soul. No deities exist.

Brenda:

So we are born to die. We live to die. Thus, regardless of our religious preference, or lack of, we should all get the most out of our lifetime.

Doris:

That's true. Richard Dawkins, in his book *Unweaving The Rainbow*, wrote: *We are going to die, and that makes us the lucky ones. Most people are never going to die because they are never going to be born.* Dawkins was an English evolutionary biologist, graduate of Balliol College, Oxford. He studied the relationship between the arts and science.

Rev:

Many believe that after death we are reincarnated into someone else—a new birth. No memory of former self. It's like hitting the reset button. Some think it happens 12 days after death. How do you know who you were before? You don't. Your memory is erased. You move into a new home and forget about the old home. You're in the new body and forget about the old body. You might have been a professor, and now you're a fisherman. If you don't have a soul, then you are the walking dead.

In short, many people believe that reincarnation is when a soul is born again and has a new life.

Tiger:

I may have a wrong take on our sensitive topic for this session. Again, using KISS—Keep It Simple Stupid; if you don't believe you have a soul, then automatically you don't believe in God. If this is the case, why do you go to church? Why do you pray?

Lars:

People tell me that they join a church group or attend meetings, like the Pilgrim meeting at our church, because they are able to talk about things that matter. To them, talk at the workplace is superficial. So, at church it's a way to open up and feel free to talk about anything.

Rev:

You could be highly religious, semi-religious, or an atheist. Or you could be just a good person, having your own faith. It doesn't matter because our thoughts for you have no spiritual preference. And we aren't going to present gooey religious stuff either. But you want to know the real truth?

Many of the people in those categories I just mentioned use sayings about the soul without thinking. A few examples, 'I won't tell a soul', 'May God rest his soul', 'Please don't tell a soul', 'She's pouring out her soul', 'She's into it heart and soul', 'Body and soul.' My point is that soul comes into play as a word we're used to.

Not to get gross, but many religious people swear. When faced with a sudden tragic situation some people say, 'Oh! God no!' 'Please,

God help me!' 'Jesus Christ! No!' They utter these words, perhaps having no solid belief in God. My main point is that God and the soul are everyday words used for one reason or another.

To give you a perspective from the standpoint of other religions, I've put together a list of what some, randomly selected, religions believe about the soul.

- Protestants - soul exists
- Catholics - soul exists, to be judged by Jesus Christ
- Seventh-day Adventists - soul returns to God
- Buddhists - does not deny soul's existence, but not clear
- Judaism - soul given by God at first breath
- Hindus - more concerned with 'self' as distinct from various mental faculties
- Jains - soul exists in every living thing (plants, any bacterium, human)
- Taoism - there are 10 souls - 3 'hun' and 7 'po.' 'Po is tied to the dead body; 'hun' to the ancestral tablet
- Islam - the soul is put into the human embryo 40 days after fertilization. After death, the soul sleeps until Judgment Day

As you can see, there are many viewpoints about the soul. The reason for giving you this short run-down is to show that beliefs differ about the soul. But in all these religions, the people believe in their philosophical and spiritual system.

As I've said before, you need to believe in something—not everything is plain and clear.

Brenda:

I'd like to know how the Muslims feel about this. But first, I have some statistics for us, since I'm the Alpha Team's journalist. There are 1.2 billion Catholics in the world, 1.99 billion Christians.

Tiger:

Yeah! And 1.3 million Catholics in the Big Easy—30% of New Orleans's population. I had to sneak this in here.

Brenda:

And here's where we get to Muslims. 2.04 billion Muslims in the world; 28% of the world's population and 53% of Africa's total population. All of this caused me to be curious about their beliefs.

Rev:

Islam is the second-largest religion and the fastest growing religion. To Muslims everything is preordained by God to include predestination per the Qur'an. The Qur'an puts emphasis on bodily resurrection. Islam philosophy encompasses four parts of the soul. But for now, you can see that the soul is of concern to most of the religions of the world.

Doris:

Shifting gears, here's a copy of a poem by Walt Whitman that is very enlightening. It's called, *Darest Thou Now O Soul.*

1
DAREST thou now, O Soul,
Walk out with me toward the Unknown Region,
Where neither ground is for the feet, nor any path to follow?

2
No map, there, nor guide,
Nor voice sounding, nor touch of human hand,
Nor face with blooming flesh, nor lips, nor eyes, are in that land.

3
I know it not, O Soul;
Nor dost thou—all is a blank before us;
All waits, undream'd of, in that region—that inaccessible land.

4
Till, when the ties loosen,
All but the ties eternal, Time and Space,
Nor darkness, gravitation, sense, nor any bounds, bound us.

5
Then we burst forth—we float,
In Time and Space, O Soul—prepared for them;
Equal, equipt at last—(O joy! O fruit of all!) them to fulfill, O Soul.

It seems to me that the soul is your golden thread. Look in the mirror—can you see your soul or just your face? The eyes are the window to the soul. Can you see your soul? The soul is deep within you. Yes, it's your engine. What matters is what's inside you—not outside, which really just focuses on unimportant material things. Your inner place is yours.

Lars:
Reverend Whitcomb has a surprise for you—and all of us here, for that matter.

Rev:
Before I start, let me remind you that some things are given—like the sun. For some other things, you just have to decide for yourself whether to believe in whatever it is—or not.

Lars:
Let me butt in. When you said given, it reminded me of my cadet days at West Point. We were graded in every class, every day. For example, in math class the instructor would say, *'Take boards'*. Then he would assign us a problem. Like, deriving a formula—you just had to go with it. Cadets dropped their chalk after one minute and you were graded on your response.

My point is that some things are given. Does $E=MC^2$? I guess so, but certain elements of the equation are given. It's a mathematics term. E is energy, M is mass, C squared is a huge number...the speed of light doubled. Albert Einstein's Theory of Relativity.

Rev:
Good analogy, Lars. Again, you have to make up your mind as to what to accept. My quick summary here will make a lot of you happy. I'm going to support the view that dogs have souls. Here are a few

random, supportive views in regards to animals having souls:

- Pope John Paul II: '*...the animals possess a soul and men must love and feel solidarity with our smaller brethren...that all animals are fruit of the creative action of the Holy Spirit and merit respect and that they are as near to God as men are.*' He talked about the divine spark of life—the living quality that is the soul.
- Pope Benedict XVI said that '*Animals too, are God's creatures...*' He also said, '*...it is contrary to human dignity to cause animals to suffer or die needlessly.*'
- Isaiah said, '*God will include animals in the new heavens and new 'earth.*'
- Ecclesiastes 3:19-21: *Surely the fate of human beings is like that of the animals; the same fate awaits them both: As one dies, so dies the other. All have the same breath; humans have no advantage over animals. Everything is meaningless. All go to the same place; all come from dust, and to dust all return. Who knows if the human spirit rises upward and if the spirit of the animal goes down into the earth?*
- Book of Enoch, chapter 58, 59: *dogs have souls*
- Monsignor Canciani welcomes dogs and cats into his Church in Rome. It is a great joy for him because, like men, they are given the *breath of life* by God.
- John, in the Revelation, included animals in his vision of heaven.
- Aristotle had 3 degrees of the soul: nutritive – plants; sensitive - all animals; rational - human beings
- From Thomas Moore, in the book we read for homework: '*An animal reveals its soul in its striking appearance, in its life habits, and in its style.*'
- Matthew 6:26: *God looks out for animals.*
- According to Professor Marc Bekoff, an animal behaviorist at the University of Colorado: *If we have souls, our animals have souls.*

And finally, to be frank, the Oxford Dictionary defines soul as '*the spiritual or immaterial part of a human being or animal, regarded as immortal.*'

From these points, **YOU** can be assured that the soul of your pet is alive in heaven. As a sidebar, pets are really important to us. So important that we have the Blessing of Pets each October in remembrance of St. Francis of Assisi, who loved all pets. If you have a pet, I'm sure you have a special bond. It's like no other relationship.

If you don't have a pet, think about getting one. It will change your life and your overall outlook on life. I can't end my little thought provoking information without ending with a saying from Anatole France: *'Until one has loved an animal, a part of one's soul remains un-awakened.'* A French poet and novelist, Anatole France won the Nobel Prize for Literature. He died in Tours, France in 1924.

Lars:

That gives us hope, Rev, that we all have a soul. We're not trying to convince **YOU**—rather, give you a mixture of views about the soul, so you can decide. I'll add a couple of thoughts here.

In 1907, Dr. Duncan McDougall determined that the soul weighs 21 grams. After six patients died, his experiment showed a small change in weight—the missing mass—from the deceased patients' body weights. East German researchers experimented with 200 terminally ill patients in 1988. They determined the soul weighs 0.01 grams. Jay Alfred, an expert in Dark Plasma Theory, says that the soul is a form of energy composed of low-density plasma of dark matter particles. You should read Alfred's article: *'What is the Weight of the Human Soul.'*

It seems that several experiments can't determine the *missing mass* after death, so that it appears to me that the soul, as a subtle body, must have weight. The Greek Philosopher in the 6th century BC, Heraclitus, felt that the soul was some rare kind of matter, a finer substance.

My faithful friend, Goddess Kali, believes the soul is a vapor. After you die, the vapor leaves you and connects somewhere else. Thus, you live for an eternity. Remember how Goddess Kali helped us on that last criminal cold case, where we all almost lost our lives? In summary, you've got to take the results of these experiments with a grain of salt.

Brenda:

You may worry about your body, but I bet you don't even think about your soul. To me, it's the center of our emotions. The soul core lives inside you. I think it's made up of your feelings, thinking, character, anxieties, desires…it's at the center of it all. The body is only temporary, so I say you should think more about your soul and take care of it.

Doris:

Perfect timing, Brenda, for us to respond to the Professor's homework assignment: *The Care of the Soul* by Thomas Moore.

Tiger:

In the book, he states that the soul path is to feel existence. And the soul is the depth of you. Think about those two thoughts. Gives me a euphoric chill. I gar-run-tee you dat!

Brenda:

I liked his statement: *Storytelling is an excellent way of caring for the soul.* And his comments about how you should figure out a way to fulfill your dreams. Going back to our earlier fireside talk, you've got to get rid of shadow feelings or, the dark shadow.

I think Thomas Moore is hitting close to what we were talking about when we discussed the dark shadow that follows all of us around. Taking care of the soul lightens the load on you, lightens the dark shadow. And that's what we all need to do.

Oh! To continue. The shadow feelings can be strengthened by feelings of jealousy and envy. As the author states—these impact the soul in a negative way. He mentioned that the soul is the pivot of our existence. Specifically, he wrote …*the soul is explosive and powerful.*

Rev:

Again, Moore stated: *There is nothing neutral about the soul. It is the seat and the source of life,* and *the power of the soul…is more like a great reservoir or…like the force of water in a fast-rushing river.*

Lars:

My favorite part of Thomas Moore's book is this: *Soul is not a thing, but a quality or a dimension of experiencing life and ourselves.*

It has to do with depth, value, relatedness, heart, and personal substance.

Another part that is a lesson for all of us: *Care of the soul requires ongoing attention to every aspect of life.*

Rev:

Of course, as a reverend, I agree with the author when he writes that the soul can benefit from spiritual awareness. Actually, some of our helpful thoughts are *soul thoughts* because as he wrote …*these soul thoughts can generate a deep-rooted moral sensitivity.* It's all about faith. Some things you have to take as *given*. Without faith, you are empty, living a splintered life. Not good.

Doris:

Good thoughts in regards to Moore's book. I'll close this part of my thoughts by stating that if we don't take care of our soul, *we suffer the loneliness of living in a dead, cold, unrelated world.*

Rev:

In Genesis 2:7 '…*and the Lord God formed man of the dust of the ground, and breathed into his nostrils the breath of life, and man became a living soul.*' I think the soul is the spiritual part of you as distinct from your physical part, or body.

Lars:

Let me check in here with Plato's dualism of the soul. He and Descartes wrote about the mind-body dualism viewpoint. The physical and spiritual. It was felt that the soul animates your body. Plato wrote: *Thinking: the talking of the soul with itself.* And Aristotle wrote: *The soul is the form, or essence of any living thing.* This means to me, Reverend Whitcomb, that your physical body is not who you are. It's your living spirit that is really you.

Some of those that have written about the immortal soul are:

• Socrates—soul is rewarded based on good deeds, or punished for evil deeds.
• Thomas Aquinas—soul is a conscious intellect. Cannot be

destroyed.

• St. Augustine—wrote about the immortality of the soul. The soul deserts the body at death. It lives after destruction of the body.

• Origen Adamantius—pre-existence of souls. Conditions at birth depend on what the soul did in the pre-existent state. Some are born poor, others wealthy for example—depending on the pre–existent state. The immortal soul has a substance and life of its own.

Rev:

Lars, this is perfect timing for me to read from Matthew 16:26: *For what profit is it to a man if he gains the whole world, and loses his own soul?* To gain knowledge about the soul, like we're providing to you tonight, is the most difficult thing to do.

Lars:

I have to refer back to the Alpha Team's first criminal case. Candance, the murdered co-ed, looked at me as if she was looking through my eyes as a window to my soul. From that point on, I was challenged to pursue her killer. And I found a poem by J. Coiner, *Window To The Soul,* which I'll pass out to each of you now.

Window To The Soul
by Jolene Coiner

They say the eyes
Are a window to the soul
Through them we see
the Past, Present, and Future.
In the eyes of the old we see knowledge and life.
Knowledge of things that were and things yet to be.
We see life as it was, full of love and sorrow
full of understanding, yet also innocence.

In the eyes of the young we see tomorrow,
We see their hopes and their dreams.

Their fears of who they are
And who they will be.

In the eyes of men we see pride
and a need to be loved.
We see the burden of family
and the little boy yearning to be free.

In the eyes of women we see determination
and a fear of a world full of harsh realities.
We see a mother's love and a daughter's devotion.
We see passion, fire, and a pride from within.

Yes, the eyes are definitely a window to the soul
but just like with any window...
there's something different
each time you look inside.

J. Coiner - July 17, 1994

Plato wrote that the soul is the essence of a person. And Aristotle felt that the soul is the core essence of a being. They both agreed on much about understanding the soul.

Yet, as I summarized the scientific viewpoint earlier, some feel we are a machine. Our thoughts are developed through electron chemical processes in our brain. Others feel the soul is metaphysical, a backup of our brain, liberated in a spirit.

Tiger:
Rev, it seems to me that religions are rather pointless without the soul having a play. All of them have their own notions that define their souls. And some don't want you to attack their views. I gar-run-tee you dat!

Rev:

Because I believe in God, I feel light—light in body and mind, the dualism. I just take it for granted. Like Lars, at West Point, certain things were 'given'; the rest was up to you to solve the equation. Right, Lars?

Lars:

Yup; right, Rev. Some of those equations were difficult to solve.

Rev:

There is not always evidence to prove everything. It's my dream. It helps me to feel secure and thwart anger. I'm not an angry person because of my beliefs. As I said before, it's an ancient question, whether there's a soul or not. Philosophers, scientists and others will debate it until the end of time. In the meantime, my happiness means more to me than remaining indecisive.

We have approached this sensitive topic from all sides to give you our thoughts about the soul. Certainly, it is not our attempt at trying to sway you one way or the other. It is your decision. Our thoughts might be passed on to someone you are trying to help, if that's the case.

However, taking care of your soul, per Moore, will help to quell depression, denial, anxiety and other topical areas we have covered in these fireside talks.

Tiger:

It works for me too, Rev. However I do get angry at times. My beliefs, as a Catholic, keep me from having my anger turn to rage.

This is a sidebar, but I have to control my anger in regards to Congress. It's so broken and dysfunctional. Sequester and government shutdowns—incredible way to manage finances. They messed up Vietnam, too. I'll never get over that. I know there are some good people in Congress, but what we need to do is to flush them all out and start over with new elections. Sorry to have vented here.

Rev:

That's okay, Tiger. Now that you've let that all out, your dark shadow just took a beating. It's a relief for you to get rid of that piece of dark baggage. *'You don't believe in the soul until you feel it straining to escape the body.'* –words by Glen Duncan, a British author, in *A Day and A Night and A Day.*

Born in 1965, Duncan studied philosophy and literature at the universities of Lancaster and Exeter.

Most of you know what Jesus said, per John 11:17-26: *I am the resurrection and the life; he who believes in Me shall live even if he dies, and everyone who lives and believes in Me shall never die.*

Lars:

Back to your comment about the financial disaster, Tiger. You just gave me an idea. We need to teach Strategic Financial Management in universities. A required course. Right now, a course like this isn't taught anywhere—to the best of my knowledge. Lack of leadership and a lack of real statesmen hurt us. But we need to get back to the soul.

Doris:

Maybe this is the soul in action—letting out your inner feelings, like Tiger did for the first time.

Rev:

This tough topic, the soul, is an ancient question about spirituality. Let's face it; birth and death are mysteries. That short summary of religions and their beliefs about the soul shows you how different people view it.

And there are over 2,000 Protestant denominations or sects with a wide range of beliefs. Some feel that the *soul sleeps*—waiting for the resurrection.

Others believe in a waiting period before judgment is made— purgatory where cleansing or purifying takes place.

Brenda:

Mahatma Gandhi wrote: *Spiritual relationship is far more precious than physical. Physical relationship divorced from spiritual in body without soul.* Some of the people in my yoga group feel that we have a third eye. When we die, the third eye takes off—it is your soul.

Lars:

Let me zip off a couple of points about the scientific side of the soul discussion. They believe that neuroscience is the only way to understand the soul, of the mind for that matter. The scientific paradigm doesn't recognize the soul. It involves quantum physics.

From a physics and chemistry standpoint, the soul is implausible and just speculation. The soul can't be seen in an X-ray, MRI or electron microscope.

The scientists rely on physics and chemistry, which shows, to some of them, that there's no survival after we die. Yet, here's what Albert Einstein wrote: *It is only to the individual that a soul is given.* It seems that the soul provides creative intelligence, which expresses your life.

I'm going to do something very different right now. I made a copy of Chapter 69 of the novel that covered our last criminal cold case. The reason why, is that Doris and I have a debating game we play all the time. She takes one side and I take the other.

You'll see what I mean when you read it. Doris audio-taped it, then wrote it up. That's what you'll see now. We can discuss it and move on to other thoughts.

[Lars passes out the chapter handout.]

***

CHAPTER SIXTY-NINE

Lars and Doris sat in a booth away from the crowd at Rock Bottom Brewery.

"Hey, Mike! Whip some wings on us with two mugs of the Red Tower Ale."

"Coming up, boss!"

"Taurus is driving me nuts, Doris. He's so clever. He may be the most clever serial killer of all time."

"He sure is smart," declared Doris.

"I'm out to avenge all these cold cases of his. I'm steaming with vengeance."

"But vengeance isn't the key."

"Yes, it is, Doris. Even my buddy, Alexander Pope said, *'On wrongs, swift vengeance waits.'* And if Pope said that, it must have merit. He's up there with Shakespeare and Tennyson as the most quoted English poet."

"Well, where is this all going?"

"I mean that Taurus is gonna see darkness or hell. He has no soul."

"Hold on. Doesn't everyone have a soul?"

"I'll tell you what we'll do. Let's play our debating game. You know, where you take one side and I'll take the other."

"You mean like we did when we talked about whether we should have invaded Iraq?"

"Yup. I took the side that we shouldn't have invaded. You took the other side. Remember about the airlines. I took the side of Federal regulation. You defended privatization."

"Taurus started all of this, but let's go," whispered Doris.

"I'll represent the scientific view. You represent the theological viewpoint. I'll start. Remember what Belissa Hawthorne wrote near the end of her letter to me? I'll see you on the other side ... *I hope there's an 'other' side.* She's right. Nobody knows if there's an afterlife. Think about this. When the brain is destroyed, how can something bring forth consciousness or personality, which dissipates? The soul can't keep the mind alive. The mind is decaying and will continue to decay until one hundred percent is gone." Doris took a swig of her ale. Lars exhaled and slugged down about eight ounces of his Red Tower.

"You say that you want to kill Taurus."

"Yup."

"But you also believe in the Ten Commandments, the sixth being, 'Thou shalt not kill.'"

"Yeah, Doris, but there are exceptions. After all, I belong to *The Guild of All Souls* at St. Paul's. Remember, I'm arguing the scientific, not philosophical side of this issue."

"When I was a Catholic, we believed in Purgatory ... a place where cleansing of the soul takes place. Most Catholics believe this is a step before you can gain entrance into heaven. Believers undergo purification to achieve a level of holiness necessary to enter heaven. Lars, this is a lot of people ... since there are 1.1 billion Catholics in the world, according to the Vatican, and 68.5 million in the US. Now that you switched me to the Anglican viewpoint, I'm not sure anymore. The bottom line is that most Christians believe that people have souls, and when they die, the soul leaves the body and goes to heaven or hell. Like it or not, Lars, that's how it is."

"I realize that, but most scientists believe that Purgatory is a bunch of horse manure. Another Catholic cop-out!" Lars scratched his head as he took another gulp of beer.

"I also know that religions look at afterlife differently ... Catholic, Hinduism, Islam, Jainism, Buddhism. Taoists believe there are ten souls. It's sort of all mixed up in the theology world. Science can't answer non-empirical questions. Science measures."

Lars continued, "Death is a plunge into darkness. The person who died is oblivious to anything because everything in that person's physical system is dead and will continue to deteriorate over time. If the person is cremated, then that, of course, speeds up the deterioration process. There is no consciousness left because the brain is dead and not functioning at all. For a short while, a person's presence could be felt, but as the energy emanates from the body, it dissipates in the atmosphere…never to be reassembled or reconfigured. Even the Bible teaches that the dead, if not cremated, lie in the grave, and have no emotions and thoughts. The dead possess no consciousness. And I …"

Doris interrupted, "Wait a minute! The Bible also teaches about resurrection to everyone who worships God and repents."

"But, Doris, the term 'immortal soul' does not appear in the Bible. Like I said before, Taurus has no soul. It will be darkness for him. In 1 Timothy 6:12–16, it states, *'You know that no murderer has eternal life abiding in him.'*"

"My dear Lars, Thomas Aquinas said that the soul is a conscious intellect and cannot be destroyed. Also, Socrates and Plato said that the soul is the essence of a person. Aristotle viewed the soul as part of the human being, not separate."

"Hold on, Doris. Do this exercise. Close your eyes." Although she didn't like the idea, Doris closed her eyes.

"Keep them closed. Play like you're asleep. What do you see?"

"Darkness. It's black."

"Now, say you die in your sleep." Doris shakes her shoulders uncomfortably.

"What do you see now?"

"It's dark."

"Okay. Open your eyes. What do you see?"

"You." She laughs.

"No, I mean now you see light, right?"

"Yes."

"But if you stayed asleep forever. I mean if you died in your sleep, you would just be blacked out forever. I rest my case."

"That was mean. Having me die in my sleep, you goon!"

"All I can say, Doris, is that darkness needs light to recover. A dying person still sees light, then shadows of gray, followed by complete and still darkness." Lars wanted to add that he still planned to kill Taurus. It's the driving force that keeps him going. *If he doesn't kill me first.*

"So what do you really believe?"

"You're the only person I've told this to. In my second year at

West Point, a bolt of lightning hit our dormitory. God was standing there with outstretched arms in my room. I sat up in my top bunk. My roommates didn't wake up. I was the only one who saw the vision. It was electrifying. He was motioning to me to be his servant, but he did not speak. Then he disappeared. So I have a strong faith. Having presented the scientific side, I must admit that I tend to believe in the soul and afterlife."

"You have to realize where I'm coming from! My undergrad degree is in engineering, then an MBA, and a doctorate in strategic management. I think in terms of logical models based on realistic facts."

"This soul, spirit, after-life, Purgatory stuff is a paradox for me. There is just no proof. It's like a criminal case where you have to prove that Elmer Fudd did it beyond a reasonable doubt. There lies the key element that is missing — a reasonable doubt. Nobody can show that we all have souls — beyond a reasonable doubt. I must say, Doris, that having faith in God gives me a stronger inner-faith that projects self-confidence. I could have been killed at least a dozen times in Vietnam, but my faith pulled me through."

Lars waved his beer mug at Doris and chugged the remaining beer.

"Oh, there's one more thing, Doris. There are a lot of phonies that go to church just to be seen. Going to church doesn't make you a Christian any more than standing in a garage makes you a mechanic."

"Let's have another beer." They clinked mugs and smiled at each other … the way lovers do.

"You had a closing statement. What about me?"

"Go ahead, Doris." She tore at a chicken wing and wiped her hands on her napkin.

"If there's no immortality, why exist at all? It's pointless for us to live at all. But the soul after death is everlasting. I'm going to pass on to Brenda your saying by Timothy … that Taurus will not have an afterlife. She might use it in one of her articles as she tries to draw Taurus out in the open."

"Bravo, Doris! Bottoms up!"

***

Lars:

There may have been some extraneous stuff in this handout, but it is a decision everyone has to make about afterlife.

Tiger:

Some people, maybe the scientific and non-believer types, think that all you leave behind are your memories. You leave a legacy of some sort to help others with their life journey. It is selfless—not selfish.

Brenda:

Thomas Merton wrote: *Every moment and every event of every man's life on earth plants something in his soul.* Merton is a Catholic writer who has written more than 70 books, mostly on spirituality. And William Paul Young wrote from his book, *The Shack: Emotions are the colors of the soul.* Young was a Canadian author, known for his novel, *The Shack.* I think that along with your dark shadow, that we've discussed, you carry ghosts with you. Maybe this is why you are sometimes bewildered. Ghostly thoughts such as anxiety, regret, depression, sadness, grief...

Lars:

Ghosts of the past haunt me. Those 41 who died in battle and I lived.

Tiger:

Me too, Doc. I play back some of those intense fire fights in Nam and it affects me deeply. I guess that's why we both have PTSD.

Rev:

The soul appears 473 times in the Bible—the body only 154 times. That might give some credence to James 2:26: *The body without the spirit (soul) is dead.* It seems as if your soul is the real you—not your physical body.

Doris:

King Solomon wrote: *Your own soul is nourished when you are kind; it is destroyed when you are cruel.* The point is to think pure thoughts per Reverend Whitcomb's earlier comments. Thomas Moore wrote about taking care of your soul. There are things you can do to keep your soul on the ball. Brenda is going to tell you about a few of them.

Brenda:
Something that nourishes the soul is for you to start doing new things. Best for the soul are: arts, gardening, cooking. Try drawing or going to art shows, museums, or to the theater. Symphonies, opera, ballet, whatever. Learn about plants and flowers. Plant them and care for them. Never cooked? Try it. Look up new recipes. Keep a card file of them. Watch cooking shows on TV. Take the focus off yourself and on to new things. The soul gives you depth and fights the dark shadow, which can cause you to feel slightly empty inside. You may be leading a rather shallow life, regardless of your job or position.

Edwin Leibfreed, author of many books such as *A Soliloguy Of Life*, wrote in his *The Song of The Soul: The Soul can hear the violets grow! It can hear the throbbing heart of God!*

Tiger:
Everyone wants to go to heaven, but nobody wants to die. So you need to be happy in this lifetime since we're not really sure of what's next. If you're not happy, you've got to do something about it. Being happy keeps your soul intact. To repeat, I like KISS: Keep It Simple Stupid. That way your soul is not confused, meaning you're not confused. Make sense?

Lars:
Yup! You're on target, Tiger with KISS!

Rev:
I know the dead can't write you a letter, but they can reach you in other ways for the rest of your life. Right after Christopher Reeves, Superman, died his wife was sitting outside on her porch. She saw a falling star out of the heavens and could feel that was a sign from Christopher. Many other people have had similar experiences. Maybe

you have too. It could be a bird, butterfly, or almost anything. *Blessed is the influence of one true, living human soul to another.* A rich passage written by George Eliot. Eliot was a pen name for Mary Ann Evans, an English novelist, known for the novel, *Silas Marner* and others.

Lars:
   Our next to last fireside talk is next week on INSPIRATION. After all, our Alpha Team's purpose is to *inspire you with our practical thoughts*—food for thought!

Doris:
   I'd like to end this one tonight with Jelaluddin Rumi's poem, *Moving Water:*

Moving Water

When you do things from your soul,
you feel a river moving in you, a joy.

When actions come from another section,
the feeling disappears.

Don't let others lead you.
They may be blind or, worse, vultures.

Reach for the rope of God.
And what is that? Putting aside self-will.

Because of willfulness people sit in jail,
the trapped bird's wings are tied,
fish sizzle in the skillet.

AMAZING FIRESIDE TALKS

The anger of police is willfulness.
You've seen a magistrate inflict visible punishment.

Now see the invisible.
If you could leave your selfishness,
you would see how you've been torturing your soul.
We are born and live inside black water in a well.

How could we know what an open field of sunlight is?

Don't insist on going where you think you want to go.
Ask the way to the spring.
Your living pieces will form a harmony.

There is a moving palace that floats in the air
with balconies and clear water flowing through,
infinity everywhere, yet contained under a single tent.

- Mewlana Jalaluddin Rumi

***

In the kitchen, the Rev told the team that he had developed a mini-sermon on Inspiration. He will present it next Sunday at the Ft. Myer Chapel. You could tell that he was very excited. The Alpha Team suggested that he cover the sermon with them next Thursday. He agreed.

Lars asked the team if they would like to hear a saying by one of Goddess Kali's devoted poets. It deals with her words about blackness. They all pounded on the kitchen table signifying a go ahead.

It's by Ramakrishna Paramhanse (1836-1886):

'Is Kali, my Divine Mother, of a black complexion?
She appears black because She is viewed from a distance; but

327

when intimately known She is no longer so.
The sky appears blue at a distance, but look at it close by
and you will find that it has no colour.
The water of the ocean looks blue at a distance,
but when you go near and take it in your hand,
You find that it is colourless.'

All applauded and cheered. Doris said she knew tonight's fireside talk would be tough so she made something special for the team: *Paris-Brest*. It's a choux pastry and praline flavored cream created in 1891 to commemorate the Paris-Brest-Paris bicycle race. It was popular with the riders due to the energy boost it gave them. That's why it's in the shape of a wheel.

Brenda was intrigued by Kali stating that all colors merge into black. She reminded everyone that the primary colors are red, yellow, and blue. Red + yellow = orange, blue + red = purple, and yellow + blue = green. So, all of these get absorbed into black. She added that the favorite color worldwide is blue. Males favorite color is blue followed by green and black—females is blue followed by purple and green. Brenda said that she wrote an article for *The Post* years ago about what women like about men. She found that women liked men dressed in blue because blue is associated with reliability and dependability. A little trivia for you guys.

They continued to talk about the Soul until midnight. They gave the traditional high-5's at 12:08 am and departed.

Helen Keller
(1880 – 1968)

American author, political activist, and lecturer.
She was the first deaf-blind person to earn a Bachelor
of Arts degree. She graduated from Radcliffe College.

"The best and most beautiful things in the world cannot be seen or even touched—they must be felt with the heart."

- Helen Keller

Fireside Talk #24
Inspiration Brings Focus To Life

"I'm living up to your request about providing you with a copy of my mini-sermon given last Sunday at the Ft. Myer Memorial Chapel."

Reverend Whitcomb passes out a copy of the sermon to the Alpha team. They encourage the Rev to read it to them.

It's Up To You
Sermon
Reverend Charles M. Whitcomb
10:30am
Ft. Myer Memorial Chapel

'These are troubled times in our country. You are faced with disappointments and problems that cause depression and anxiety. Based on talking to people all over the USA, coupled with intensive research, I've determined that these are some of those difficulties: unemployment (loss of job), loss of home. Iraq and Afghanistan wars, health care, poverty, homelessness, drugs, college tuition costs, unfair taxes, dysfunctional government, distrust of Congress and local politicians, and the declining, unstable economy.

In a macro sense, people are upset about: the huge debt, spending billions in other countries, irresponsible sale of US companies to foreign ownership, inflation, illegal immigration, and rampant fraud inside and outside the government.

Some people are seriously affected by traumatic situations, such as disappointment with a family member, relative, or friend; combat loss of a loved one; shocking results from an earthquake, flood, tornado, or fire. Many people are faced with struggles against unspeakable odds.

Here are some thoughts for our congregation to think about…in regards to the importance of inspiration. It helps you to: focus on positive outcomes, remove obstacles, speak directly on tough issues even if you risk personal and business relationships, develop situational courage, gain life-enhancing wisdom, avoid making excuses, increase your inner energy, get rid of rigid ideas of who you are.

Just remember that enthusiasm brings out the fighter in you. My point is that to handle your struggles, you should be self-inspired. It's inspiration from within yourself.

You have to be self-inspired in order to inspire those around you. The key is being true to yourself, which is the heart and soul of self-inspiration.

You can change discouragement to excitement. The spill-off effect will inspire others. Many people lean towards conflict avoidance. However, it's best to get out of the comfort zone and open our minds to dissent and criticism. This is a way to learn about yourself. Trust your instincts and do what you feel is right. Avoid what makes you unhappy.

Frankly, I feel that we don't need to rely on external stimuli because self-inspiration emanates from our inner heart.

Think about it…we spend most of our time at work or doing things that are external (outside). That's sad, because much of our time should be spent examining our inner-self. The true you.

The Bible is good for all of us as a guidepost because it challenges our hearts to reach new heights. Self-inspiration is a dazzling revelation, an awakening guided by divine inspiration. It's the spark that carries our vision along a lifelong journey.

Through inspiration, we receive and record truth. I would like to conclude with two important Biblical verses that relate to this matter.

2 Timothy 3:16: 'All scripture is inspired by God and profitable for teaching, for reproof, for correction, for training in righteousness.'

2 Peter 1:21: 'For no prophecy was ever made by an act of human will, but men moved by the Holy Spirit spoke from God.'

We all have the seed of God within us. That's why it's important to keep looking inward rather than outward. It's up to you whether you grow the seed or let it just lie there. **It's up to you.**

And also, it's up to you to develop self-inspiration. You can do it.

God bless everyone. In the name of the Father, Son, and Holy Ghost. Amen'

The Alpha Team murmured 'Amen'. Lars, Doris, and Tiger crossed themselves. Brenda held her arms skyward, pointing to Heaven. Brenda was ready to kick off tonight's topic. Everybody was excited and inspired by the Rev's sermon.

***

Brenda:

We need to be sure that we know what inspiration means. After all, the purpose of this book is to inspire **YOU** and/or help you inspire someone that needs to be awakened.

Tiger:

Yea, you right!

Brenda:

The Oxford Dictionary states: *The process of being mentally stimulated to do or feel something, especially to do something creative. The drawing in of breath; inhalation.*

Merriam-Webster Dictionary: *Something that makes someone want to do something or that gives someone an idea about what to do or create.*

Doris:

I know we're going to cover why inspiration is important, how to inspire, and results of inspiring yourself or others. But first, let's start with Rudyard Kipling's poem entitled *If*. It is considered to be the *most famous poem in the world*. He won the Nobel Prize in Literature, 1907. Kipling, the English poet, displays wisdom, insight, breadth and depth in this poem. The bottom-line is he shows that you have potential no matter what your situation is. 100% inspirational. I thought this poem could jump-start our discussion tonight on inspiration.

If—

*If you can keep your head when all about you
Are losing theirs and blaming it on you,
If you can trust yourself when all men doubt you,
But make allowance for their doubting too;
If you can wait and not be tired by waiting,
Or being lied about, don't deal in lies,
Or being hated, don't give way to hating,
And yet don't look too good, nor talk too wise:*

*If you can dream - and not make dreams your master;
If you can think - and not make thoughts your aim;
If you can meet with Triumph and Disaster
And treat those two impostors just the same;
If you can bear to hear the truth you've spoken
Twisted by knaves to make a trap for fools,
Or watch the things you gave your life to, broken,
And stoop and build 'em up with worn-out tools:*

*If you can make one heap of all your winnings
And risk it on one turn of pitch-and-toss,
And lose, and start again at your beginnings*

And never breathe a word about your loss;
If you can force your heart and nerve and sinew
To serve your turn long after they are gone,
And so hold on when there is nothing in you
Except the Will which says to them: 'Hold on!'

If you can talk with crowds and keep your virtue,
Or walk with Kings - nor lose the common touch,
If neither foes nor loving friends can hurt you,
If all men count with you, but none too much;
If you can fill the unforgiving minute
With sixty seconds' worth of distance run,
Yours is the Earth and everything that's in it,
And - which is more - you'll be a Man, my son!

Lars:

That is an incredible poem, Doris. To me, inspiration is key because it is what can give you a lift. In other words, it causes you to tackle something new. Gets you out of your comfort zone. It gets you moving forward—per Walt Disney, *'Keep moving forward.'* It gives you a source of new energy. It will spill over to others. Makes them better too.

Doris:

One thing that will make a difference in **YOUR** life is to expose yourself to a role model—a genuine one. Not a rabble-rouser or phony motivational speaker who may be, in their real life, shallow. Typical examples are some evangelists, pastors, politicians and others who are phony.

Rev:

The 'why' of what makes inspiration important, is that it causes us to challenge the routine or status quo (status quo is a Latin term meaning the existing state of affairs). Also, the quotes, sayings and poems that we are providing to you keep you going during tough times. That's why it's important to keep this book close by. It's your Personal Troubleshooting Guide.

Tiger:

You know the old saying, *'When things get tough, the tough get going.'* I agree, Rev—these thoughts from others via quotes are a super source of energy. They push me a little harder each day.

Brenda:

By the way, that saying is credited to *Joseph P. Kennedy*, father of our former president.

Rev:

Lots of enlightenment. Inspiration gives us the intestinal fortitude to do better. It's in your mind and gut. Inspiration can turn your dream into a reality. Without it, you will tend to lack enthusiasm and excitement.

Brenda:

I agree with Lao Tzu, *'A journey of a thousand miles must begin with a single step.'* And the Japanese proverb, *'Fall seven times, stand up eight.'*

The importance of inspiration is that it tickles our creative spirit that is just waiting to be unleashed. With inspiration putting thought into action, we've gone to the moon, made a better vacuum cleaner, coffee maker, iPhone, chair, table, home improvements…

People had to be inspired to do all of that. Someone inspired them to tackle the challenge or they were self-inspired. They challenged the routine or status quo.

Rev:

Inspiration can come from a thing or from a person or group. For example, the waterfalls and powerful rushing water at Great Falls here near Washington DC is euphoric. Usually there is an artist drawing the falls—totally inspired by the scene.

In school, I was a sprinter but many years later, I bumped into a friend who I hadn't seen for a long time. She was into marathons.

Betty inspired me so much that I got excited and read nearly every book on running. Ended up qualifying for the Boston Marathon and ran it a year after I started training. Actually, I qualified for it by running a qualifying time in the Marine Corps Marathon. Her enthusiasm and excitement spilled over to me. Then I wound up inspiring others to run competitively. As mentioned before, it's sort of a spill-off effect.

These are just two examples of hundreds, but you get the point. Inspiration causes you to be more creative, enthusiastic, and excited about doing something. You can be inspired or you can inspire someone via your passion. Really, you have to go for it, per Jack London who said, *'You can't wait for inspiration. You have to go after it with a club.'* It takes focus. London, author and journalist, was one of the first recognized fiction writers. He wrote two famous novels: *The Call of the Wild*, and *White Fang*. He died in 1916. Actually, I went to the Jack London Grill in Carmel, California while I was going to the Defense Language Institute in Monterey for Vietnamese language training.

Doris:

If you feel hopeless or totally bored it might pay off to list the obstacles in your way. What will make you feel good? Maybe cleaning up and bringing stuff you don't need to Salvation Army or Goodwill will boost your own self-inspiration. Get rid of the obstacles that are in your way. No matter what you're faced with, by chipping away at it you'll start seeing a glimmer of light at the end of the tunnel.

Lars:

If you're trying to inspire someone, to pick them up, it's best to let them know you are here to give advice and support. That attitude is what you radiate by setting a good example.

Tiger:

I guess we're into the *how to inspire **yourself** and others*. Recently, a buddy of mine who has his own small landscape business, told me that his wife has a boyfriend. This guy loves what he does—is excited and passionate about his work, whether it's taking down a large tree, pruning or replacing bushes. Now he is downcast, but still puts energy into his work, which spills off, onto his crew. It's sad because this guy is so nice. A wonderful person who cares about doing a top-notch job. Maybe you or your friend is faced with something like that, or a serious medical condition, victim of a shooting or bombing, deep grief.

However, *you've got to re-inspire yourself.* It ain't easy. I gar-run-tee I you dat! I think words are important. An old, familiar adage dates back to March 1862. It was printed in the African Methodist Episcopal Church bulletin, *The Christian Recorder.* The Church had a large black following. It's what children used to reply to someone calling them names. Maybe you have used it: *Sticks and stones can break my bones, but words can never hurt me.*

Wrong, words *can* hurt you. But on the other hand, just one thoughtful word, a pat on the shoulder or a nice smile is enough to buck up a sad person. I got that thought from Saint Therese of Lisieux who said: '*One word or a pleasing smile is often enough to raise up a saddened and wounded soul.*' I use this when I meet with my Wounded Warriors. I've mentored them all: no legs, one arm and one leg, shot up organs, PTSD…the works. By the way, Saint Therese was a French nun, called The Little Flower of Jesus. Pope Pius X called her, 'the *greatest Saint of modern times.*'

Lars:

I do the same thing with my Wounded Warriors and other people in distress. It's something that people miss because they are out of focus. And somehow, through osmosis, it causes yourself to be more inspired. Maybe that's because you feel good about what you're doing—it's internalized. Tiger is right on. I'll piggyback his comment by adding that if you say 'hi' or 'how are you' in an automatic, dull, flat voice—then you don't greet genuinely at all. You have to add spark to it. You should tackle everything with energy and vitality. Gardening, cleaning house or washing the dishes, packing the car for a trip, loading grandma's wheel chair in the vehicle, whatever! I've learned to share my passion with the Wounded Warriors. I'm all for them—all the way. We need to treat everyone this way. Volunteering or helping someone causes us to share our passion. And you become more enthusiastic yourself.

My big point on how to inspire deals with listening. Letting the other person talk makes them feel that you feel that they count—they are important. That's good. If everyone took the safe path, life would be boring.

[For the break, Brenda had everyone stand up. She guided them through 10 repetitions of arm circles. Finger tips on shoulders, rotate elbows backward and then forward 10 times. She had them do three sets of ten repetitions. Although not mentioned, usually Brenda has the team do a quick exercise at each fireside talk session.]

Rev:
Maybe some of the Alpha Team's thoughts will change your thoughts, which could change your life. Your comments, Lars, reminded me of a saying by Yogi Berra: '*When you come to a fork in the road, take one.*' Berra was the New York Yankees catcher and won the American League award for Most Valuable Player 3 times. And Robert Frost's poem: *The Road Not Taken*. Frost was an American poet who won three awards of the Pulitzer Prize for poetry.

The Road Not Taken

Two roads diverged in a yellow wood,
And sorry I could not travel both
And be one traveler, long I stood
And looked down one as far as I could
To where it bent in the undergrowth;

Then took the other, as just as fair,
And having perhaps the better claim,
Because it was grassy and wanted wear;
Though as for that the passing there
Had worn them really about the same,

And both that morning equally lay

AMAZING FIRESIDE TALKS

In leaves no step had trodden black.
Oh, I kept the first for another day!
Yet knowing how way leads on to way,
I doubted if I should ever come back.

I shall be telling this with a sigh
Somewhere ages and ages hence:
Two roads diverged in a wood, and I—
I took the one less traveled by,
And that has made all the difference.

I just think **YOU** should do something different that separates you from the *pack*. To be inspired makes you feel happier. You're awakened to something new, which might move you closer to your vision. *You need to pay attention to your inner voice—it is talking to you.* Your best advisor.

Doris:
Another way to inspire is to expose yourself to role models and others that are genuine inspiring people—not rabble-rousers or motivational speakers who, in their real life, may be shallow or superficial. This was mentioned before.

Tiger:
Boy! You hit my button. Evangelists, rabbis, priests, pastors, and others that are fakes. They make me sick, Rev. Look at the Catholic Bishop who authorized a $43 million renovation of his church residence. Thank goodness Pope Francis nailed him. Pope Francis is a great dude, gang! Great person! He loves to help the poor.
There are plenty of examples of manipulators. The Rabbi's divorce-torture kidnap gang. They beat up a guy to cause him to agree to a divorce. These are Orthodox Jewish married women that the husbands didn't want to divorce. Rabbis charged tens of thousands of dollars for the husbands to give the *get divorce* paper. A divorce requires the husband's permission, called *the get*. These Rabbis should be put in prison for life. Dregs of the earth. Who do they think they

are?

Rev:

I agree. Religious leaders should live a modest life…live humbly. This is reverse-inspiration. So be cautious as to who you choose as a role model. Not to get on my religion bandwagon, but some consider inspiration as divine or spiritual, leading us to new possibilities or challenges.

Lars:

I have a few rules I've shared with my students and companies I have helped.

- 80/20 Rule—The law of the trivial many and the critical few. 20% of something is responsible for 80% of the results. 20%-vital, 80%-trivial. You need to concentrate on the 20% of the main things you need to do, let the 80% slide. If you have 20 things to do, only four are top priority. The others can be done later.
- Be willing to change: unfreeze, change, refreeze. If you want to change someone, or yourself, you have to unfreeze them. If it's an attitude problem, for example, then the person needs to recognize the need for change—unfreezing. Then the changeover needs to take place by storytelling, sharing experiences, or by educational means. Finally the change is made, a new atmosphere. It's like comparing yourself to an ice cube. It needs help! So take it out of the freezer, let it melt—the change—then remold it into the form you want. Put it back in the freezer so it can refreeze into the desired shape. So, you are building motivation for change (unfreeze the current state), then moving or transitioning (change), to reestablishing equilibrium—the desired state (refreeze).
- See the whites of their eyes. You can't help somebody via telephone calls, emails, letters, or other communications. You have to meet them, preferably on their turf. Those types of communications, especially emails, are cold and impersonal. But all communications are good in between the times when you see the whites of their eyes.
- Connect the dots. Again, if you're helping someone try to connect

things—that way you'll form a clearer picture. Like in my case—I was doing certain things and thinking about various weird stuff. With the dots connected, it was obvious I have PTSD. The dots are there. Think of how many bombings and shootings in this country could have been avoided if the perpetrators had connected their dots. Those are a few things you might think about.

Brenda:

We cheated on **YOU**, the reader. We met two days ago to discuss the approach to provide you to inspire people.

We beat it up for three hours and finally agreed that Marc Chernoff's post on www.mardandangel.com was the best we could provide. If we discuss the *how to inspire* our usual way, it would consist of piecemeal thoughts. Chernoff's written article provides principles to live by. Lots of wisdom. Everyone has a copy. I'll read them now.

18 Ways To Inspire Everyone Around You

1. **Be authentic and true to yourself.** – In this crazy world that's trying to make you like everyone else, find the courage to keep being your awesome self. Embrace that individual inside you that has ideas, strengths and beauty like no one else. Be the person you know yourself to be – the best version of you – on your terms. Above all, be true to YOU, and if you cannot put your heart in it, take yourself out of it. No it won't always be easy; because when it comes to living as a compassionate, non-judgmental human being, the only challenge greater than learning to walk a mile in someone else's shoes, is learning to walk a lifetime, comfortably in your own.

2. **Stick with what you love.** – Take part in something you believe in. This could be anything. Some people take an active role in their local city council, some find refuge in religious faith, some join social clubs supporting causes they believe in, and others find passion in their work. In each case the psychological outcome is the same. They engage themselves in something they strongly

believe in. This engagement brings happiness and meaning into their lives. It's hard not to be inspired by someone who's passionate about what they're doing.

3. **Express your enthusiasm.** – Passion is something you must be willing to express if you want to inspire others. You can gain a lot of influence just by publicly expressing that you are excited and passionate about a topic. Expressive passion is contagious because of the curiosity it stirs in others. You'll get people wondering why you love what you love so much. Naturally, some of them will take the time necessary to understand what it is about the topic that moves you.
Read How To Win Friends and Influence People
(http://www.amazon.com/gp/product/1439167346/).

4. **Excel at what you do.** – People watch what you do more than they listen to what you say. Be someone worth emulating. Most people are inspired by GREAT musicians, writers, painters, speakers, entrepreneurs, engineers, mothers, fathers, athletes, etc. There's only one thing they all have in common: They excel at what they do. There's no point in doing something if you aren't going to do it right. Excel at your work and excel at your hobbies. Develop a reputation for yourself, a reputation for consistent excellence.

5. **Focus on building your character.** – Be more concerned with your character than your reputation. Your character is what you really are, while your reputation is merely what others temporarily think you are. A genuinely good character always shines and inspires in the long run.

6. **Care about people.** – People don't care about how much you know, until they know how much you care.

7. **Challenge people to do their best.** – As Ralph Waldo Emerson once said, '*Our chief want is someone who will inspire us to be what we know we could be. If people know we expect great*

things from them, they will often go to great lengths to live up to our expectations.'

8. **Lead by example.** – Practice what you preach or don't preach at all. Walk the talk! Be the change you want to see in the world. If you really want to inspire others to do something, then this 'something' should be a big part of your life. You don't necessarily need to be an expert at it, but you do need to be passionately involved.

9. **Articulate what everyone else is thinking.** – We are very connected to each other in various ways, the most important of which is our thoughts. Out of fear, or passive shyness, lots of people hesitate to articulate their thoughts. If you take the risk and say the things others are holding back, you become the glue that brings people together.

10. **Make people feel good about themselves.** – People will rarely remember what you did, but they will always remember *how you made them feel.*
(http://www.marcandangel.com/2012/01/29/20-things-to-start-doing-in-your-relationships/).

Start noticing what you like about others and tell them. Go out of your way to personally acknowledge and complement the people who have gone out of their way to excel. As von Goethe once said, Treat a man as he appears to be, and you make him worse. But treat a man as if he already was what he potentially could be, and you make him what he should be.

11. **Help people heal.** – Instead of judging people by their past, stand by them and help repair their future. In life, you get what you put in. When you make a positive impact in someone else's life, you also make a positive impact in your own life. Do something that's greater than you – something that helps someone else to be happy or to suffer less. Everyone values the gift of unexpected assistance and those who supply it.

12. **Share lessons from your successes and failures.** – When you can, be a resource to those around you. If you have access to essential information, don't hoard it, share it openly. You have more to share than you realize. Mine the rich experiences of your life and share your wisdom from your unique point of view. Be vulnerable. Be willing to share your failures as well as your successes. Others will relate to you. They'll understand that they're not the only ones with challenges.
Read The 7 Habits of Highly Effective People
(http://www.amazon.com/The-Habits-Highly-Effective-People/dp/1455892823).

13. **Keep your cool in tense situations.** – What you do in a tense situation says a lot about your limits. People take note of how far the pressure or social discomfort around you goes until you lose control of yourself and the situation. President Obama, who often displays a calm and collected persona, had a joke in his speech at the White House Correspondent's Dinner awhile back where he said, *'In the next 100 days, I will strongly consider losing my cool.'* Obviously this made him appear even more calm and collected. Bottom line: Keeping your cool in tense situations lets people know you have a mind of steel – a personality trait most people are drawn to.

14. **Focus on the positive.** – Be happy with who you are now, and let your positivity inspire your journey into tomorrow. Everything that happens in life is neither good nor bad. It just depends on your perspective. And no matter how it turns out, it always ends up just the way it should. Either you succeed or you learn something. So stay positive, appreciate the pleasant outcomes, and learn from the rest. Your positivity will help encourage those around you.

15. **Keep your promises and tell the truth.** – Inspire people with your dependability and commitment to the truth. If you say you're going to do something, DO IT! If you say you're going to be somewhere, BE THERE! If you say you feel something, MEAN IT! If you can't, won't, and don't, then DON'T LIE. It's always

better to tell people the truth up front.
Read The Four Agreements
(http://www.amazon.com/gp/product/1878424319/).

16. **Listen intently to what others say.** – Make people feel important, and inspire them by showing them that they are. Eyes focused, ears tuned, mobile phone off. In a world that can't move fast enough, someone who can find time to listen to others is always appreciated.

17. **Communicate clearly.** – Mystery does not inspire. Say what you mean and mean what you say. Share your vision and ideas often with those around you. Also, be sure to maintain eye contact when communicating; it's one of the most alluring forms of personal communication. When executed properly, eye contact injects closeness into human interaction, which captivates attention.

18. **Be faithful to your significant other.** – There's nothing more inspiring than the *unwavering love and commitment between two individuals. Furthermore, your sustained fidelity in a long-term intimate relationship creates a healthy foundation for everything else you do.*
(http://www.marcandangel.com/2011/11/20/60-tiny-love-stories-to-make-you-smile/)

I really like the 18 points. This is something you should keep close by so you can refer to it occasionally—as needed. I do like #14 because I know a lot of my friends focus on things they don't have.

Tiger:
 Also, Doris—those kinds of people, who focus on things they don't have, usually are the ones who focus on negatives—like what's not working for them.

Doris:
 These helpful thoughts from Lars and Brenda remind me of Helen

DR. CHARLES N. TOFTOY

Steiner Rice's poem, *Climb 'Til Your Dream Comes True'*. She was a religious and inspirational writer .Pope John Paul II and President Jimmy Carter were admirers of her writings.

Climb 'Til Your
Dream Comes True

Often your tasks will be many,
And more than you think you can do.
Often the road will be rugged
And the hills insurmountable, too.

But always remember, the hills ahead
Are never as steep as they seem,
And with Faith in your heart start upward
And climb 'Til you reach your dream.

For nothing in life that is worthy
Is never too hard to achieve
If you have the courage to try it
And you have the Faith to believe.

For Faith is a force that is greater
Than knowledge or power or skill
And many defeats turn to triumph
If you trust in God's wisdom and will.

For Faith is a mover of mountains.
There's nothing that God cannot do,
So start out today with Faith in your heart
And Climb 'Til Your Dream Comes True.

AMAZING FIRESIDE TALKS

Lars:

You know…inspiration causes you to yearn for something. Like a coach at halftime, firing up his players to go back out there with renewed energy, yearning for victory. When you unfreeze yourself or someone else, the trigger can be something you yearn to do. Then you are unfrozen from your current state. That's important for anybody to include those that need to shrug off drugs.

I just thought of this. You remember the Wounded Warrior that I helped who had PTSD so bad that he was on a suicide watch. I used the 'unfreeze-change-refreeze' approach with him. He was sad. When he said that he was interested in helping kids…the change occurred by writing a business plan. When he became the CEO of his own company, he was refrozen and locked in. A brand new person…more like his original self.

Again, our thoughts are presented to guide you through a tough problem or rugged condition you're faced with. Hopefully you can apply some of our practical ideas to enhance your life or the life of someone you're concerned about.

Next week we wrap it all up with a fireside talk on LIFE IS A PARADOX. We decided to conclude with this topic because, regardless of our thoughts provided over the past six months, there are many self-contradictory statements made out there in our world. Less is more, living death, and so on. Next time!

***

They all puttered around in the kitchen, still affected by Whitcomb's sermon. Lars said that inspiration lives inside all of us. It can be the painter who goes to the mountains to gain inspiration about what to paint. Making your own creation, like needlepoint or Doris who inspires herself to be creative in the kitchen. Tiger injected that Doris's creations are divine…finger lickin' good! He added that if you're not inspired, you're a dud!

Living up to her kitchen creativity, Doris brought out Poire Belle Helene. She explained to everyone that it is pears poached in sugar syrup with vanilla ice cream, chocolate syrup and sliced almonds. It was created by Auguste Escoffier in 1864. He named it after the operetta *La Belle Helene* by Jacques Offenbach.

Once again, Tiger shouted Ooh, La La. The team smacked their lips and agreed that Doris definitely was self-inspired. They all danced around the Rev like little children. They stayed until 1am still talking to the Rev about self-inspiration. Also, they all discussed Marc Chernoff's *18 Ways To Inspire Everyone Around You.*

Abraham Lincoln
(1809- 1865)

16th President of the United States, serving from
March 1861 until his assassination in April 1865

Fireside Talk #25
Balancing Life's Paradoxes

This is the first time, since they've been doing the fireside talks, that Brenda, Tiger, and the reverend arrived at the same time...8pm. Brenda drove her red and white Mini Cooper into Doris and Lars driveway, followed closely by Tiger's black ford Explorer SUV, and the Rev's red Dodge Challenger.

Brenda took Tiger's right hand with her left, the Rev's left hand with her right, and skipped up the front sidewalk...just like Dorothy following the yellow brick road in *The Wizard of Oz*. She was obviously getting sentimental since tonight is the next to last fireside talk. They heard piano music as they entered the front door.

Everyone stood behind Doris as she hammered out the beautiful composition, *La Campanella*.

As usual, Doris filled the team in on some details as she played. She said that *La Campanella* is the final movement of the Violin Concerto No. 2 in B Minor, Op.7, by Italian composer and violinist

Niccolo Paganini. You could tell that all of this was Greek to Tiger.

La Campanella means '*The Little Bell.*'

Composed and written by Franz Liszt in 1826. He was a Hungarian composer and pianist. Liszt is considered the greatest pianist ever. He wrote more than 700 compositions. In 1842, Liszt found out about the *Great Fire of Hamburg*, which destroyed 1/3 of the city leaving 51 dead and 20,000 homeless. Liszt gave concerts to create aid for the thousands of homeless. *La Campanella* is really an Italian folk song with bell-like effects. The team observed Doris's flashy finger work. She told them that this piece requires a brisk pace. Your right hand jumps between intervals. She said: '*Not easy to play by someone like me.*'

Brenda's eyes welled up and tears streamed down her face. Tiger handed her a used paper towel from his pocket.

Rather than applaud, the team picked up Doris, all 100 pounds of her, and hoisted her over their heads… marching into the living room. Then, they let all 4' 11" of her down carefully. Brenda hugged her tight for about 3 minutes. The team was primed to dig into the last important topic…life is a paradox.

***

Brenda:

I have a handout to give to everyone. It's from Poetic Expressions website in the UK. They are a group of writers that work together to collect words and put them together to form an expression that is useful. Also, they support Marie Curie who has nurses that provide free nursing care to cancer patients and others that have terminal illnesses—in their own homes. Here it is. I'll read it.

Paradox of Life

The paradox of our time in history is that we have taller buildings but shorter tempers, wider freeways, but narrower viewpoints. We spend more, but have less, we buy more, but enjoy less. We have bigger houses and smaller families, more conveniences, but less time. We have more degrees but less sense, more knowledge, but less judgment, more experts, yet more problems, more medicine, but less wellness. We drink too much, smoke too much, spend too recklessly, laugh too little, drive too fast, get too angry, stay up too late, get up too tired, read too little, watch TV too much, and pray too seldom.

We have multiplied our possessions, but reduced our values. We talk too much, love too seldom, and hate too often. We've learned how to make a living, but not a life. We've added years to life not life to years. We've been all the way to the moon and back, but have trouble crossing the street to meet a new neighbour. We conquered outer space but not inner space. We've done larger things, but not better things. We've cleaned up the air, but polluted the soul. We've conquered the atom, but not our prejudice. We write more, but learn less. We plan more, but accomplish less. We've learned to rush, but not to wait. We build more computers to hold more information, to produce more copies than ever, but we communicate less and less.

These are the times of fast foods, and slow digestion, big men and small character, steep profits and shallow relationships. These are the days of two incomes but more divorce, fancier houses, but broken homes. These are days of quick trips, disposable diapers, throwaway morality, one-night stands, overweight bodies, and pills that do everything from cheer, to quiet, to kill. It is a time when there is much in the showroom window and nothing in the stockroom. A time when technology can bring this letter to you, and a time when you can choose either to share this insight, or to just hit delete.

Remember: spend some time with your loved ones, because they are not going to be around forever. Remember, say a kind word to someone who looks up to you in awe, because that little person soon will grow up and leave your side. Remember, to give a warm hug to the one next to you, because that is the only treasure you can give with your heart and it doesn't cost a cent.

Remember to say, I love you to your partner and your loved ones, but most of all mean it. A kiss and an embrace will mend hurt when it comes from deep inside of you. Remember to hold hands and cherish the moment for someday that person will not be there again. Give time to love, give time to speak, and give time to share the precious thoughts in your mind.

Life is not measured by the number of breaths we take, but by the moments that take our breath away.

Tiger:

Wow, Brenda! We always give credit for quotes, sayings, and poems we use—where did that one come from? It's up-to-date and right on target.

Brenda:

The author is unknown, Tiger. It was written by a Canadian man who wrote it on a greeting card for Carleton Cards in the 1970s.

Before we get rolling on this complex topic, let me give you a couple of definitions of paradox. That's part of my job as our team's journalist.

- Merriam-Webster: *A tenet contrary to received opinion; a statement that is seemingly contradictory or opposed to common sense and yet is perhaps true; one having seemingly contradictory qualities or phases.*
- Oxford Dictionary: *A statement or proposition that, despite sound (or apparently sound) reasoning from acceptable premises, leads to a conclusion that seems senseless, logically unacceptable, or self-contradictory; a seemingly absurd or self-contradictory statement or proposition that when investigated or explained may prove to be well founded or true; a situation, person, or thing that combines contradictory features or qualities.*

So you get the full meaning of paradox, I've lifted three paradoxical statements from Mark Manson's list of 20 in the Psychology of Life:

DR. CHARLES N. TOFTOY

The more you try to keep someone close, the further away you'll push them.

The only certainty is that nothing is certain.

The less you care about others, the less you care about yourself.

[Manson is an author and life enthusiast who writes wonderful thoughts about life.]

It just seems that you can make a paradoxical statement that is self-contradicting, yet possibly true. *It's irony in action.* We deal with paradoxes every day, even though we may not look at it that way.

Tiger:

Some of the old favorites are: wise fool, bittersweet, the beginning of the end, what came first–the chicken or the egg, when a tree falls in the forest, does it make a sound? We've all used these paradoxical expressions before.

Another paradox is a sad one for me. I know guys in prison in New Orleans who are afraid to get out—not wanting to be paroled. They are satisfied within the prison walls rather than face the terrifying world outside. I call it the inside-outside paradox.

I went to Vietnam to do good for my country. Upon my return, I was treated badly, like all my buddies. An ugly paradox.

Rev:

We are all jugglers from birth to death. Some say being born is a death sentence. We have to get the most out of our life's journey. Robert Louis Stevenson wrote: *Live life to the fullest.* As jugglers, you have to juggle all the paradoxes in your life to bring balance because life, in itself, is a paradox. Life is full of contradictions. But you have to grip paradoxes; respond to them—they give us insight. They awaken us and cause us to be aware so we can find balance. That includes balancing our time and choosing to do one thing over the other. As already mentioned, you face these every day. It's like cause and effect, which is another paradox.

So in short, you need to juggle your paradoxes during your life's journey. And to end my thoughts on a good note—if you're faced with a bad situation, it can lead to a good outcome later on. Just hang in there. That's a paradox, too. Oh! You all remember Stevenson, right? Famous Scottish novelist who is known for *Treasure Island, Kidnapped,* and the *Strange Case of Dr. Jekyll and Mr. Hyde.*

Doris:
Gandhi said that there are seven things that will destroy us. All are paradoxes:

'Wealth without work;
Pleasure without conscience;
Knowledge without character;
Religion without sacrifice;
Politics without principle;
Science without humanity;
Business without ethics.'

One thing he left out is assassination. He was assassinated in 1948 in New Delhi, India. As the leader of Indian nationalism, he was *Time's* Person of the Year.

There are people I've met during my work life at the FBI who can't seem to trust anybody. The paradox is that those kinds of people can't be trusted either.

Tiger:
Here's a well-known funny paradox: *The sentence after this is true. The sentence before this is false.* Another funny one is that Tarzan lives in the wild jungle, yet he has no beard. And from school, I can admit that the more I learned, the more I realized how little I knew. It's just that paradoxes permeate our lives. It's kind of a dynamic interplay. Do you want to be creative or stay stagnant? A paradox. Take a risk or stay the routine course? And there's the famous Murphy's Law: *Anything that can go wrong will go wrong.*

Back to my peeve about Congress. Supposedly, we are a free democratic country, yet we create laws that prevent us from being free. A sad, disappointing paradox in action all the time.

Another realistic paradox is that we sell, trade, or give weaponry to other countries and later they use them against us or our Allies. Man, that really upsets me, but it's true. Also, we can sell a machine gun to Iraq, or some other country and it winds up being used by rebels in Venezuela.

Lars:

Let me piggyback that Tiger using our academic institutions. We have certain foreign students graduate from our very fine universities, then they go back and lead revolutions against us. I wish we could stop this unfair practice.

[At the break, Tiger showed everybody three good back exercises. Since he has curvature of the spine these exercises are critical. Then, he briskly walked to the restroom. Everyone chuckled. They talked more about *La Campanella* with Doris. Mainly, that it's difficult to play, yet beautiful. Brenda teared up again, just talking about it.]

Doris:

To continue this bigger picture, if our country is dysfunctional and is in a state of paralysis much of the time, then what do we expect at the family unit level? That's right—dysfunction. All families are dysfunctional; don't worry—it's just one of the paradoxes of life.

Brenda:

'The only real prison is fear, and the only real freedom is freedom from fear.' This is sort of a paradox, stated by Aung San Suu Kyi, who was born in Yangon, Myanmar, 1945. She was the Chairperson and General Secretary of the National League for Democracy in Burma. In 2012, she received the Congressional Gold Medal, the highest civilian award given by the United States. She won the Nobel Peace Prize in 1991.

Tiger:

Dat's right gang. After all, look at Congress. It's dysfunctional and can't make timely decisions. So they're set in paralysis too. In Nam, they let me down and it continues to this day. But for you it's different.

AMAZING FIRESIDE TALKS

You can make your own decisions and move forward with your life.

Brenda:

Just to follow you up, Tiger. I watch *House of Cards* and *Scandal* on TV. Those two TV shows portray what you are talking about. In regards to the Hill and the White House, scandals prevail all over the place. In *Scandal*, Kerry Washington and her group protect public images of the elite. In *House of Cards* with Kevin Spacey, real situations are representative of our political turmoil.

Examples: manipulation, using influence, ruthless actions for one's own good, cold-hearted decisions regardless of outcomes, conspiracies, and doing whatever it takes to destroy others that are in the way. Most of these activities are based on personal greed. It is true today in our political system.

The paradox is that we elect these political officials, then when elected some of them turn to applying some of these actions mentioned. Makes me feel stupid to have voted for those that follow the *Scandal* and *House of Cards* misdoings.

Plenty of paradoxes here. Another one is that we elect a person to an elective position based on campaign promises, only to find out later that many of those promises are not kept.

Rev:

Here's a revelation for you. A Bible paradox: *You're made in the image and likeness of God,* and then we read that we are *made from dust and to dust we return.* Your main power is inside you. It's not outside. If you're always trying to show off your outside, then you're sort of kidding yourself in a phony way. A paradox for sure, inside-outside revisited here.

I talk to a lot of parents who have a soldier in the Army. Many times I've heard them say that they don't see anything of their son in them. One mother said about her daughter: *'I don't see anything of her in me. A stranger, yet she's my daughter.'* That is certainly a paradox of life.

Brenda:

Let me piggyback the reverend with a saying from Buddha:

'Do not believe in anything simply because you have heard it. Do not believe anything simply because it is spoken and rumored by many. Do not believe in anything simply because it is found written in religious books. Do not believe in anything merely on the authority of your teachers and elders. Do not believe in traditions because they have been handed down through many generations. But after observation and analysis, when you find that anything agrees with reason and is conducive to the good and benefit of one and all, accept it and live up to it.'

I take Tai Chi. There's a picture on the wall of our exercise room of a warrior monk teaching Tai Chi and meditation to others. How paradoxical is that?

Lars:

It's a challenge to deal with daily paradoxes but without them, you will find yourself stagnated. Again, it's a juggling act. A game of balance that you must play or you may remain rather idle. We have more leisure time, but less fun. Couples with two incomes, more divorces. Faster communications yet we don't communicate well with each other. Back to juggling and balancing. You have to balance logic and the failure of logic. Sorrow and joy. Despair with hope. And quite frankly, life and death. We have multiplied our maternal possessions, yet reduced our own values.

Rev:

It has been said that increased affluence causes a decline in morality. A gloomy paradox.

Doris:

We've all agreed to provide you with some paradoxes that are food for thought. Our opinions, so you may disagree with some of our thoughts. I'll start. CNN reported that now that the war in Iraq was won, we can…blah! blah! blah! Won? Are they kidding?

The paradox is that George W. Bush sent us there, supposedly to win. That's one side of the spectrum. The other is that 6,000 Iraqis were killed in 2013, two years after our withdrawal; 600 this month, 880 killed last month. It's a deepening crisis. The paradox is we think we've won, yet the crisis is deepening and they were better off before we attacked them. A terrible paradox.

Rev:

Another terrible, disappointing paradox is the attitude of our citizens. Ball players, movie stars, host and hostesses of TV shows get huge bucks while the important people get meager salaries in comparison. The people that should have substantial pay are teachers, police officers, firemen, and others that really make up our infrastructure.

A player the other day was granted $10 million for next year. Nobody in this country is worth more than $1 million annually. It's a lopsided paradox. We're the best country in the world, yet we're known as greedy capitalists. Makes me sick.

Brenda:

Yeah. Like the Mafia. They go to church on Sunday and are really maggots that eat away at our morality.

Tiger:

Take Vietnam. A sergeant in my platoon was taken out of the bush—back to the rear, fire support base, two weeks before he was to rotate back to the States. That was a common practice to reward a soldier for his hard-duty time. One night the fire support base got hit by mortars. One landed in his bunker and blew him to kingdom come. Nice looking guy, newly married, with a beautiful wife waiting for him in the USA. He was safe, yet not safe.

Lars:

Similar story in 'Nam. My classmate had one day to go before he was to return to the US. He decided to go on his last patrol—against everyone's advice. He wasn't required to go, but he wanted to help the officer who was his 'turtle'— (replacement). Stepped off the path and blew his left leg off. True paradox.

DR. CHARLES N. TOFTOY

Brenda:

My grandfather told me about this story. The Coconut Grove, Boston's premier nightclub, had a fire in 1942 that killed 492 people. The paradox deals with Clifford Johnson who went back in the nightclub four times to find his girlfriend unsuccessfully.

He suffered third-degree burns over 55% of his body, yet Johnson survived. He had several hundred operations during his 21 months in the hospital. Married his nurse, returned to Missouri. He burned to death in a fiery auto crash a year later.

Rev:

The Jihadists wage war against non-Muslims, yet they are obliged to pray five times a day—*'May the peace and mercy of God be upon you.'* Less than 1% of Islamists are Jihadists.

They pray and then attack unbelievers. I've read the Quran, which does not refer to suicide. It is forbidden in the traditions attributed to the Prophet.

So what they do is use propaganda to fill their ranks with those unfortunates who believe they will become a martyr with heavenly privileges if they sacrifice their lives via suicide bombings. Some of the baloney they extol is that you will get 72 black eyed, bosomy, virgins.

Tiger:

What about the women suicide bombers? Do they get 72 young men as their heavenly privilege? My gosh—what a gross paradox, Rev!

Doris:

Most parents break their butts taking care of their children. You know the drill: changing diapers, rushes to hospital, fevers, worry, school, runs to practices. Then later, kids give their parents a hard time: being thoughtless, selfish, self-oriented…lacking broad understanding. An unfortunate, unfair paradox.

Another paradox is vegetarian friends of mine, who I see occasionally coming out of KFC, McDonald's, Elevation Burger, Wendy's, etc.

AMAZING FIRESIDE TALKS

Lars:

The Japanese blindsided us with the attack on Pearl Harbor. US casualties were 2,402 KIA, 1,282 WIA. The worst atrocity of WWII was the Bataan Death March, in which 1,000 US and 9,000 Filipinos died.

Buried alive, shot, beheaded, bayoneted, beatings with shovels, hammers, pick axes. Yet today the Japanese own many US companies; Nissans, Toyotas, and Hondas are all over the place. Wow! What a paradox!

Tiger:

Another one is the US-USSR Cold War. We both won WWII. So we were the victors, yet we end up in a cold war. Paradox.

Brenda:

Paradoxes can be turns of events. The Nazis operated the concentration camps. But when the war was won, it was them, as POWs, who became inmates of their own death camps.

Doris:

Everyone is athletic on the Alpha Team. Try this paradox. Any top sports team can be beaten by the lowest rated team on a given day.

Brenda:

The most bizarre and absurd global paradox of this century is the Russia versus Ukraine quagmire. Ukrainian defense factories still supply parts for helicopters, missiles, and airplanes to Russia. These defense products are then used by Russian invaders to kill Ukrainians.

Lars:

I'll end our sharing of paradoxical thoughts by an amusing one. We had a barbeque in my backyard for officials from the largest company in Russia. The CEO and his number one man got into a poetry argument:

'If you are in Lars' garden, around the corner from the patio, then you don't exist because I can't see you.'
'But, I do exist—here I am.'

'I would not know that if you were in the garden, so you don't exist.'

So does a tree make a noise, or not, if it falls in the forest?

Rev:
These thoughts about life's paradoxes are a good way to end the fireside talks. We've tried tonight to merely make **YOU** aware and awaken you to some thoughts to build your strength in living a better life. It's all about balance. You are your own juggler.

Lars:
Our last meeting is next week. Not a fireside discussion, but each of us is going to give **YOU** our five favorite thoughts to remember. In other words, it will be like a summary of all of our meetings. The Alpha Team's best thoughts.

Tiger:
It's gonna' be good, my friend. I garon-tee you dat. But before we leave paradox, let me give you two favorites: *'The sentence at the bottom is true. The sentence at the top is false.'*
And another one. *'It's announced: Ignore all the rules.'* Yet that is a rule itself!

Brenda:
You're on top of your game, Tiger.

***

Doris led them down the hallway to show them another favorite painting of hers by Claude Monet. The team huddled around her like a football team huddles around the quarterback. The diminutive Doris looked up at them and provided some background.

The *Water Lilies* painting is actually one in a series of oil paintings by Monet. He completed many paintings while suffering from cataracts. Monet undertook a large landscaping project around his home that included numerous lily ponds. Claude Monet was one of the most famous impressionists in the world. He liked to paint in series. Another very famous series are his *Haystacks.*

One little known fact about Monet was that he served in the First Regiment of the African Light Cavalry in Algeria. He died in 1926.

They filled their mugs in the kitchen with Mexican Spiced Hot Chocolate, made especially for Tiger, since he's the New Orleans 'spicy guy' on the Alpha Team. Cocoa mixed with ground chipotle and cinnamon.

Doris served Punitions, which she had to explain to the non-French group. It's really French shortbread cookies.

They dove into the Punitions like there was no tomorrow.

Reverend Whitcomb wanted to add one last paradox. The Rev studied Moliere in college and remembers one of Moliere's famous sayings: *'Trees that grow slow bear the best fruit.'* Moliere was the greatest master of comedy. His stage name was Moliere but his real name was Jean-Bapiste Poquelin. He wrote *Tartuffe, The Misanthrope, The Learned Women, The School of Wives.* His works will lighten up your day. He died in 1673.

Before they departed, everyone topped off their mugs and snared a few more Punitions.

Lao Tzu
(Laozi: 604 BC – 531 BC)

Philosopher and poet. Author of *Tao Te Ching*.
Legendary figure and founder of Taoism

"If you do not change direction,
you may end up where you are heading."

- Lao Tzu

Afterword

They were all seated around the long kitchen worktable. Doris had a surprise for them. After all, it's the last meeting. Doris explained that it's the French Upside-Down Apple Tart. Invented by accident in the 1860s at the Hotel Tatin in the Sologue Region of France. She filled their mugs with hot apple cider. Each mug had a cinnamon stick, a sprinkling of ground cinnamon and a slice of Granny Smith's apple. They headed for the fireplace in a good mood.

***

Lars:

Many people are in despair and thinking about giving up. You may be in that situation yourself or someone you're trying to help fits that mold. A medical condition or personal relationship can cause you to feel down in the dumps.

Examples are: heart disease, cancer, living disease, Alzheimer's, diabetes, stroke, pneumonia, liver disease, Parkinson's disease, PTSD, bullying. Other troubling areas are: grieving over a loss due to an accident, someone who committed suicide, loss of limbs, traumatic brain injury, and various forms of mental illness. A broken personal relationship or divorce can do it, too.

People around the world are faced with all kinds of these situations. Of course, job loss and having to mortgage your home is another factor that causes depression and anxiety. We feel our thoughts can inspire you to overcome personal challenges.

The Alpha Team has composed a list of some thoughts. Each of us has five thoughts, derived from our fireside talks that we would like to share with you. You might consider this as a summary of our amazing thoughts. Looks as if Tiger wants to go first.

Tiger:
- Never give up
- Hang in there
- Keep moving forward
- Keep your promises
- Count to 3 before you say anything

Doris:
- Take one day at a time
- Stick with happy people
- Turn you dark shadow into a gold one
- When you're in a jam, count to 10, then backwards 10 to 1
- Find your Sacred Space

Rev:
- Do unto others as you would want them to do to you
- Think pure thoughts
- Don't waste energy
- Better to give than receive
- Be yourself; don't try to be someone else

Brenda:
- Believe in yourself
- There's always hope

- Run to the roar
- Be very patient
- Follow your heart

Lars:
- You are worth more than you think
- Work at something you love to do
- Give credit to others
- Learn by listening
- Balance your paradoxes, as a juggler

We have provided common sense thoughts that the Alpha Team hopes you can apply in your daily life. Nobody should feel alone in this world. Try to develop a good friend that you can trust. Just remember, these *Amazing Fireside Talks* provide **intriguing thoughts to awaken you** to different approaches in handling difficulties you face in your daily life.

A good sign-off for these fireside talks is a quote from William Shakespeare: *'A friend is one that knows you as you are, understands where you have been, accepts what you have become, and still, gently allows you to grow'.*

And finally, I must be frank:

TOMORROW CAN BE BETTER
IF YOU TAKE ACTION
TO RESCUE YOURSELF,
OR SOMEONE ELSE, TODAY.

Winston Churchill
(November 1874 – January 1965)

Former Prime Minister of the United Kingdom

"Now this is not the end. It is not even the beginning of the end. But it is, perhaps, the end of the beginning."

- Winston Churchill

Author's Closing Comment

"This book is for **YOU**, written to **YOU**. In my little way, this is an attempt to inspire you. We're all living in tough times, economically and socially.

Thus, the timing is right for a book like this, with thoughts to help you overcome whatever obstacles you are faced with.

The reason I used the four major characters from the two previous mystery/thriller novels is because they live inside of me. I can't let go of them. They talk to me. They are my invisible friends.

The Alpha Team was perfect to use as a discussion group. I didn't want the thoughts, or practical suggestions, to be one-sided, me to you only.

There's no real expertise intended here, but just practical suggestions that you can apply in real life, or modify to suit your needs.

Please read this book at least twice. It's a slow read. That's the best way to have the material work its way into your internal system. Then, if you are seeing some results from the thoughts, you might keep it handy and not shelve it like other books.

Feel free to contact me at www.charlestoftoy.com."

"Knowledge is in the end based on acknowledgement."

- Ludwig Wittgenstein

Acknowledgements

"First, I want to thank you, the reader, for reading *Amazing Fireside Talks: Intriguing Thoughts to Awaken You.* Hopefully, the Alpha Team's intriguing thoughts inspire you, which may change your life for the better. Or, someone you care about.

I am most grateful to all of the people who supported and provided insights for this effort, which took over three years of research and study. My acknowledgement list is too long, in the hundreds. It includes books, personal one-on-one interviews, over 50 small group discussions with people of diverse backgrounds, journal articles, internet articles, websites, and blogs. I respectfully appreciate all of these resources from which I gained vast amounts of knowledge forming the foundation for this heavy-duty research effort. I'll point out those who strongly influenced me. Others know who they are."

- Charles N. Toftoy

Primary Editor, Cover Design, Interior Formatting:
Cindy Bauer (http://cindybauerbooks.com)

Typing and Editing:
Maggie Leak, Senior Secretary of the Department of Management, School of Business, The George Washington University

Creative Thinking and Sharing Ideas:
Jeff Duval, Sergeant E-5, USA (ret), Disabled Combat Vietnam Veteran (1st Cavalry Division)

Patricia Toftoy, author's wife

Research Support and Cooperation:
One-on-one live interviews, small group live discussions (diverse groups), journal articles, articles on internet, posts and blogs on internet. And those living and dead whose quotes, sayings, or poems I selected. Because of them, we gain wisdom.

Special Support:
My two Yorkshire Terriers, Sasha and Zoe, who supervised me. Especially Zoe, who would lie down on top of my desk, less than two feet away from where I was writing—watching me with one eye open.

Lastly, it would be only fair to bestow my gratitude to Peter Hyich Tchaikovsky, whose music played continuously as I wrote. A real inspiration, which denied me of any writer's block whatsoever.

This book could never have been completed without the extraordinary efforts of Cindy Bauer and Maggie Leak. Finally, I thank my wife, Patty, for suggesting that I switch from the mystery/thriller genre to the self-help/motivational genre.

"Books are for nothing but to inspire."

- Ralph Waldo Emerson

About the Author

Charles Toftoy has four books published. He has worked in the military, corporate, and academic sectors.

A highly decorated US Army Infantry Officer. Served two one-year Vietnam tours as a Ranger/Paratrooper. Awards include two Purple Hearts.

Graduate of West Point and has an MBA and Doctorate in strategic planning. He taught in The Business School, George Washington University, for 17 years and is now emeritus from GWU. He has received numerous academic, corporate, and military awards and honors. Currently, he serves as a business advisor to several local companies in Northern Virginia.

Charles lives in Arlington, Virginia with his wife, Patricia, two Yorkshire Terriers, Sasha and Zoe, and an African Grey Parrot, Sancho.

Dr. Toftoy is available for readings, lectures, group discussions and signing sessions. Learn more by visiting: www.charlestoftoy.com

"Life is a journey. When we stop, things don't go right."

Pope Francis
(Born December 17, 1936)

266th and current Pope of the Catholic Church – A humble Pope, who cares about the poor. Maintains a simple approach to the papacy.

IT'S IN THE EYES
by Charles Toftoy
August 2009 (Thriller)

A Psychopath Is Stalking Co-Eds In Washington, DC

It's spring in Washington, DC - a beautiful time of year in the nation's capital, yet its citizens are uneasy. Their heightened restlessness is reminiscent of the recent 9/11, sniper, and anthrax scares. But this time the enemy is a psychopathic killer responsible for the deaths of four local university co-eds - raping and murdering them using rituals practiced by the Thuggees, killers for the Goddess Kali who were responsible for the deaths of more than two million travelers in India in the 17th and 18th centuries.

It's up to Lars Neilsen, a college professor and part-time sleuth, and his highly skilled Alpha Team to find out who is committing these atrocious murders. But Lars and his team are in for a few nasty surprises along the way.

EYES OF COLD CASE KILLERS
by Charles Toftoy
December 2011(Thriller)

Cold Case Killer Haunts Washington, DC Metro Area

Lars Neilsen, a professor-sleuth, and his highly skilled Alpha Team put their lives on the line to catch the cold case killer of twenty victims.

Taurus, nickname for the killer, has a track record of murders from Buffalo, Albany, Philadelphia to the Washington, D.C. Metro area. His modus operandi is mostly strangulation—placing a plastic bag over the head of his victims.

D.C.'s heightened restlessness is reminiscent of the post 9/11, snipers, and anthrax scares. Everyone is walking on pins and needles, particularly in the Northern Virginia region. The entire nation watches.

THE BOTTOM LINE

Do you see the glass as half full (optimist) or half empty (pessimist)?

I sure hope that our thoughts have caused you to become a solid 'glass half full' person. That enables you to think that you'll overcome any difficulties or hurdles. There is hope and a bright side in any situation, so try to look for the good in everything. Think of the Wounded Warrior that we mentioned during the fireside talks. Even though he lost all four limbs in the war, he is a 'glass half full' person.

'Glass half empty' people are complainers that look for the worst in any situation they face.

Eighty percent of the people in the world see their glass as half full. I'm sure the pioneers, inventors, and explorers were 'glass half full' people. Where would we be without them who struggled through tough and daring challenges?

In short, take inspired actions to self-motivate and stick with positive people...the 'glass half full' ones.

The Author (2014)

'God saves Noah, his family and the world's animals. The Ark is 450 feet long, 75 feet wide, and 45 feet high...built according to God's instructions. When the flood recedes, the Ark comes to rest on Mount Ararat. The Ark, or teba which is Hebrew for Ark, is mentioned twice in the Bible. There is no evidence to confirm the Ark, but still we think the 11 lessons are good final thoughts for **YOU** to take away from our journey of intriguing thoughts to awaken **YOU**.'

The Alpha Team and Reverend Whitcomb - 2014

**Everything I need to know,
I learned from Noah's Ark**

ONE:
Don't miss the boat.

TWO:
Remember that we are all in the same boat!

THREE:
Plan ahead. It wasn't raining when Noah built the Ark.

FOUR:
Stay fit. When you're 60 years old, someone
may ask you to do something really big.

FIVE:
Don't listen to critics; just get on with
the job that needs to be done.

SIX:
Build your future on high ground.

SEVEN:
For safety's sake, travel in pairs.

EIGHT:
Speed isn't always an advantage.
The snails were on board with the cheetahs.

NINE:
When you're stressed, float awhile.

TEN:
Remember, the Ark was built by amateurs;
the Titanic by professionals.

ELEVEN:
No matter the storm, when you are with God,
there's always a rainbow waiting.

AUTHOR UNKNOWN